Dearly Beloved

Letters to the Children of My Spirit

VOLUME THREE

1974 - 1983

by
Catherine de Hueck Doherty

MADONNA HOUSE   PUBLICATIONS
Combermere, Ontario   Canada   K0J 1L0

PRINTED IN CANADA

Cover: Catherine at the shrine on her island where these letters were
written.

Nihil Obstat: Rev. Robert D. Pelton

Imprimatur:

J.R. Windle
Bishop of Pembroke
Dec. 14, 1990

The Nihil Obstat and Imprimatur are a declaration that a book or pamphlet
is considered to be free from doctrinal or moral error. It is not implied that
those who have granted the Nihil Obstat and Imprimatur agree with the
contents, opinions or statements expressed.

Canadian Cataloguing in Publication Data
Doherty, Catherine de Hueck, 1896-1985
Dearly beloved: letters to the children of my spirit

Includes bibliographical references.
ISBN 0-921440-10-3 (v. 1) −
ISBN 0-921440-11-1 (v. 2) −
ISBN 0-921440-21-9 (v. 3)

1. Christian life − Catholic authors.
2. Doherty, Catherine de Hueck, 1896-1985.
I. Title.

BX4705.D64A3   1988   248.4'82   C89-090000-0

DEDICATION

To all the Children of my Spirit,
those who are with me now and those
who are as yet unborn.

INTRODUCTION

This third and final volume of *Dearly Beloved* contains two sets of correspondence. The first set completes the Staff Letters that Catherine had been writing to her 'spiritual children' for almost thirty years. The second set contains selections from her Letters to Local Directors, written especially for her 'elder children,' challenging them to become leaders for Christ.

* * *

The Staff Letters in this volume, which Catherine wrote in the final decades of her life, continue the theme enunciated in her very first letter:

> I pray much these days, as *the vision of the whole* opens widely before me, and I see the immense possibility of the vocation that God has called us to. ... All of us sometimes lose sight of the overall picture. I can't, because it is my duty to look at the Apostolate as a whole, and at each of its parts. (Vol. 1, page 1).

The human heart yearns to be creative in many facets of life – artistic, intellectual, emotional, spiritual, physical, social, familial, historical, economic, etc. Catherine realized this. She wanted the light of the Gospel to illuminate *every* part of human existence, to have the Author of Beauty and Truth dwell there, in the *whole* of life, in all his fullness.

The vision she embraced was not an intellectual one. Her view of life was not that of an urbane twentieth-century cosmopolitan thinker (though her mind could operate on that level). Her understanding came not so much from human wisdom as from mystical insight. She tried always to see the fundamentals *through the eyes of God,* and to put on the 'Christ-Mind' when dealing with each day's realities:

> All of us must begin in God, continue in God, depend on God, and be led back to God, all the while attending to our outward duties and responsibilities. ... We must be flexible [and] objective, [and] pray much ... (Vol. 3, p. 332-333).

But salvation — whether of society or of an individual — does not come by way of intellectual thought, nor even by prayer. *It comes by love.* Catherine was a woman deeply in love with God; and her day-to-day existence was that of love-in-action. She longed for her followers to 'burn' with the Madonna House vocation: to love God *passionately* ... and to love the world around them (and within them) with *the Heart of Christ.*

This urgent longing runs through Volume One, as she pushes her followers to 'get cracking' and create the Apostolate which God has asked her to form. It grows more urgent in Volume Two, as she sees both Church and society torn apart by a lack of love, a lack of obedience, a lack of commitment ... an unwillingness to share in the pain of Christ, a reluctance to accept His Cross as a source of salvation.

She begins Volume Three by exploring the mystery of pain, both human and divine. She continues to write of Love, and she recognizes that it does not journey the pathways of life alone; two handmaidens walk alongside it — Faith and Hope. She takes time to observe how these traveling companions move, and to meditate on three questions: how to *love* ourselves, no matter how bitter the past; how to have *faith* in God's Plan for us, no matter how dark the present; how to *hope,* and keep on hoping, and continually to forgive ourselves, no matter how mysterious the future.

Catherine thinks back to her childhood. She looks forward to her own inevitable death (which occurred in December 1985). She ponders the deaths of others: Alma Beauchamp, in 1971; her husband, Eddie, in 1975; her brother, Serge, in 1976; Paul Lussier, in 1977; her beloved friend, Dorothy Day, in 1980. She is aware of the possibility of death for her spiritual director, Father John Callahan, who suffered from a heart condition for many years; and Janet Lukos, who underwent a number of cancer operations. (They died in 1984 and 1985, respectively.) Catherine sometimes makes reference to these thoughts; often, she does not. But their presence is there, between the lines.

In 1971, Catherine heard the word *sobornost* spoken in her heart, and she shared it with her family. Madonna House began to build a Byzantine-style chapel, a 'sacred space' to embody that concept of 'unity with God' and with one another. Catherine listened silently to her own growth in faith, and watched that mystery of faith unfold in others. Then she began to reveal her inner life – the dreams and images and voices that came to her.

Sometimes she'd get so excited about sharing these insights that her tongue would become 'all thumbs' so to speak. Though she herself absorbed ideas better when they were expressed in symbols, she wasn't sure that her imagery was understandable to others. Too many grown-ups left their imagination behind when they became adults.

She wanted her followers to use the imagination God had given them. To become like children. To celebrate their own existence. To see life with an innocent eye. To wander, and to wonder. To discover Christ, *personally.* To develop a deep trust in his 'pity' for them. She knew that this return to the simplicity of childhood would give more than comfort; it could heal as well. But it requires a great effort to let this healing happen. To face the reality of one's being, the mystery of self, is never easy.

Catherine hoped that, if only people would get close enough to God to touch the hem of his glory, if only they would stop for a moment and listen to the sound of his voice, they would respond to the strange *Game of Love* he wants to play with them. If only they could enter that game with childlike abandonment, their excitement would become so great that they'd begin to glow with love; even, perhaps, become a bonfire of love.

Catherine so wanted for *everyone* to be inflamed with the Love of God!

* * *

The second set of correspondence in this volume was written in the ten-year period between 1958 and 1967. Because a number of these letters began with the word *Carissimi* (Italian for 'Dearly Beloved'), the editors have chosen to use this salutation for all of them. It reminds the reader that these letters were directed toward a select group of people; the advice they contain may or may not apply to every situation.

The date on each letter indicates when it was transcribed or mimeographed, not the date on which it was composed. With the exception of the final few pages of the book, the letters have been rearranged into their probable order of creation.

Catherine dictated these messages with

unflinching honesty, and unfailing charity, sharing with her 'eldest children' the many problems that confronted her in the Apostolate. She analyzed her own emotional fears, and dealt with them vigorously. She looked with compassionate understanding on those who could no longer dedicate themselves to the 'committed' life. She challenged those who remained with her to *aim always at sanctity,* and to carry on the work of the Apostolate.

The comments she makes in these Letters to Local Directors are sensible and realistic. Any Christian can incorporate into his or her life, directly, much of the advice that Catherine offers in the areas of planning, organizing, delegating, and directing. Her other admonitions may be regarded as a springboard for discussion and further examination, and adapted to each reader's unique situation.

However the insights in this section are used by the individual reader, it is all part of the great 'Game of Love' (as Catherine called it). To the person who has an especially childlike heart, it may seem a sort of divine peek-a-boo, an infinitely delightful session of hide-and-seek. Somewhere in each human soul is a Torch, yearning to be enkindled. Somewhere in each is a passionate longing for Christ, who is the Fire of the Father, and who came to bring each one back into the blaze of Love that is God – Father, Son, and Holy Spirit.

The Editors

CONTENTS

LETTERS TO LOCAL DIRECTORS

PAIN – THE CHALICE OF LOVE

January 11, 1974

Dearly Beloved,

I have been praying very much about all of our fieldhouses, or shall I call them the 'rooms' of Madonna House? It came to me that whenever you write to me, from whatever room, you state something so obvious that it almost doesn't need to be said. At the same time, it has to be expressed because we must share with one another whatever happens to us. For if we don't share, our existence loses its meaning.

From your letters I 'hear' with my heart what you are saying over and over again; namely, that in each of the houses there is pain. What did you expect, dearly beloved? An absence of pain? "There is much pain in the place." How could it be otherwise when we are following a crucified God whose whole Incarnation (to say nothing of his crucifixion) was not exactly without pain? Consider the prayer of St. Francis of Assisi:

Lord, make me an instrument of Thy peace.
Where there is hatred, let me sow love;
Where there is injury, pardon;
Where there is doubt, faith;

Where there is despair, hope;
Where there is darkness, light;
And where there is sadness, joy.

O Divine Master, grant that I may not so much seek
To be consoled as to console;
To be loved as to love;

For it is in giving that we receive,
It is in pardoning that we are pardoned,
And it is in dying that we are born to eternal life.

These words are a cry of pain that conveys the hurt of a soul. He is asking God *not* to be consoled, *not* to be understood, *not* to be loved. Just these few sentences are pain – terrible pain that hurts almost beyond the ability to express. Even if you pray this prayer – and mean it – you are already allowing pain to enter your soul; and, of course, it will also enter your fieldhouse.

But this is a beautiful pain, my friends, because it is a pain offered for the world. It is the pain of abandonment, of surrender to God. Did you really expect to have a house without pain? That is an impossibility, my dearly beloved ones, because it is through this pain that you will resurrect. It is through this pain that each one of you will share the lot of humanity.

What kind of Apostolate would we be if there were no pain among us? Expect it, therefore, and welcome it. Know that this pain is like a fire sent by God to cleanse your soul, your heart, your mind. Because of it, you cease to be self-centered, and can go out to all your brothers and sisters in a given 'room' of Madonna House. You do not rest there; you take upon yourself the pain of others for whom your fieldhouse has been opened.

There is a heavy pain in the hearts of all of the prayer houses, because they have 'taken on' their own pain, the pain of their neighbors, and the pain of the world. To carry that in the poustinia of the marketplace is not easy, my dearly beloved ones. But because they return constantly to prayer, their spiritual feet already walk in the resurrection.

So when you share with me that there is pain in your house, please try to add the words: *Praise be to God for the pain!* It is the path that leads higher into the mountains of the Lord. It is also the tool that makes you straighten out the path of the Lord in your own heart so that you level out its hills and fill in its valleys. Then you yourself, and your brothers and sisters too, can walk on a smooth path to the Lord – the path that you have made with the tools of love, of hope, of pain.

But do not dwell on this pain as if it were something that you have to carry in utter loneliness; that's something which doesn't belong to our Apostolate. Just look at our Little Mandate and you will see that it is filled with pain; and yet the chalice of that pain is joy. As St. Augustine said, *a Christian should be an alleluia from head to foot.* That is so true.

Through your pain, you will people the Church with holy souls, that is, souls in love with God. Take St. Paul's Letter to the Hebrews for instance: "Son though he was, he learned the meaning of obedience through all he suffered" (Hebrews 5:9). Jesus came to do the will of God; and to be obedient to the will of God is to suffer. But where does that suffering lead? It certainly doesn't lead to depression. No. It leads to joy, to love, to faith.

As I prayed about the pain that you express, it came to me that much of the pain in each house is the pain of hurt. Sometimes this pain might have begun in the womb; or it might have begun before the womb, for man carries tribal memories in his soul. Some of these hurts may have been inflicted in babyhood, childhood, adolescence, or even in adult years.

Some person or persons of importance may have rejected you. Society also had a share in inflicting hurts and pain and sorrow and anger, creating in you the hostile symptoms of either aggressiveness or withdrawal. So there is Pain! Pain! Pain! Many of you have come to Madonna House carrying this burden of pain and not even knowing that you did. When people are in pain, they sometimes say that pain 'blinds' them.

Yes, sometimes pain does blind us to all the beauty of community life. Because we haven't been trusted, we don't trust others. Since people haven't been open with us, we are not open with ourselves. And so on down the line. So, instead of being bearers of the Good News, we start singing dirges in a low and minor key!

As I kept praying about this, some words came into my heart: *Tell them about the healing of memories.* I began to understand why God gave me these words at this time. He wanted me to bring this thought of 'healed memories' to you because this means forgiveness. And forgiveness engenders understanding, tenderness, generosity, and deep healing.

We must forgive the society from which we came; we must forgive the ways it has hurt us. We must have forgiveness for all the pain that we have unknowingly experienced, even in the womb before our birth. We must forgive those who may not have understood us, or have seemingly neglected us, or perhaps even rejected us. It is especially important that we forgive our parents for their human frailties. If we can generate that first impulse of forgiveness within ourselves, then – like lightning going through a darkened sky – our forgiveness will cover everything! It will flash across our memories as a lighthouse scans the sea, so that whenever its rays illuminate anything that we think has hurt us, the touch of that light will bring forgiveness into our hearts and bless those whom we forgive.

As I pondered what God had given me yesterday, another word suddenly came forth: *reconciliation*. In a flash, I understood that forgiveness will bring reconciliation; and I knew then that there had to be reconciliation among nations, among peoples, among us. We have to be reconciled to God first, then to ourselves, and then to the whole world ... including whoever has hurt us.

But we have to do more than that! If our forgiveness isn't accepted, we have to turn the other cheek. That is what is meant by the two Beatitudes of the Lord: "Blessed are the meek, for they shall inherit the earth" and "Blessed are you when men revile you and persecute you and utter all kinds of evil against you for my sake; rejoice and be glad, for your reward is great in heaven." If we implement these two Beatitudes, we shall inherit the earth as well as heaven.

We have not yet reached the blessedness of heaven or of immense sanctity, but we are on the way; and Christ who is the Way found the going pretty rough. So if we are walking with him, that is what we can expect also. Isn't that true?

I think that we should ponder these things, for there is no such thing as a 'sad saint.' (If he were a sad saint, he would be a sorry saint!) What I mean to say is that I want you to share with me your moments of pain, and to acknowledge the fact that in each of your houses there is pain. But I also want you to realize that *without this pain* there would be no houses, or missions, or rooms of Madonna House.

Pain is the chalice of love. Love is the chalice of pain. Let us face it. There will always be, I hope, pain in every house. And I hope that we will understand *why* God gives us a share of his pain: it is so that we may imitate him and be led by him to his Father.

Lovingly yours in Mary,

PRAISING GOD IN SONG

February 12, 1974

Dearly Beloved,

I rarely discuss music with you because, though I love music profoundly, I suffer from the inability to carry a tune. I have been surrounded with music for much of my youthful life, however; and I had a mother who taught me to appreciate it. But this letter has little to do with music as such; it is a letter in which I want to pass on to you my ideas about how our family should praise God in song.

There is no need for me to remind you of the biblical injunction to praise the Lord with timbrel, lyre, harp, and various other instruments. You know all about that from reading the Psalms. But there is one thing that worries me, and that is an undue attachment of some of our members to one form of music or another. In Madonna House, as we learn more about Eastern spirituality, and some of our members delve into and experiment with some of the lovely thousand-year-old music of the Eastern Rite churches, it becomes evident that we are getting rather one-sided. I confess that the singing at the Holy Eucharist and at all the Offices of the Russian Church truly 'sends me.' It brings back thousands of memories of my own life and reechoes in my soul with a familiarity that brings me an intense joy. But that's personal.

We of the Madonna House Apostolate are not Eastern Rite, however. We are Roman Catholics. I feel like saying that we are Christians and Catholics – which means that we are universal – and must encompass all the ways of singing that are available to us; but we must emphasize especially our own Roman Catholic heritage.

I would very much like to see the breviary sung. Not the modern breviary (we haven't the money to be buying the new version), but we have a lot of copies of pre-Vatican II breviaries and we have a lot of psalm books. (I'm talking here about *A Short Breviary for Religious and Laity* from Collegeville, Minnesota, and *The Psalms* from the Grail.) The singing of these psalms could be taken from some of the Trappists' simple melodies, or that of Gelineau, or from other sources of the same type. And I am not averse to 'trying out' some of the latest guitar songs, the ones that are suitable. But I have noticed that they don't seem to 'wear' well; we tire of them rather quickly.

Perhaps you are beginning to see the accent of this letter, and to understand what I am presenting for your meditation and consideration. Let us open our musical horizons as we try to open our spiritual ones, for the two are connected. *Music, after all, is the echo of God's voice.*

What I am coming to is that, although we should have the freedom of the children of God, such a freedom is nevertheless always disciplined. That is because there is no freedom without discipline. And we must not abandon the old for the new just because it is new, nor discard the old just because it is old. We must blend the new with the old because it is part of our heritage and our tradition.

There should be harmony among the priests and the laymen and women of our family, and each should try to bring this harmonious whole together: the East and the West, the old and the new, the plain chant of the Trappists and the more modern chant of Gelineau, etc. We should blend our voices in joyous praise to the Lord without too much discussion about when, whether, and how to sing this or that.

I am sorry to say that many clashes come into our family through music, and it shouldn't be so. If we have clashes, if each wants to have his or her own idea, if we forget to blend into a joyous and harmonious whole when we sing to the Lord, then our songs will fall flat and will never reach him. For it is important to sing with our whole minds, our whole hearts, and our whole souls, lest our songs be rejected by the Lord.

I wonder how many of you remember the legend of the little monk who belonged to a French Monastery that was celebrated for its marvelous singing. He couldn't sing; he just couldn't carry a tune. So he used to sit in the corner behind the choir and weep a little that he couldn't praise the Lord in song. Well, one day the abbot told the assembled community that a great honor was going to be bestowed upon them; The King of France was coming with all his retinue to assist at Mass, so the singing must be 'perfect.' The monks practiced and practiced so the singing would be as perfect as possible.

Finally the great day arrived and they began to sing. Their choir seemed like a heavenly one. Suddenly, into this harmonious whole came the voice of the little monk who, carried away by the beauty of the singing, could not resist joining in with the rest of the choir. Of course, he was completely out of tune! There was consternation among the choir members, and it took time to get the monk removed.

That night the abbot was so angry he could barely contain himself. He ordered the little monk to spend the next twenty-four hours on his knees on a very cold floor in a very cold cell. Then the abbot became calmer and began to prepare for bed. Suddenly he was startled by a growing light which seemed to fill the room. And there, standing before him, was the Mother of God. Though always gentle and tender, she was on this occasion rather stern – as a good mother might be with a wayward son.

She said: "Heaven was filled with a terrible sound this evening, a harsh grating noise full of self-centeredness, pride and vanity. It was the sound of your evening prayer, which you sang for an earthly king. It was almost unbearable. And just as all of us were wondering if we could possibly listen any longer, we heard a faint sound of such sweetness and purity that it began to transform the disharmony into something almost pleasant. As your little monk lifted his heart to the Heavenly King, his voice grew stronger. It permeated the terrible noise the rest of you were making, and what finally reached our ears was more beautiful than anything we have heard from this monastery in a long time. So, my son, I suggest you go to your brother and offer him your bed for the night. Perhaps you will take his place on your knees for the remainder of the twenty-four hours; for it is he, not you, who has greatly pleased the King."

The moral of the tale is *true singing is love singing,* while 'perfect' singing can be filled with pride. It was especially so in this story. The little monk had sung from his heart with great sweetness because he loved passionately. Perhaps we should think about this, because we all love God. And I know that whether we have an good ear for music, or a imperfect ear, whether we can carry a tune or not, isn't important. What matters is that into our singing goes the passionate love for the Lord and Our Lady that fills our heart.

There is another point to mention. Let us not concentrate on one way of singing. *All good songs are echoes of God's voice.* Let us try them all out, but let us always remember that the majority of us are Roman Catholics. Though we may and should sing the songs of all nations and all ways, nevertheless, we should remember the songs of our ancestors of the Latin Rite.

Above all, in all of the rooms of Madonna House, the only true way to lift our voices to God so that he will hear is for the choir director and the choir itself to be always in loving peace and contentment with one another. I don't know whether or not I have made myself clear, but I have tried to.

Lovingly,

ON PURITY OF HEART

February 18, 1974

Dearly Beloved,

Often a thought comes into my mind and it won't go away until I pray about it and think about it again and again. Then finally from the depth of my heart comes a meditation on that sentence or word which had entered so subtly into my mind. I call it 'receiving a word from God.' The word that came to me throughout the last weeks of quiet at my cabin was *purity of heart.*

I prayed a lot about it because it was such an important word. It belonged to the Beatitudes, for it says that "the pure of heart shall see God." As I prayed more and more about it, I connected purity of heart with the words of Christ about who is going to enter heaven. Remember how he set a little child in front of him and said: "Let the children come to me, and do not hinder them, for to such belongs the kingdom of heaven."

So now I had the two words of God blending. I understood little by little that the pure of heart are the innocent ones. In our language the word *innocence* has just one connotation, but in God's language it has many.

Innocence and simplicity go hand in hand. Slowly, I was drawn back into my past and I began to see people who really were pure of heart. They weren't saints (though I am sure all the saints had purity of heart); they were lay people, just the 'ordinary garden variety' like you and me. Then again, not quite like you and me.

I thought of the retarded boy who used to come to Friendship House in Toronto. He was actually about nineteen, but who knew his psychological age? He was a slum dweller like us, and few people paid attention to slum dwellers in those days. Every day this boy used to go through the garbage cans of the neighborhood. And somehow he would find a piece of red paper, maybe a bit of tinsel, a paper flower, or something like that; and he would bring it to me. He would put it on my desk and say: "I went and looked to find something pretty for you because I love you." He was exceedingly pure of heart.

I remember the man who was so drunk he could barely stand up. In fact, he didn't stand up; he would weave his way around and come to me, and in his hand he had a withered bouquet of some sort. They might be gardenias, dark and smashed, or other flowers that had been thrown away. He would hand me the decaying flowers and say: "Give these to Mary for me. I promised to bring something for her." And then he would fall flat on his face. I knew at that moment that I was looking at a pure heart. Yes, these people and many like them were pure of heart. They had simplicity; they had innocence, the kind that God loves so much.

Still, I kept thinking about purity of heart, and what it really is. Slowly, very slowly, I realized that it is faith – simple, childlike, innocent faith – a faith that makes of a human heart a shield against all attacks upon it. I realized that purity of heart is a light that shines in the darkness of faith and always lights the next step that men have to take to be one with God. I realized that purity of heart is folding 'the wings of the intellect' and opening wide 'the doors of the heart' so that everyone can come through!

Purity of heart is an inn where everyone is welcome: the ugly, the beautiful, the young, the old, the crippled, the mentally retarded, the rich, the poor and all in between!

The prisoner, the parolee, the prostitute, the nun, the priest – everyone! Yes, purity of heart is an inn that accepts everyone because in its simple, innocent, childlike faith, it sees God in each one.

For a while I was content. I felt I had really begun to understand this beautiful idea given by the Beatitudes: *The pure of heart shall see God.* As the days passed, I wanted to know more about this purity of heart. The whole area of sex came into my mind. I thought of the many discussions people are having about sex being the 'fulfillment' or 'non-fulfillment' of the person. As I thought about all of this, I suddenly understood that this whole area of sex hinged upon being pure of heart. For sex has two faces: the normal, direct approach to the natural aspect of sex in marriage; and the life of celibacy, often freely chosen because of dedication to some cause.

I thought of the young communist in Harlem who was incensed when someone asked him why he wasn't living a life of 'free love.' He bluntly said that he didn't indulge in any form of sex, nor did he smoke or drink, because he was dedicated to a cause. Many have chosen this way: doctors, scientists, explorers, and many others who were not even in any organized form of dedicated life. They have chosen celibacy in order to give a greater dedication to some cause.

It came to me that Christian continency was quite easily achieved by those who were pure of heart, and hence 'saw God.' For then, sex in all its aspects fell into the beautiful hands of God. And once human beings beheld all these aspects resting in those divine hands, their whole attitude changed. They placed their sexuality and their whole lives in the heart of him who makes all things new, exciting, simple, childlike, innocent, and pure. This time I felt I was sure that I had entered a little into the mystery of the pure of heart.

After a few days, however, something else was added, and I understood that when one became pure of heart one *surrendered* to God. One had to surrender the totality of oneself. On this I rested. I saw that surrender was a deep, immense, profound, incredible word. To totally surrender oneself to God is painful – terribly painful. It frightened me, but only for a moment, because the last word on purity of heart was the sight of a cross – a huge cross toward which I had been walking. When I approached it, however, it suddenly became a door; the wood of the cross became a door, and I went through it, and entered the ineffable light of the resurrection! Then I understood that purity of heart was the totality of my surrender because I wanted to see God. And because I wanted to see God, he brought me to the cross, to the resurrection.

All this, beloved ones, was in faith; but it was as vivid, as real, as if faith had become a thin veil. Yes, that's what purity of heart is all about!

Lovingly yours in Mary,

POETIC CHASTITY

The theologians spoke
In learned words – chastity,
They said, was continency ...
It was aloof. It kept itself apart.
It lived on pinnacles ... snowy white ...
Hard of access, and reached by few.

They pondered further
Amidst the cold rooms of ancient cities
And the comfy ones of new metropolises.
They took chastity apart
And when they were finished with it
They put it all together.

It seemed so lustrous ... so cold ... dead
Somehow ... perhaps from too much handling.

A prostitute was walking down their street.
The mascara'd eyes were kind.
The painted mouth, tender and soft.
The swaying body, young.
A small child came up to her and said,
"You smell so nice; I like you."
The girl blushed and bent to kiss the little face
So pure, so innocent.
It was the kiss of chastity itself.
It shone like blinding light.

A singing, pony-tailed woman child
Was walking by. She sang a jazzy song.
A man stopped, turned, and followed her,
With heart full of greedy lust.
But then, she turned ...
He looked into her eyes
And quickly walked away ...
For chastity had smiled at him
In the fullness of its purity.

A mother of a brood came next ...
Heavy of body and of step ...
Burdened with a lot of bags,
And with one chubby infant.
Men smiled, and women too ...
For chastity was passing by –
Fruitful and full.

The theologians did not know
The face of chastity ...
For they had cut her up
To see what made her click.

LOVING ONESELF

March 29, 1974

Dearly Beloved,

During my long 'poustinia' in bed, one idea kept running through my heart. During my three weeks of sickness, I constantly meditated upon it. It was a grace and a clarification which I want to share with all of you. It was simply the obvious need for us to *love ourselves!*

What does that mean, and why do we have to love ourselves? It is because, my dearly beloved, you must begin to realize that you are, in your person, *an instruction, a catechism, an icon, a light* to your neighbor. And in order to be all of these things, you have to love yourself. Madonna House has been founded to witness to Christ, to listen to the Spirit. That is all! Witnessing to Christ means, first of all, being able to love. You are called to witness to the Good News, and that witnessing is not so much in speech as through *being yourself.*

But you must realize, dearly beloved, that loving oneself requires effort. It is very difficult thing to do, at least initially. The commandment of love, when 'lived out,' leads to a flexibility and an adaptability that a few of us are just beginning to understand these days! First, we have to understand *why* we are lovable. When we understand *that,* we will touch God again. We will begin to love ourselves when we think of how beautifully we are created, and how lovingly. Our love for ourselves will grow because we will constantly see God in ourselves.

Christ died to make us like God. All of this will daily come to us more and more clearly if we beseech the Holy Trinity for growth in faith. If we do not grow in faith, we cannot love ourselves or anyone else. But this faith has been given to us in baptism, and throughout our lives we must 'listen' to our growth in faith. We must constantly pray to the Trinity to give us an increase of faith. God is our Father from whom that faith stems. Jesus Christ is our brother who came to save us and to bring us that faith through his life, death, and resurrection. The Spirit is given to us by the Father just for that purpose – to make us grow constantly in faith. Fundamentally, then, faith envelops us! There is God and there is the human soul, and the two mysteries meet – Creator and creature. Now that is what loving oneself is all about ... *letting these mysteries unfold.*

As we grow in faith, we also grow in prayer. If you try to 'explain' the mystery of faith or the mystery of prayer, you will get absolutely nowhere. But we human beings will always try (as you only too well know), and we don't get anywhere at all. That is one of the reasons why we neither know ourselves nor love ourselves. We don't believe in mystery – *the mystery of ourselves.* Oftentimes, this leads us to lose part of our faith, or all of it. But when we begin to grow in faith, when we enter this strange mystery of the encounter between God and man, we become bereft of words and our hearts will be wide open to 'see' God. That is contemplation. That is prayer. And we grow in our relationship to God.

Prayer leads us to accepting anything that happens as part of God's plan for the consummation of all in Christ. By 'consummation' I mean that strange, mysterious Fire that goes with the Wind of the Holy Spirit and consumes without consuming. It leads us beyond the speculating of events, beyond trying to understand how they fit into God's plan (or our own) as we 'say our prayers.' Prayer becomes a simple act of faith, which – before any explanation or contact arises with the mind – bows down and adores the mystery of God. We realize that, no matter what happens to us, *we must begin to love ourselves.* That Wind will teach us to love ourselves as God wants us to love ourselves. Factually, what we are going to do is to love God in us!

Yes, we must work toward this, and this is a tremendous work! It is almost staggering to think that one must engage in it. Yet it is a strange thing ... if I begin to love myself, spiritually speaking ... if I turn inward and look at myself in Christ, at that very moment I have already turned outward and loved somebody else! To the extent that I believe in God, I believe in myself, for God is in me. Then I can trust God, and myself. When I believe in God and myself, I can believe in everybody and trust them too. Therein lie the roots of loving my neighbor – even 'trusting the untrustworthy!' For I have begun to love myself in the right way. If you would ask me who I am, I would say: "I am a person loved by God." Fundamentally, that's who we are!

One of the great difficulties that we have in beginning to love ourselves is that we are filled with *guilt and shame*. That should never happen to a Christian. What is guilt? It is our feelings about the past, our reaction to an act in which we have broken the law of the all-merciful God. When this happens, we go to confession. And once we have confessed it, we become reconciled to God. Once we have received the kiss of Christ in the Sacrament of Penance, God forgets all our wrongdoing; he erases it away completely. It doesn't exist! So why be guilty about something that doesn't exist any more?

Shame is an embarrassment that others should know of our failings. It is part of the effect of guilt. When we go to confession, there is no reason why we shouldn't be somewhat ashamed of being so weak, of this failure or that; but this shame should disappear with the guilt. God no longer remembers it. (He is very delicate about shame, you know; consider the woman taken in adultery.) Our God is a merciful, lovable, tender God. So why should we carry guilt in our hearts when he doesn't?

The remedy for both shame and guilt is faith. We must begin to realize that *faith encompasses all things*. Life in Christ is a life of faith from beginning to end, reaching into the most minute details of man's existence. St. Paul says that the righteous man shall live by faith. When our faith is deep and true, there is no real problem in our Christian existence; for all things that appear insurmountable can be overcome by faith. Again, St. Paul said: "In all these things we are more than conquerors, through him who loved us." This does not mean that there is no place in the Christian life for suffering. Certainly there is. But faith is precisely that Divine Force which took

Jesus from Gethsemane to the resurrection.

The intellect (and our whole being) is subject to faith, or should be. Faith is a deep mystery of God, and he alone can give it, and we must constantly ask for an increase of it. Faith is directed toward the *invisible*, St. Paul tells the Hebrews. And here the word invisible means beyond the range of the mind as well as beyond that of our external senses. God is invisible. Yet God is not hidden, in the sense that he hides from us deliberately or withdraws his presence from us. He is a loving Father who desires to draw all his children to himself as closely as possible. If God is hidden, it is because he is out of the reach of our senses, our imagination, our mental perception. It is to his most sacred and hidden abode (symbolized by the clouds which covered Mount Sinai) that God calls his beloved children. The words of Jesus in the Gospel exactly express the Father's will: "Father, I desire that they may be with me, where I am."

Faith is the only way of penetrating that hidden abode; and in faith lies our answer to what we are seeking – how to fall in love with God so that we may fall in love with ourselves (in the way he wishes us to), and so that we may fall in love with our neighbor. Then we can fall in love with all humanity, and truly become people of the towel and the water. For only those *who love themselves in Christ* can bow low and kneel before the feet of the dirty, the stinking, the old, the young, the wise, the foolish, and wash the clay feet of humanity.

Lovingly yours in Mary,

PRIESTHOOD DAY

April 27, 1974

Dearly Beloved,

During Holy Week I gave some talks at noon and I thought that some of them could be a Staff Letter for you. I shared deeply with the Madonna House staff and I want to share the same with you.

———————

Today is Holy Thursday. Today is Priesthood Day. Yes, it is a strange, mysterious, unfathomable day, if you stop to think about it. It is the day when Christ brought forth the priesthood.

This statement is simple and yet incredible, for the Gospel tells us that Jesus, after his resurrection and before his ascension to his Father, berated the disciples because they weren't too happy to see him go to his Father. That seems like a contradiction because, in reality, Jesus himself didn't want to leave us either! It stands out clearly all through the Gospel. And because he didn't want to leave us, we have the priesthood now. In his immense love for us, he chose men from among those with whom he had walked and talked, men who would 'lift him up' and who could share with us that Bread and that Wine which Jesus said would give us life everlasting. Yes, and through those men he gave us 'living water' to drink – the water that he spoke of to the woman of Samaria. Once more, his incredible love for us is made visible.

You who come wandering into Madonna House seeking God ... seeking something, at least ... or simply out of curiosity: Do you ever wonder why we have this tremendous love for priests? Why do we rise when they come to the table for meals? Why do we relate to them with 'respectful informality'? The answer is simple: it is because when a priest walks into this house, *Christ walks in.* We know that in faith. At ordination, an ordinary man (probably with a normal sinful background) walks up three steps to an altar. Another man who is older and who is a bishop lays his hand on the head of the one to be ordained. There are prayers and ceremonies, and eventually the man descends and mingles with his brethren – a priest of God. Can anyone touch the mystery of this strange act?

Once, when I was visiting in Rome, a priest of a religious order told me that one of their bishops went to Moscow and ordained three men in a lavatory! So we don't need to have three steps and choirs and elaborate rituals – just a human being who desires to be a priest and a bishop to ordain him. In that immense fullness of the power of Christ which the bishop possesses, he can ordain a man in a men's room if he has to!

It isn't astonishing that, upon realizing this, one falls to one's knees, enveloped and absorbed in the mystery of God's love for us. *He didn't want to leave us orphans!* He wanted to give us someone in whom we could see his resemblance. I don't mean his physical resemblance, but the resemblance of that which he really is – the Lover, the Tender One, the Forgiving One, the Servant – one who would do what he did: wash the feet of humanity. But he did more! He gave the priest a special power so that, when he utters a few words, Christ washes our soul and embraces us in love and reconciliation. Christ comes to us, therefore, in such tremendous simplicity of love that our breath should be taken away. He comes to us in the guise of a priest!

But you will say, "What of the priest who is sinful and unholy, who 'leaps over the wall' to escape his commitments, who marries without dispensation?" You ask this because, in this country, you haven't been given the fullness of knowledge of what priesthood really is. Therefore, you don't realize that the 'seal of priesthood' has been *etched* into the soul of this poor sinful man. It has been placed there by the Fire of the Holy Spirit and the touch of the Father's hand; and that he can never lose that gift, that mark of predilection.

Seeing the Inner Man

In Russia, when the last Roman Catholic priest in my city died (he was killed before my very eyes), if there had been a priest who I knew had committed every mortal sin in the book (and who was, perhaps, living in the house of his mistress), I would have *crawled on my belly* to that man to receive the divine gifts he could give me. I couldn't have cared less about his mistress, or his other sinful ways. Because faith penetrates these things; it tears off the outer facade – that which I would have seen, the physical presence of a priest in sin – and it shows me the inner reality. Suddenly, in faith, I would have seen this man transfigured in divine glory. I would know that on his ordination day – in a strange, incredible fashion that cannot be explained at all because it is a mystery – this man was transfigured into Christ. I would know that, whether he is a sinner or not, *Christ in him* would absolve me.

We are dealing here with intangibles, with a mystery beyond our kenning. So remember this if you are faced with death under any circumstances, as I was faced with it in the Russian revolution. I would have crawled to that man to say: "Father, please hear my confession. Give me the Viaticum ('food for the journey' – the word we use for Holy Communion received when we are in danger of death)." And I wouldn't have worried about the man, for I would have seen the Christ in him.

You ask an awful lot of questions about priests, and a good many of them are irrelevant ... why do they get married, or do this or that or the other. Well, that's the humanness of them. But in them is Christ – always Christ!. They can bind him, for they are human beings just as we are; just as we can bind Christ by our sins, and scourge him, and crown him with thorns. But there is one thing in the priest which is very different from anyone else's soul; and that is: Christ will unbind himself in them *if anyone else needs him.*

We have to remember that the twelve apostles weren't perfect men. One left; one denied him for a while. One stuck around for the crucifixion, but the rest just turned their backs and kept running away from Golgotha as far as their legs could carry them. They were pretty ordinary guys.

Oftentimes we judge priests by human appraisal (their winning smile, their great knowledge, their savvy about one thing or another). All this is a lot of 'baloney' if I may say so! We should not judge a priest by his good looks, education, and so forth. We should just look at him and say to ourselves, "Thanks be to God he is here," because he is one of the greatest signs of God's love for us. (I still don't understand why Madonna House has fifteen priests when thousands of parishes throughout the world have none. But, of course, the Lord has his own ways, incomprehensible to us). So then, approach a priest with the understanding that he has 'God in him' in a special manner through his ordination. Approach him as you would approach Christ.

You who are women, guard your heart, your mind, and yourself, in a profound purity. When a priest leaves his priesthood duties to marry someone, that someone is almost more responsible than he is. We are all vessels of clay, but the woman has to carry her vessel of clay in what I would call 'the towel of Veronica.' According to legend, this woman wiped the face of Christ with a towel. For this act of kindness, she received the imprint of his Face on that cloth of hers. So we wrap our vessels of clay in that 'towel'; because if Christ is within us and shines forth from us, we will not tempt priests. So it is a good thing to remember that our heart faces the heart of Christ directly in the priesthood; and that we should not, in any way, seduce the man who through ordination has taken a vow of chastity. Just saying the name *Jesus* should be a balm to our hearts and a total restraint of our senses.

Addressing the Outer Man

Why do you want to criticize priests? Why should we criticize anyone? Christ told us, "Judge not and you shall not be judged." Priests deserve our deep respect. In Madonna House we stand when a priest comes into the room. We don't get up for the man; we get up for him who is Christ. This takes faith, deep faith. Here is a human being like you or me. But he is a special human being, someone before whom you can kneel and have your sins washed away. He is someone who can give you the Bread and Wine, which Christ died to give us so that we might have life everlasting.

The way to treat a priest is with *respectful* informality, and the accent is on the word respectful. I remember one time a priest arrived here and he was very drunk; so I put him to bed to 'sleep it off.' In the morning I brought him some coffee. He was bleary-eyed, and sort of 'lost'; but I knelt by his bed and asked him to bless me. He looked at me and said: "Do you realize who I am and what I did? Do you realize that I am a bum?" I answered, "Yes, but you are a priest also and I ask for your blessing, for *it is Christ's blessing!*" He blessed me, and then he started to cry.

I remember another time when I was ten years old, and our family went to Poland for a vacation. I was walking down the road when suddenly, there in the mire, I saw the parish priest of this village. Now I had been brought up from babyhood to love and reverence priests, and this just completely shattered my little heart! I ran away from the place as though the devil were chasing me. I ran home to my mother and said: "There's Monsignor, and he is drunk, drunk, drunk! The priest is drunk!"

Mother looked at me and said: "Is that so? Then let's go to him." With her holding my hand, we retraced my steps in silence. When we came to the priest, still lying there in the mud, my mother said: "Catherine, you are a big girl. Help me to lift him up." Before we did so, however, she kissed his dirty hand. Then we carried him into the presbytery where, still silently, she handed him to the woman in charge.

In silence we walked back home. When we got there, my mother asked me to go into the baby's room and get his little potty, fill it with water, and bring it to her. While I did so, she gathered a bunch of beautiful white lilies from the garden. When I arrived with the potty, she put the bouquet into the potty and said: "Look at that. The white lilies don't change, though they sit in a potty instead of in a beautiful vase. Always remember that, Catherine. The potty might be the priest. The white lily is Christ, the

Christ who never changes, the Christ who is in the priest in a special way. Yes, the priest might be the potty, but the 'Christ in him' always remains just like those lilies. Never in your life make the mistake of mixing the two together!"

I wish that I could truly tell you what a priest is. I remember when I was twelve and living in Alexandria, in Egypt, and going to a convent school. A priest came and gave us a retreat. And at the end he said to us all, "When you grow up, you can begin to pray for priests." I was an impatient person, however, so I sought an interview with this holy Jesuit. Immediately I asked permission to start praying for priests now, at the age of twelve, instead of waiting until I was twenty or so. He granted me that permission and blessed me, and I have been praying for priests ever since.

Holy Thursday is to me a gift beyond all measuring, for God has given us the Blessed Sacrament – the Last Supper. Each year I remember vividly that, on that day, the Lord didn't want to leave us, and so chose priests to keep reminding us that *he is with us in a human body.* A priest is a lover of God. A priest is a lover of men. A priest is a holy man because he walks before the face of the Almighty! The Russians say that the face of God is reflected in the face of the people; so the priest who offers the Eucharist must reflect the Eucharist.

A priest understands all things. A priest forgives all things. A priest encompasses all things. Perhaps he doesn't intellectually understand many things better than you or I do; but he understands much more than we think he understands, because Christ is his teacher. Look at St. Jean Vianney, who is now the 'patron' of parish priests. He was almost thrown out of the seminary because he couldn't do well in his studies; yet he became a saint, and a great confessor. That is what I mean by 'understanding.'

Getting a Sense of Direction

Incidentally, this is the whole essence of spiritual direction. A priest isn't a person to whom you go with all of your psychological hang-ups. He isn't a man you just 'run to' because X,Y, or Z was unkind to you. You go to a priest to say: "Father, I have sinned." You go to a priest to be absolved. You go to a priest to say, "Father, show me the way to God." The Holy Spirit teaches him, and it is through him that we find God more easily than we would alone.

What do I mean about his knowledge? A priest stands before a directee and – first and foremost – he is the great listener. His heart has two ears: one is listening to the Holy Spirit and the other to the directee. (The Lord who is in him makes this possible.) St. John of the Cross, a magnificent saint, says of the spiritual director: "He doesn't do anything. He just watches the work of the Holy Spirit in the souls of his directees, and gets the infinite grace from the Trinity to move those who come to him further along the road toward their union with God."

I have been baptized into the death and resurrection of Jesus Christ, but my baptism is only a first step to that union with God. The spiritual director helps me to be more and more united with God; without him I could reach my goal only with difficulty, because the heat of the day would crush me. There is no denying that all of us need the help of spiritual direction to move along the road to heaven. It is *the essence of my soul* that I open up to him! I do this so that he might lead me by a 'shortcut' (as it were) to God!

The heart of a priest is pierced like Christ's with a lance of love. But all of us must pray that this love in their hearts keeps on growing. With hearts pierced as Christ's heart was pierced, they will lovingly lift you and me up. And it is this that we are seeking – this 'lifting up unto Christ.' So that is what we seek from our priests, this spiritual direction.

The love of a priest is a benediction, for it is God loving you; and because God knows that we are human and frail and sinful, and full of doubts and fears, he has given us *people* to show us love – his love! The heart of a priest is the resting place of human and divine love. This is a truly beautiful thought: his heart is a chalice where man and God meet in him whom God has ordained to show his Christ-love to the world. Truly, this should make one's faith soar into the cosmos!

A priest is a man whose goal is to be another Christ.

A priest is a man who lives to serve. A priest is a man who has crucified himself so that he, too, can be lifted up and draw all things to Christ. A priest is a man in love with God. A priest is a gift of God to man, and of man to God. (Once upon a time, I hoped that my son might be a priest; I thought that would be my greatest gift, if God desired it. But God did not desire it.)

A priest is a symbol of the Word made flesh. A priest is the naked sword of God's justice. A priest is the hand of God's mercy, and a priest is the reflection of God's love. Nothing in this world can be greater than a priest – nothing but God himself!

This is Holy Thursday. On this holy day, in this most holy of weeks, the priesthood (as we understand it) was born into the world. On this day, the Holy Eucharist was instituted to feed us. The Last Supper became the beggar's meal, nourishing us poor sinners in the divine life. Therefore, the greatest gift that a priest can give to our world is to offer that Divine Sacrifice and to feed us with God!

I know that when I try to say something about the priesthood, I just get 'all thumbs' as far as my tongue is concerned. There is nothing I can say, really. What can one say of the love of God in the shape of man?

Lovingly yours in Mary,

OUR STRUGGLE WITH FOOLISHNESS

May 22, 1974

Dearly Beloved,

In the beautiful and incredible week of Easter – the week of Christ's resurrection – I made a poustinia. It was a very special day, and I have a most extraordinary word to bring to you, my beloved ones. The word is *foolishness*.

All day long, the words Christ said to St. Francis kept coming to my mind: "... for the Lord said to me that he wanted me to be a simpleton the like of which was never seen before." It occurred to me that these words blended with Easter week, for Christ exhibited a greater 'foolishness' than St. Francis did. Probably he told St. Francis about it because he himself had experienced it.

Can you imagine, dearly beloved, anything more foolish than dying on a cross? I had been thinking of several other ways in which God could have saved us. But then I 'understood' the depths of *sin*, in a manner of speaking. I recalled that the word sin in Hebrew means 'to forget.' Because we forget God, Christ came to make us remember!

Had he not chosen this pathway of suffering and agony, we would too easily 'forget' that we had been saved; or else we would disbelieve that we were ever 'saveable.' And in this remembering is our salvation. He has achieved it through his incarnation, life, humiliation, and death.

As I contemplated these thoughts, I realized that foolishness and wisdom are interchangeable. I realized also why I had to bring that word to you. Nevertheless, I wanted to know its real meaning, so I kept asking myself throughout the day: "What does it really mean?" I couldn't answer it immediately. There was something that eluded me. I didn't know what it was, but there was something that I couldn't grasp.

It was only toward evening that I began to understand that to be a fool for Christ's sake is to love him passionately, to leave all things to be one of his companions, and – forgetting all else! – to be concerned with serving him alone. It also means to have an immense courage. I suddenly understood that my beloved prayer – "Give me the heart of a child, and the awesome courage to live it out as an adult!" – is somehow part of all of this. Because only a child, or an adult with a childlike heart, can be a fool for Christ's sake.

Christ was a fool in men's eyes, and we have to have the courage to be as foolish as he was. We must have the courage to be a nonconformist (as he was), to appear singular, and to be willing to face the ridicule which that brings. Each one of these things, until we absorb them slowly and lovingly, are like a sword in our heart. They are the essence of our struggle with God.

There is more to this 'being a fool.' We must be willing to speak the truth, as jesters of old spoke the foolishness of truth to the kings. We must speak the truth to all whom we meet. That is going to be difficult, for our manner of speaking the truth must be varied. At times the truth will frighten us, for it will demand a courage which may lead us almost to death. Who can tell? Jesus said: "Go and preach the Good News to the world." That is the truth we must give to others. Only recently, a nun told me that she couldn't face people who weren't Christians. She was afraid of proclaiming the truth. So many of us are afraid of speaking the truth to each other!

Yes, we have to practice foolishness for Christ's sake. He wants us to be fools the like of which the world has not seen before, and he gives us St. Francis to show us the way, to help us expose ourselves to ridicule. St. Francis took two branches from a tree and pretended that he was playing music on a violin. That sort of thing requires courage. It isn't necessary for us to cut off any tree branches. We just have to cut off 'the strings of our heart' and let them play the music – the foolish music of one who follows Christ until the end. (It is all sort of inconceivable, and yet it stares me in my face. It stares me in my heart.) We must turn to God in prayer:

Lord, how can I be a fool for your sake? I thought that I was being a fool for you. What more do you want from me, my Love? What more do you want? You always want more, Lord, always more. You want it not only from me but from the community also. We must be fools about money. We must receive it in order to give it away. We must rely entirely on you. Here is where foolishness becomes wisdom, and wisdom gives us the key to faith ... or perhaps it is the other way around. Perhaps faith is the key to wisdom, and wisdom is the face of foolishness, which is your face, O Lord!

Yes, we must *give away* money. We must not only give it away, but detach our heartstrings from it. Yes, foolishness enters even into the financial aspect of Madonna House. Foolishness must also be in what we do; anything and everything we 'work at' must be approached with the foolishness of God. There must always be prayer, and an identification with the Lord. We must ask:

Lord, what would you do in a case like this or that? You want us to be foolish like St. Francis; in other words, you want us to be "foolish with your wisdom." Then give us the grace to accept it, because *we are so afraid of your wisdom; so very afraid!*
Lord, your wisdom is based on the darkness of faith, so give us the courage to walk in that darkness. Give it now, Lord! Give us courage to walk in that darkness of faith, and to let our 'foolishness' be the light to guide our way. It is not easy to make it into a lantern to light our path and that of our neighbor. But we accept to do so ... simply because we love you, because your voice is heard in our hearts, because you are calling us to the 'impossible' (which with you is always possible).
Today, Lord, while I was in the poustinia, I faintly heard your call to me to 'move on' to a greater faith. But your voice was disguised to me, in your words to St. Francis. But now I understand, and I answer you with a *yes!* Let us of Madonna House be fools for

Christ's sake – greater fools, perhaps, than St. Francis – for all things are possible to you, Lord. In your 'foolishness' there is wisdom, and this is the wisdom that alone will conquer the world.

In our daily 'world' of Madonna House, that nitty-gritty life of ours, there are a thousand possibilities a day to be fools for your sake. Help us to see those possibilities, and to act on them. Keep us in your 'foolish' heart, O Lord!

I suggest to you, my dear ones, as you read this letter from my Easter-week poustinia, that you discuss it 'wisely.' In your spiritual conversations, enumerate the various areas in which one can be 'foolish' in Christ's way.

Take *forgiveness,* for instance. In such a setting, you expose yourself to ridicule for his sake, but you are not afraid of any hurts because you remember that the Lord has been so terribly hurt for us. And in that deep wisdom (which to the world looks foolish), you wish to share his pain and sufferings as closely and as fully as possible. You do so because you love him so intensely, and because you have learned to be unafraid of rejection. This attitude may be seem foolish to most people, but it is wisdom according to the Lord.

Yes, in the nitty-gritty life of the Madonna House Apostolate there are a thousand ways of being foolish for his sake, of being a simpleton, of being a child at heart (even though we are adults).

Help us, Lord, to see the wisdom of that foolishness. For by entering it we shall bring wisdom to the world. Amen.

Lovingly yours in Mary,

JOY IS THE KEY TO FREEDOM

June 6, 1974

Dearly Beloved,

Whenever charity permits, I go to my little poustinia every Friday. I like my little poustinia very much. It is simple and small; originally it was a little barn made of logs. It has only a wood stove, a table, a chair, a bed, and a Bible, just as all of the other poustinias do.

Remember, however, that one does not go to the poustinia for oneself only but for the community. If one is married, then one goes for the family, the parish, the neighbors, as well as for the whole world. Therefore, one must be ready to share with others the key thought that God has revealed in the poustinia. The Russians call it the word that God has left in one's heart after spending twenty-four hours alone with him in fasting and prayer.

Last Friday, the word that I came out with was *joy*. It seemed like a very strange word to me because it appeared to be rooted in pain. I couldn't fathom how this was possible. People strive desperately for peace, happiness, and joy. In our minds, all of these mean the total absence of any kind of pain, whether emotional, intellectual, or what-have-you. Yet in my poustinia the word joy seemed to have deep roots in pain.

Still wondering, I began to leaf through the Bible and to look at the concordance. Then a phrase came to me from Psalm 126: "They who sow in tears will reap in joy." I remembered that in Isaiah (29:19) we read that "the meek will increase their joy." And Matthew speaks again and again of the "joy of the Lord." John says that "his joy is fulfilled" and "that your joy also may be filled." In Romans 14:17, the kingdom of God is joy.

Having considered it further, I began to understand this 'poustinia word' that the Lord was giving me to share with the community of Madonna House. Christ spoke of the immense joy of eating the Pasch with his disciples just before he died. He died after being tortured, and it was a terrible death on the cross – let's face that fact! – and yet that, too, was an act of joy.

Slowly, like a child learning to walk, I began to understand the meaning of this word given to me in my poustinia. This joy was *the key to freedom.* If one enters this kind of joy, then one is truly free. So, God was giving me the key to freedom.

I looked back on my life, and I saw that there was much pain in it. Ever since I left my parents and went with my husband through the first World War and the Russian Revolution, ever since I became a refugee and a stranger in so many places, I had (in a manner of speaking) 'put forth roots' into the domain of Lady Pain. But the Lord had given me the gift of *fiat.* So I allowed my roots to grow more and more deeply into that land of pain. Slowly, it cleansed and healed me. It healed me of memories, healed me of many things that could have wrecked my life. I was healed and given peace. Slowly again, imperceptibly, I began to know joy and freedom – freedom from all of the things that people seem to find so very important, and I entered into the freedom of God. Don't ask me how it happened, but on that Friday in May, in my poustinia, I knew freedom ... and a joy beyond any understanding! And, my friends, I knew a peace that is also beyond understanding.

There is nothing of myself in all of this; it is of God. I wish I could impart to you the fantastic state that this freedom and joy gives, even though the roots of both are still growing in the land of pain. One thing I know is that those who pass through pain, in faith and love, receive from God what I think are 'the keys of his Kingdom' – peace, joy, freedom.

I wish that I could share all of these with you because with them go tenderness, compassion, and understanding. Can I share them with you? I really don't know. I simply bring it to the family of Madonna House and leave it in your hands ... and in your hearts. That is all that I can do.

If you desire to talk about it, don't hesitate to ask. It will be a difficult question to answer, however, for it has to be experienced.

Lovingly yours in Mary,

THE DESERT OF THE HEART

November 26, 1974

Dearly Beloved,

It is time for us to enter into emptiness! All around us, in my heart and in your hearts, there is confusion. In fact, there is terrific violence and tragic confusion throughout the whole world. The Lord says to all of us, "Where is your brother Abel?" And we keep answering in so many words, "Am I my brother's keeper?" Today we, the people of God, are not murdering one person (as Cain did to Abel); we are murdering hundreds, thousands, with hijacking, bombs, and other forms of violence. That is why we must enter into *emptiness.*

The desert is emptiness. It is a strange emptiness. It is not ugly. It is not really a total emptiness because one sees flowers, insects, and all kinds of creatures there; but for human beings it is emptiness. It isn't a physical desert that we are asked to enter, like that of the Sahara. It is the desert of the heart ... my heart and your heart. We have to enter it in order to see ourselves, for that is the function of the desert, its 'vocation' so to speak. It is there to strip us of all illusions, of all the wrong images we have about ourselves, of all that is a sham within us. It will strip us and show us to ourselves as nothing else can.

The moment of this 'facing oneself' is a difficult and excruciating moment because it is here – in this desert of our own hearts – that we meet the Evil One. The Lord has created us 'free.' The Lord has created us 'good.' Nothing that the Lord did binds us or hinders us. We are totally free *to choose good or evil.* And it is in this inner desert, this 'emptiness of heart,' that we begin to understand that God didn't cause the Vietnam War (or all of the other evils that besiege us). Human beings have caused them to happen! We ourselves do this whenever we choose evil against good.

Yes, at various times, throughout our whole lives, we choose so many 'Vietnams'! This is our answer to God whenever he asks what we have done with our brother. We keep repeating the words of Cain, "Am I my brother's keeper?" Before this constantly repeated answer of man to God, there is only one place to which we can go, and that is into the emptiness of the inner desert. It is there that we face the human condition and we begin to examine our individual conscience, which seems to be so totally asleep.

If we really undertake this 'journey inward'* into our hearts – that journey which every mortal must undertake – we will meet God. And if we do not enter our inner desert to find the Triune God who dwells there, we shall face *another* emptiness. It is 'the emptiness of desolation' – a desolation that we have created for ourselves through our Western arrogance, our Western avarice. It may well be an emptiness with few survivors, an emptiness we have created by flaunting our technology – the atom bomb. Unless we enter the 'desert of God' to become empty of all that is not God, we will know the 'desert of despair,' whose emptiness is terrifying. Which one are we going to choose?

Yes, we must enter the desert of our own heart. We must empty it as thoroughly as a room is emptied so its

* Also the title of a book by Catherine, published in 1984 by Alba House, New York.

wooden floor can be sanded and waxed, its walls and ceiling washed and replastered and freshly painted. Everything must come out; and most of the knickknacks and clutter must never be allowed to return to that room of ours. We must go deeply into our hearts *today,* for time is short.

If we do not go into the desert of our own hearts and allow this emptiness to cleanse us, others will do it for us! But then it will lack that 'creative' emptiness of sorrow, and of compunction. There will be no contrition. There will be only the emptiness which must have filled the hearts of the women of Ramah as they cried over their children, the Holy Innocents,* lying dead in their arms.

Is our emptiness a quiet, holy emptiness? Is it the emptiness of waiting? There *is* such an emptiness, you know, and it is beautiful. It is the waiting for a Child to be born within us. He will make our desert bloom with beautiful flowers, a place where everyone can come to enjoy a divine fragrance, where many will gather blossoms to carry on their pilgrimage.

Or has our desert become an arid land overrun with thorn bushes, its prickly tendrils tearing at clothes and skin, a place where we seek the fulfillment of earthly desires for wealth, power, and things? Is it filled with those desires? No matter what price we might have to pay for them? Yes, we can 'kill' ourselves without any other hands intervening, without Herod's soldiers descending upon us seeking to destroy our offspring. We do it by letting our hearts be cluttered with urgent desires for useless things, none of which are of God.

How empty can we make ourselves? For emptiness is like a net, a fisherman's net, one that is woven out of humility, out of love, tenderness, gentleness. It is the emptiness of a womb, one that is preparing for a better world, by having us become pregnant with God. We prepare for this as the Virgin Mary prepared, by becoming lovers of God, by cleansing the desert of our hearts of all wrongful desires, by creating a resting place for a Little Child.

---

* An allusion to Matthew 2:16-18 and Jeremiah 31:15.

That kind of emptiness becomes an 'inn' where my brother can rest and be refreshed. It is a lodging place where he comes to sleep peacefully, not to die in agony. Like Cain, we too can murder our brother! We can do it in a thousand ways, not just with revolver, shotgun, knife, or bomb. We can murder with *words,* which are worse than all the array of modern weapons. We can suffocate our brothers and sisters by giving a beautiful speech at some world assembly. The spoken word is a powerful arsenal; it can engineer the euthanasia of an entire nation. There are many ways we can murder, while seeming to help those around us, if our hearts are not filled with love, tenderness, gentleness.

Yes, the desert awaits us, within ourselves, calling us as only a desert can. Shall we begin that 'journey inward' which all men must take to meet the God who dwells within? It is the most important thing we should think about just now. On entering that desert, in allowing ourselves to become cleansed and renewed by it, we will begin our union with God. And those who are united with God are also united with their fellow creatures. Such a one brings peace – God's peace – to all creation.

But how are we going to do all of this? It seems so utterly impossible! Emptiness? Desert? Surrendering all that we have (or most of it)? Pilgriming within our own soul toward the Absolute? Seeking to be united totally with him? How 'on earth' are we going to do all of this?

The answer comes simply, humbly, clearly: by prayer. *Only by prayer.* The world today is filled with such confusion that the human mind just can't absorb it; neither can the human heart. People are finally beginning to suspect that, without God, they can do nothing! So this is the time to become that pilgrim. This is the hour to enter the emptiness of the inner desert, to clear some land and build a little poustinia,* and there to truly learn how to pray. For prayer alone will remove

* A Russian word that means both 'desert' and 'place of prayer,' so named in memory of the early Christians who went into the deserts of Egypt and Palestine to pray for themselves and for the world.

whatever does not belong in that desert of the heart.
Listen! Listen! Emptiness calls you, just as it keeps
calling me. Our hearts ache to become free from the clutter
which fills them now, that burdensome clutter of 'self.' Let
us listen to the soft wind which blows across the desert
wastes. We will hear the voice of God saying: "I am
coming to the desert of your heart. When it is empty, you
and I – together – will make it bloom, and save the world
once more!"

Lovingly yours in Mary,

Catherine

A CHRISTMAS OF ATONEMENT

December 1974

Dearly Beloved,

This year I come to wish you a Christmas of poverty.
For he who was born on this day so many years ago,
whose birthday we celebrate again with a gratitude beyond
all kenning, was born in poverty. *He who was God was
born naked.* He was naked in a cave, and he died naked on
a cross for love. For the love of us all!
Today the same scene reenacts itself from sea to sea,
from mountain to mountain, from city to city, from village
to village. For there is no wealthy or underprivileged
country which does not have its 'caves' where children are

born naked (as all babies are), but whose parents have nothing to put on their newborn infants. Jesus, at least, was wrapped in swaddling clothes.

I needn't go into the specifics of the great poverty in today's world; it is already brought to us in all its gory details by the media. Because God loves us, he uses these incredible and forceful pictures to draw the world's attention to what the poor are suffering. Do you see, dearly beloved, why I come to wish you a Christmas of poverty? What other Christmas can I extend to you in this Year of Grace, 1974?

Yet there is another Christmas Wish I can offer you. It is one that I can lay in your hearts: Let this Christmas be *a Christmas of Atonement.* Let us fast for those who have nothing to eat. Let us pray for those who don't pray. Let us cry out to God with an ever greater faith so that all around us can 'catch the fire' of faith. May they be moved by the flames of compassion, tenderness, gentleness, and service toward those who have no earthly goods – and those who have too many of them! – beholding how both are caught in the pain of it.

Having offered you my wishes for this Christmas, I call you to a celebration because the feast is so immense; the joy in our hearts should be so great as to overwhelm us! Our gratitude, like a rare perfume, should be spilled, not at the feet of Christ only, but on 'the whole Christ' ... which means on all of our brothers and sisters. Let us bring our great joy to this tender feast. Let us celebrate it with song and dance.

This year, fasting and feasting must go together. Yes, tears and joy must mingle to make an offering for the Infant, an offering of diamonds and pearls and other jewels – all kinds of atonement! For today's Infant is every child who is born in shacks and in streets, or discarded in garbage cans or sewers; and we must take the place of the Kings.

Here at our training center, we have tried to implement this in one particular way. We are going to put on display the dolls of a hundred different countries, each dressed in native costume. But there will be no sweets of that country in front of them. We are going to have our

38

usual collation,* but without such confections. We are
making cookies, of course, but not for ourselves. They are
for others in this rural area, a token of friendship to those
who otherwise might not have much in the way of
presents. We have given our jams and jellies away, too, as
well as half of the apples which had been donated to us.

We intend to dance around the crib and the manger.
Our fasting and prayer will make us more graceful
dancers. Our joy and pain will be combined, as at
Golgotha, and so the joy of the Resurrection will also be in
our hearts. We shall celebrate the birth of our God and
King, and we shall pray:

> *Lord,*
> *Give bread to the hungry,*
> *And 'hunger for you'*
> *To those who have bread.*

Thus we will embrace the poor and the rich, and
everyone in between. He was born for us all, and for all of
us he died, and for all of us he was resurrected. A joyous,
tender Christmas to you. Personally, I ask for you a heart
ever more united to his. Alleluia!

Lovingly yours in Mary,

Catherine

---

* "A light meal, especially at an unusual time." Catherine refers to the meal at 2
a.m., after Midnight Mass on Christmas.

A LONG JOURNEY

March 21, 1975

Dearly Beloved,

It began with a phone call. From faraway Arizona, a blurred voice stated in stark words that Father Eddie* had had a heart seizure and that his lungs were filling up. Now there was only one question: how long would he last? Death seemed imminent, so the voice on the phone said.

It was at that moment that I began my long journey. It was a strange journey. You know, you can walk very far, standing still. You can go on pilgrimage along many paths, by just waiting. I stood still; and I waited. In that waiting, I realized that I was truly starting on a long journey into faith. The whole, immense scene of faith was set forth before me, and I looked at it with new eyes. A mystery that I cannot explain took place in my heart.

Father Eddie and I had discussed death quite often – death in general, and our own deaths in particular. We were always peaceful about it, for both of us felt that "death was but a door to life." Now, confronted over the telephone with the reality of having to accept Father Eddie's death, I remembered our conversations. And I asked myself whether I really believed that "death is the door to life."

Time seemed endless in that standing, and waiting, and inner journeying. At a certain moment of this timelessness, I realized that I did indeed believe ... *Credo!* Yes, I believed. I believed with a faith that was transformed, filled with joy; it brought me peace beyond any ability to put into words. There was within me a 'total acceptance' of Father Eddie's death and (strange as this might seem) a joy over it, a joy that surpassed understanding.

---

* Catherine's husband. In 1969, two and a half months before his 79th birthday, he became a priest in the Melkite Rite (a part of the Catholic Church which allows married clergy).

I have always believed in the resurrection of Our Lord Jesus Christ. After the phone call, for some unaccountable reason, this resurrection suddenly stood in the middle of all my thoughts. Jesus was born for us, he suffered for us, he was crucified for us, he died for us. *And he resurrected!* Because he did, I had this utter sense of faith within me. It was a deep, immovable, definite faith that began to make the waiting easy and the journey light.

Then came the next day, and the next step of my long journey. Again the telephone rang and told me, not of the death of Father Eddie, but that his lungs had cleared and his heart was okay. Nevertheless, he was to remain in that hospital in Winslow, Arizona. (As you know, he has been spending the winter months at our house there because our rugged Canadian climate is too much for his heart to take.)

So I went to Arizona. This meant going to Toronto, then a series of cars, planes, trains ... simple, pleasant things. It was the second step of my journey, the inward journey that I was traveling along with the outer one. It was something else again. I asked myself if I was afraid of the darkness that surrounded me; for when one walks in faith one walks in total darkness, the darkness of a mystery beyond one's kenning. I asked myself if I was afraid. Again, I had to answer that I wasn't, even though I knew that the strange miracle of Father Eddie's being still alive was perhaps but an interlude, and that I was hastening to be present at his bedside, just in case ...

No, I wasn't afraid of the darkness. The darkness, though a mystery, though dark to me, was not really a darkness in faith. It was light, for faith is a gift of God; and anything that comes from God's hands is never dark. It is always light, though at the time I couldn't 'see' the light (in the way that one can look up and see the moon). Not at all. But I did see the *effect* of that light – an infinite peace as though I were reposing in the arms of Christ, and hearing the heartbeats of God. And so, through what was darkness, I saw light. That was the second step of my journey.

Then came the third step. I was met by our staff in Winslow and whisked away to the hospital and into the Intensive Care Unit. I walked into Father Eddie's room. He was awake. We looked at each other, and our hands touched. I asked him how he was and he replied: "Full of peace and contentment. All is well." Then he fell asleep. I sat for a while by his bedside. There, in a hospital room, once more I faced death. And I knew her to be a friend who, someday, would take me also by the hand and lead me into the heart of the Father.

As I often say, we come from the 'head' of the Father to return to the 'heart' of the Father; and it all came together in that hospital room. There was Jesus Christ, who is the Way to the Father's heart. (For he said, "I am the Way.") There was the Holy Spirit, who is there to remind us of everything that God said, so that we might walk with assured steps along this Way (who is Jesus). Yes, in the dead of the night, in the Intensive Care Unit of a little hospital, death led me to the Trinity. Strange as this might seem, my heart leapt with joy. The third step of my long journey was achieved.

I stayed in Arizona a week or so, visiting Father Eddie every day; and our love of many years came to perfect fruition. Our strange 'tree' of marriage bore this lovely 'fruit' ... a deep, profound, peaceful love, one that lived in the heart of the Lord. I remembered that it was almost twenty-one years since we had taken a vow of chastity, Father Eddie and I. I thought of how, in 1969, with the permission of the Holy See, he was ordained a priest. And it now was 1975.

My journey into faith had opened a new vista, a view of life so filled with God's graces that, in this humble hospital room, I knew the fruit of our lives together. Strange, isn't it, how death can lead you to the appreciation of life, how it can make your heart overflow with gratitude to God. It did mine!

Then it was time to return to Canada. Father Eddie said that, indeed, it was time for us to go about our Father's business – for me to go back to my work in Madonna House, while his 'apostolate' was to be in that bed. So I turned around and retraced my steps to Combermere again. My other journey – that long, long journey into faith which I seemed to have undertaken along with the geographical journey – was not turned around, however. I was not going back in exactly the same way. On the contrary! I was going forward – forward into the 'arms of faith' – to be embraced, to be held so tightly, so warmly, so wonderfully, so much at peace!

But the terrain had changed. The 'hand of faith' now led me along a path that went winding upwards to a beautiful mountain. I hastened to climb it. I was still 'waiting upon' the Will of God; I was still standing still, silently holding onto the 'hand of faith' (for faith is also in stillness and silence). But, somehow or other, I was rushing up that mountain! I returned to Combermere, and my inward life settled onto two levels – waiting for a telephone call from Arizona about Father Eddie's condition; and rushing up that strange mountain, so vivid before my eyes, so totally unseen by others.

One day, I heard that Father Eddie was coming back to Combermere. He came by mercy flight, then by ambulance, but finally he arrived! Today he is here, getting better, having no pain, sitting up, recovering; and I think I have reached some height on my mountain. The Lord shows us things from mountain tops; he showed me death. I knew her to be a 'smiling child' waiting to bring me to the Christ Child. I knew her to be beautiful because she wasn't really death but life – life renewed, life exploding, life lived in the heart of the Trinity!

I share with you my long, long journey. If any of you are afraid of death, stop it. Stop being afraid. Enter into faith. If your faith seems small, cry out to the Lord that it might increase! Then you, too, will see death for who and what she really is – someone conquered by Christ on the day of his resurrection, and delighted with being conquered!*

Lovingly yours in Mary,

Catherine

---

* Father Edward J. Doherty died May 4, 1975, six weeks after this letter was dictated.

OUR CABLE TO CHRIST'S HEART

October 14, 1975

Dearly Beloved,

I have been praying quite a bit about poverty. As you may have noticed, it was one of the big themes of the local directors' meetings. This time we approached it from a sort of 'depth' angle. At the same time, we realized that it also includes the question of physical poverty (which I call 'kindergarten' poverty), though we presume that most of our members already have passed that stage of it.

In our discussions, however, many questions continued to surface regarding this 'physical' poverty as well as that of the deeper kind. I have been praying about it constantly these days, because *poverty is the fruit of faith, of love, and of hope.* I have had a strange feeling lately that, somehow or other, the beautiful and immense 'cable' that moors our little 'barge' to the Heart of Christ was slowly being 'chewed up' by rodents, 'mice or rats' sent to us by Satan.

You know, dearly beloved, you are beautiful people! We all are. We persevere minute in and minute out; hour in and hour out; year in and year out. In our perseverance, we exhibit the beautiful virtues of love, of patience, of prayer. I need not go into the rest of the virtues, many and wonderful as they are. You know them as well as I do. But Satan does not like this picture at all! And he knows that he cannot always attack us by the 'simple and ordinary sins' to which the human condition is constantly prey. So he tries to attack each of us by little peccadillos, the little human failings that seemingly "don't matter." These are the tiny faults, or not so tiny ones, that we take for granted. Let us look carefully at those tiny things which, like mice and rats, can eat through the tremendous and strong cord which binds us to Jesus Christ.

This may be tiny question, but it is of the essence ...

may I ask you: How many of you have reported money received from your relatives and friends? Our 'way of life' (our Constitution) is easy, gentle, loving; but, in accordance with its rule, each of us has taken a promise of poverty (either yearly, or for two years, or for life). What does that promise mean to us?

Yes, we are allowed to possess money, to have an individual bank account; for we are lay people, not Trappist monks or nuns. Our promise of poverty, then, is one of *permission* – meaning that we cannot 'spend' one penny without asking permission from our director. If you have received permission in the past, you should not take that guideline for granted; you cannot always 'presume' permission. Tell your director how much you have received, and abide by his or her decision about what to do with the money. Otherwise, you fail in your promise of poverty. That is what our Constitution says; and I think it is time we examined our consciences on that. Do this prayerfully – very prayerfully! – because it is of tremendous importance.

Because of our benefactors, we are able to have 'treats' occasionally. We should go into this question thoroughly and see if we are allowing the little mice of 'self-indulgence' – or the big rats of 'fulfilling all our non-needs' – to gnaw away at the cords which bind us to Jesus Christ. Are those cords beginning to fray? (If they are not broken today, they will be tomorrow.) Those strands need to be rewoven and made secure. I would suggest a fast day to be established, once a week at least, even if it is only for one meal.

We are too comfortable. When you consider what is happening in the world, it looks as though we live not only like suburbia but like 'rich' suburbia. Very few of us could afford what we now have, if God had not brought us to Madonna House. We *talk* about poverty, yes; but we are very far from 'identification with the poor' ... even, sometimes, on a spiritual basis. We continue to eat better and better as we are given good food. But 'just around the corner' if I may say so, grown-ups and children are dying from hunger.

I speak mostly of the situation at the training center in

Combermere; but let us look around at our mission houses. We should keep them cozy and pleasant for our visitors, but they could be a little less 'cute' or what-have-you. Let us make them a little more stark, somewhat as our poustinias are. *Let us keep them more simple, a little more poor.*

Unless there is a need for immediacy or urgency, let us use buses as a way of 'pilgrimage.' The bus line is the resort of the poor who can't afford railroad tickets or air fare. Yes, there is a grave danger that, while discussing poverty with everybody else, we may indulge in an almost total lack of it. These have been our discussions, and these have been my prayers. I share them with you.

Lovingly yours in Mary,

LISTENING

October 17, 1975

Dearly Beloved,

At night, after I have walked across my footbridge onto the island and entered St. Kate's cabin (which I call my 'igloo'), I often pause before a half-finished jigsaw puzzle and try to figure out where to 'fit in' a few pieces. Sometimes I sit down and start to read a good detective story. But often I fall asleep for a couple of hours. Then I wake up, with a great desire to pray. In Russia – because we think that it is God who wakes us up in order to 'talk to us' – we say these are *the vigils of God.*

It is about this 'talking' that I want to write today. I feel that there is a great deal of noise in our hearts. We have to learn to reduce it to a gentle silence that listens to God. We need to do what the Gospel says: "Make straight the paths of the Lord" in our own hearts. To do this, we need to pray to the Lord for a 'bulldozer' to push away the rockfall and the debris. God will do this for us if we stop the swirling dust of our own mutterings, the constant using of the pronoun *I,* our thinking that we are always right and someone else is wrong, our non-listening to our own brothers and sisters.

The world which ebbs and flows around us today is a hungry world, and not necessarily for food. People are hungry for friendship, for understanding, for someone to talk to, for someone who really listens! But who of us ordinary mortals can 'really listen,' with the ear of our heart wide open, taking in every word that other person says?

The weight of listening is heavy. That is why we need to pray for a spiritual bulldozer to make straight the ways of the Lord in our hearts. Then God himself might walk these paths, unencumbered. He can come into our hearts and do the listening there. He can listen to others through us, talk through us, understand through us, help through us. He can console those who come to us. If the paths of our hearts were made straight, he would 'come running'! He wants to be with us until the end of time, as he said in the Gospel, and he still desires to serve. And what better service could there be than to have a listening ear of God in our hearts?

It is time, dearly beloved, time to pray so that we might listen to the hunger of others. Usually people don't want us to do too much for them. They want us to listen because *listening means love and friendship,* for which there is such a great hunger today.

Yes, I wake up in the night to these strange vigils of God. They don't last long, but they are etched powerfully on my heart and I want to share them with you. My words might be clumsy; they may not convey what I wish to convey, but share them I must.

Lovingly yours in Mary,

PERSEVERANCE

November 5, 1975

Dearly Beloved,

Lately I have been thinking a lot about perseverance. The dictionary gives a short explanation. Of the word *persevere* it says: "To be steadfast; maintain an endeavor; to persist in following a course to a definite goal, especially a spiritual one." This is a cold sentence which doesn't mean much, but gives some sort of essence of the word.

But in my heart, as I prayed about it, its meaning became so much deeper. Perseverance is the flowering of the love of God. It grows and grows and grows, descending upon a soul like a cascade of flowers, like bougainvillea in the West Indies. As time goes on, both the flowering tree and the flowers hanging from it become big enough to offer shade to oneself and to many others. The perfume of those flowers draw countless thousands to the tree; or rather, to the human heart in which this 'tree of perseverance' is growing.

When your heart has made a commitment, a surrender for life, you begin to sense that the words of the poet are true for you, too: "Lord, I throw my life at your feet, and sing and sing that I bring you such a little thing!" Stop for a moment. Let your heart become very still and open. Now you can begin to listen. *Listen to yourself first.* Slowly, you will find – if you persevere – that you exist and think in two layers.

The first layer is your normal thinking. Your intellect can conjure up in your mind all sorts of thoughts (secular or spiritual ones, as the case may be). It is in your mind that these thoughts flow in sequence, and have a semblance of logic about them. It is in your mind that questions arise about whether to allow that 'tree of perseverance' to grow very high, whether to let those 'fragrant flowers' fall upon the earth and bring their beautiful perfume to it.

I know whereof I speak. Seventeen times, my mind told me to leave this vocation (which, factually, was my life's goal)! I thought of a hundred reasons for leaving the Apostolate, the God-given mandate that I desired yesterday but was considering rejecting today. Yes, my mind did that seventeen times, and almost won.

The second layer of thought is deeper and more intuitive. This 'thinking with the heart' is a mysterious faculty, one quite different from 'thinking with the head.' As we begin to 'really listen' to the thoughts of our heart, we must learn to quiet the thoughts of our head. To use my well-known phrase, we must 'fold the wings of the intellect.'* I know you're tired of hearing my repeated statement about this, but it is a necessary condition for learning to 'think with the heart.' To fold the wings of one's intellect isn't easy! It takes time; the wings of the intellect are that powerful. They are tall. They refuse to fold themselves. They resist. It is *through prayer alone* that we can fold them.

But once we do this, then the doors of our hearts will be open to us. We can enter in and begin to 'think' on a secondary level. The strangest thing happens because we don't really 'think' (in the way we do when we use our mind). It more a 'sense of listening.' What do we listen

* Catherine defines this phrase more fully in her Staff Letter of April 8, 1965. See *Dearly Beloved,* Vol. 2, pages 108-109.

for? We listen for the footsteps of the Lord. When the doors of our hearts are open, he may come and sup with us. He will break bread with us, and then we will know him as the disciples of Emmaus did. But he will not disappear; he will stay with us.

He and he alone will give us the key to the mystery of this strange and awesome gift of perseverance. After that kind of experience, *perseverance* will become clear to us. We will realize, then, that it is one more virtue we need to pray for. It must be a constant prayer, a continual prayer, because its crown of beautiful flowers will be laid on our heads only when we are in a coffin.

Ah, but what a crown it is! ... Alleluia! Alleluia!

Lovingly yours in Mary,

A YEAR OF FAITH

January 5, 1976

Dearly Beloved,

This a sort of New Year's Letter to you. We should be most grateful for another year that God has given us. We should approach this year 'on tiptoe' as it were, for it holds much of God's mystery within its months. It is of this mystery that I want to speak to you.

To me, this is The Year of Faith. Somehow or other, I feel very deeply that God is giving us an increased gift of this precious virtue because he knows that we shall need it.

Yes, an increased gift of faith, and of increased hope; for without these two, there will be no love. *And without love the world will die!*

It is truly extraordinary, dearly beloved, that a tiny little Apostolate of our size – certainly not 'important' as far as the Catholic world is concerned (much less the larger Christian world) – seems to be selected by God to bring a renewal of faith, hope, and love to the world. Crazy, isn't it? But then the Lord said to St. Francis of Assisi to go and become a fool such as had never been seen before. Even Christ himself was a fool in the eyes of men. So I think that God is giving us an increase of faith so that we might truly become fools for his sake.

Do you realize, dearly beloved, what I mean when I say *faith?* I mean a land of darkness; in a sense, a land of pain, for it is not easy to walk in darkness and not be concerned (for we are human) about the abysses and crevices and pitfalls that might open wide at our feet! It is not easy to walk in faith, in total belief in the Trinity; in the love of the Father; in the sustaining, warm, divine love of the Son; in the strange, incredible love of the Holy Spirit who is both Wind and Fire.

No, dearly beloved, it is not easy. But this is the only way that is open to us in this year of 1976, when one can almost hear the world cracking apart, the trembling of the Church which seems at times sitting astride an earthquake zone. No, it is not easy. But God will give us that faith, dearly beloved, and we have to continue to pray for it so that, full of hope, we might love.

Here let me enter into a question often asked in Madonna House, especially by the young ones, those who are as yet inexperienced in the ways of faith. Because many still evaluate life by 'results,' they wonder at our 'effectiveness' and ask, "What has been achieved?" Or they ask, "What needs to be achieved?" They refer to social problems, such as they read about in newspapers and magazines. Some feel that the routine of everyday life isn't enough; other *things* should be added.

Stop here. Please stop! Fall on your knees, and pray and listen in the darkness of faith. We walk slowly because we believe in the Trinity; for no other reason, we walk slowly because we hope and we love. This, my friends, is the essence of Christianity. This is the heart of the Church. The rest flows from it. But this has to come first.

Strange as it might seem to you, it is the 'fruit' of that faith and hope and love that the Lord bends and picks up. He picks it up and changes the world! He allows his Church to expand because one or two or three (or more) people believe, hope, and love! That, my friends, is the true secret of it all. It is a simple secret which the saints understood well; but as I said, we have to approach it on tiptoes or on our knees.

Our daily tasks are part of that secret, whether the work be exciting, or ordinary, or simply a monotonous routine. Work is, in itself, part and parcel of that faith which I talk about, that hope, and that love. This workaday world of ours is the outer shell of a deep inner grace that God gives us. It is *because* we believe, we hope, and we love that we can do the things we do. Don't forget that. As St. Paul said, we must "make up for what is wanting in the sufferings of Christ." And the incredible thing is that *we can!* But again, this brings us back to faith. The impossible becomes possible because of that faith, and hope, and love.

Dearly beloved, this New Year is going to test your mettle. During this year, God will quietly 'call out' as he did in the Gospel when someone asked, "Master, where dwellest Thou?" He will say to you, "Come and see." And you will have to 'step out' and begin your walk in faith, in hope, and in love. That is the only way you can reach him, and that is the way it is going to be this year. So then, let us start now to use the gentle fruit of those three magnificent virtues.

So many of you desire to console the world, to ease its pain, to do 'something' to help it. But I suggest, humbly and simply, that you begin *by loving yourself.* Unless we love ourselves, according to God's decree of love, we cannot love anyone else. Let us pay attention to our own; there are so many lonely people among us. Let us drop the barriers of fear, the threat of possible rejection, etc. Let us cross the divide and offer ourselves to others in our own family of Madonna House. I repeat: *There are so many lonely people.* Let us go toward them. Let us reduce their loneliness with the warmth of our faith, our hope, our love. Then, and only then, can we console the rest of the world.

Dearly beloved, this is the year of faith, hope, and love. Please! Please listen to God pleading within your hearts.

Lovingly yours,

[signature]

PRIORITIES

January 7, 1976

Dearly Beloved,

After Christmas, as you probably know, I went into a sort of 'poustinia,' one of the Lord's own making. I caught the flu and had to spend quite a few days in bed. This letter is to share with you some of the things I meditated upon while there. The main subject of my meditations concerned *priorities*.

It came to me that things have changed very much since the early days at Madonna House, Combermere, as well as in most of our 'rooms' – that is, in our fieldhouses. We have enough members to fill the needs of every mission house, thanks be to God. We have, for the moment, more money than we've had in the past, and so we can give more away. The rhythm of our lives is more established and secure. We are moving, if not all at once (some of us are faster than others!), toward inner priorities ... spiritual priorities. There is still a lot of talk about work, but it isn't as pressing as it was in the past.

For instance, here in Combermere we were discussing when to begin a series of lectures in First Aid. Suddenly the whole group – almost at once, in true sobornost – blurted out: "Why should we have First Aid courses? Those courses were imperative in former years, when there was no hospital in the area, and very few doctors or nurses. Right now, it is no longer imperative. We could use that training time to absorb the spirit of our Apostolate, to go more into its depths."

So we discussed other priorities. Perhaps some of our members who work together could take a half hour (or even an hour?) away from the tasks of their department, and use that time to really go into the depths of our spirit together, and to get to know each other. It is a very wonderful priority and it would make it easier for the general courses on the spirit of Madonna House. Yes, it's time we discussed our priorities. It's fine to attend to the laundry, the clothing room, and all the other work; but if we really sit down and consider the matter, we will discover a lot of time in which we could, separately and together, enter more deeply into the spirit that is ours.

Why should I write a letter on priorities such as this? Because over the holidays I have been speaking from the heart about these meditations and about the fact that Madonna House, small and inconspicuous as it is, unimportant as it is, seems to be chosen by God to help to restore the Church.

By the grace of God to me, and to all those who have been with me in Friendship House and Madonna House, we have been upholding the Church. We have been obedient daughters and sons of the Church. No matter what persecutions were directed at me personally, *I never, in any way, let the Church down.* Friendship House and Madonna House have always upheld the Church. But now something new has been added. There are so few Christians these days; and, even among those few, so many of them reject the Church or harm it in various ways.

So few Catholics today are truly devoted to the Church. Thank God, we are part of these few. In a manner of speaking, we 'stand out' as preaching the Gospel with our lives; and that makes a difference to many people. I am sure you have realized this yourselves, because numerous people come here to be consoled and strengthened, and often to be brought back to the arms of God and his Church.

Well, then, what are our priorities? True, those who pray must wash the feet of Christ, just as Christ washed the feet of his apostles. That act of washing was his way of incarnating what he said: "I have come to serve." Now we must do likewise, for 'washing the feet' of others means *serving them in every possible way:* politically, economically, spiritually, (name it, and it will fit!).

I think that God is showing us our priorities. They are of the spirit – the spirit of Madonna House which he has given us – and it behooves us to go deeply into that 'fire and flame.' Let us make no mistake; our God is a consuming fire! And what we have to do is to enter into that fire, to be cleansed by it, and to catch fire ourselves so as to give light to the feet of our brethren, who walk such a dark and treacherous path in today's world.

I am not going to suggest how each of our mission houses, how each of our hearts, might do this. I simply call you to examine *the real priorities* which face us today. These are, I repeat, priorities of the spirit! Let each of us, in each of our fieldhouses, arrange the rhythm of our day-to-day life according to those 'new' priorities. Actually, they aren't so new; but they demand our urgent attention because the world is on the eve of tragedy, and we have to be prepared for it.

Lovingly yours in Mary,

THE MANY FACES OF STEWARDSHIP

February 3, 1976

Dearly Beloved,

Time and time again, Jesus spoke to his followers about the need for stewardship. His parable of the talents in Matthew 25:14-30 is an especially powerful example. If we study the Gospels carefully, we ourselves will come to realize the immensity and all-pervasiveness of that word *stewardship.*

Let us take baptism, for instance. When we are "baptized into the life and death of Jesus Christ," we receive a tremendous stewardship. We receive the keys of the Kingdom; and we have the responsibility of opening its doors and of finding out all about it. Because we are the stewards of it, we must seek to penetrate every corner of this Kingdom of ours. We have entered it, not for ourselves alone, but for the whole world!

In Mark 16:16, Jesus said: "Go out into the whole world. Proclaim the Good News to all creation." Here begins the stewardship of being baptized; of being members of the Kingdom of God; of being members of his body. This is the stewardship of the word.

There is also the stewardship of the heart – my heart. I must use all the talents God has given me to penetrate more deeply into his laws. In Matthew 22:37, when asked what was the greatest commandment of the law, Jesus replied: "You must love the Lord your God with all your heart, with all your soul, and with all your mind." This was the first and greatest commandment. The second one resembled it, Jesus said. "You must love your neighbor as yourself." What a tremendous stewardship this is! As I become the steward of my heart, in order to grow in God's law of love, *I become more and more like him.* I become an icon of Jesus. Through my presence in the world, through my example before others, I open the door of the Kingdom to many souls.

This concept of stewardship comes slowly down from its cosmic and dynamic immensity; it enters into the nitty-gritty everydayness of my life. I am responsible for so many things. The pollution of the earth begins with me. Do I use sprays that change the atmosphere? Do I misuse the ways of feeding people who are under my care? It is so easy to use modern chemical preparations in food. In the face of these everyday challenges, my stewardship can fragment into small pieces, and concern itself with only minor problems. If I am not alert, my sense of stewardship will become nonexistent.

If I do not listen, if I do not read, if I do not inform myself, I may feed my brothers and sisters with 'food' that hurts them. And I will hear the words of Jesus, as written in Matthew 25:29, saying: "Take the talent and give it to the one who has five talents. For to everyone who has, more will be given more; and he will have more than enough. But from the one who has not, even what little he has will be taken away."

Stewardship grows deeper. I am the steward of everything that I use: utensils in the kitchen, books in the library, files in the office, beds in the dormitory. Name it, and it is my responsibility. Everything must be kept in apple-pie order, no matter how shabby or poor it seems to be. Everything has to be kept in good repair. I am a steward of this watchfulness; and it must go deeply into my being. *It demands great inner discipline.* That is why I always talk about order. Outward order is the sign of inward order.

In the old days, when the young ones of Madonna House asked for more responsibility in the running of the house, I used to say to them: "When you put your winter boots in the proper slots in the basement, you will indeed have more responsibility." One time, shortly after I had said this, one of our members tripped and fell over someone's boots, almost breaking her leg. The boots had been left half-out in the aisle. So I confronted the group and asked them if they were ready to accept responsibility. They got the picture.

Once, when I was absent from Friendship House in Harlem, Clare Boothe Luce, the publisher of *Life* magazine, came to visit us. She intended to make a donation, and had a cheque for $25,000 in her purse. She was given a tour through the place, and saw a great amount of disorder and untidiness. She remarked to the person in charge: "If you cannot keep a storefront clean and orderly, how can you be orderly in interracial justice?" She departed without giving us a penny. And rightly so. Whoever was in charge at that time was not a good steward.

Something is wrong with our stewardship if we have dirty kitchens, cluttered clothing rooms, or messes of any sort lying around. Yes, our stewardship should be over *everything* around us. We should be watchful over details ... like a pharmacist who must be very careful in dispensing medicine, lest someone be accidentally poisoned.

There is also a stewardship over our bodies. God has created us to be icons of Christ. We can blur the image of Christ in ourselves by being sloppy in our appearance, by having a slouching posture, by not eating properly, by not disciplining ourselves in all the ways people think they find comfort. If we avoid this self-discipline, then we fail to be stewards over the first and most important gift God has given us – our own incarnation. How we care for our bodies, how we conduct ourselves, is terribly important. Think about that.

We must also be good stewards of our own hearts, and careful to give Christian example to others. From this springs stewardship of our speech, stewardship of our attention, of our thoughts, of our emotions. This form of self-discipline begins in the heart, but it moves into all areas of our subconscious and conscious life.

As we learn to 'guard our hearts' properly, we become stewards of our brothers and sisters, of our 'neighbor' (whoever is sitting next to us). Suppose that one of our family members talks to me, and my mind begins to wander. If I do not take myself in hand and refocus my attention on the person before me, it will soon become obvious in my face and eyes that I am not listening. Then my stewardship is broken into pieces! And the Lord will demand an accounting of it. Suppose I pass on some gossip, some remark that is detrimental to someone. A deep spiritual bond is broken because I have not exercised stewardship of the tongue. (That type of stewardship is something we must pray for constantly.)

I have started this letter by speaking of baptism, in which we die and resurrect with Christ, and I have tried to give you an idea of what a dynamic thing stewardship is. I have tried to show how high it soars, and how simple it can become at the base, only to return to the heights again. Do you understand what I'm getting at? A sense of stewardship is so very important because our lack of it can easily destroy a family relationship, or an entire Apostolate ... especially if we fail in *spiritual* stewardship. We must become like those stewards who spend the money of their master wisely. We are entrusted with the 'money' of love, understanding, unselfishness. *Especially unselfishness!* He gives us these gifts out of the great storehouse of his treasures. Let us 'spend' them wisely, not foolishly.

Let us not be like the seemingly transparent plastic that we place on our windows in the winter. It keeps out the wind, but it also blurs and distorts the image of things. Yes, stewardship consists of such little things, like washing the supper dishes well. Yet it is as immense as the heart of a creature uniting itself with the heart of the Creator, and becoming an icon of the Steward of the Universe.

Lovingly yours in Mary,

Catherine

HOSPICE OF THE HEART

February 4, 1976

Dearly Beloved,

For four days, while I have been resting on doctor's orders, I have undergone a 'poustinia' of sorts. I don't think I have ever gone that deeply before, in order to meet the God who dwells therein. Or perhaps I should say that I have never gone that high to meet God there. I kept hearing God's quiet voice repeating constantly:" Come higher, Catherine. Come higher."

The nights recently have seemed endless. Their loneliness I couldn't begin to describe. Their pain was so intense that it beggars words. I will just let the loneliness come to you, who also experience loneliness in all of its stark simplicity, and who often cannot communicate it.

The year 1975 was a strange one for me. There was the trip to Arizona to visit Father Eddie. There was the realization that he was close to death. Then the agony of leaving him at his own request, because he said: "Catherine, we promised God when we got married that the Apostolate would always come first. Now is the time for you to go back to Madonna House."

My whole body desired to stay in that little hospital in Arizona; but I knew that we had made that promise, and we had to keep it to the bitter end. There was no escape (if escape was what I was thinking about). It was a promise made forever and forever; *unto death and after,* for love is stronger than death. We both were in love with God, but Eddie was the first to carry this strong love to heaven.

I know now, for certain, that love is stronger than death. We were in love with each other, but we both were in love with God! And so I left Arizona. I knew that Eddie would be traveling back to Canada to die. On my own journey toward Combermere, I kept looking at cemeteries as I passed them; they were all part of the promise. A few weeks later, Eddie arrived home. Then came his death. After that came the long illness of Father Briere, whom I also love very much.

In my sleepless nights, I realized that I was very lonely. I realized that I was lonely in a most ordinary way, in the way that every human being is lonely when he or she has reached the 'golden age,' the 'twilight zone' ... call it what you will. I had a sudden desire to share with all of you a thousand little things: my childhood, youth, preteens, teens, etc.; how we did this or that in the old days in Russia. A thousand things of no importance kept returning to my mind during those nights.

I was lonely because three of my key senior staff had left Combermere, at least temporarily, to seek spiritual or psychological or physical healing. All three were my friends, and I missed them terribly much. In addition, they had been in essential positions and had held in their hands the training of future members of this Apostolate. I turned to younger staff to help me deal with this, and with the thousand-and-one other details of running Madonna House. It was good that I did so, for I met the 'second generation' of staff and we got to know each other well.

Indeed, it was good for all of us to learn that, fundamentally, we are expendable creatures. Any of us, at any time, can get up and leave Madonna House for various other places; and the Apostolate (with God's help) will carry on. All this was rather tough on me, and it was just a little bit foolish of me to make such a 'big deal' about the matter. (I apologize for that, for I might have hurt somebody's feelings in expressing my thoughts on the subject.)

I knew that loneliness was with me mainly because Eddie was gone. In my sorrow, I thought of you who are my spiritual children. How many of you there are, the ones who are lonely with the same sort of loneliness I have experienced, who want to share the type of things I've wanted to share, but who find it hard to do so because of a lack of communication. (That is less true nowadays, I admit, but communication is still not what it should be.)

Suddenly, in the early mornings of my sleepless nights, one thought kept flashing before my mind: *Madonna House is a house built by God.* And the only type of community that can survive, as you well know, is one that is founded on God. Yes, our foundations are deep and well-constructed, for it is the Lord of Pain who has taken our sufferings and used it to make these strong foundations. The basis of any group dedicated to The Crucified God is pain. Do you remember the opening sentence of The Song of Songs? "Let him kiss me with the kisses of his mouth..." Somehow that sentence became deep and pregnant for me. In a sense, he has kissed me with the kiss of his mouth; and because of it the Apostolate was born.

I understand the sentence: *Pain is the kiss of Christ.** And I think that, now, I can offer you this thought for your deep meditation. (I trust it will bear great fruit.) The pain that we all experience is varied. It is mostly physical or psychosomatic. In the beginning it is often the latter, because we are 'holding back' from one another. But Holy Communion, received each day, should help us communicate more easily.

I considered all of these things prayerfully during my sleepless nights. Then it hit me! What was Madonna House? Madonna House, I began to see, was a very special place. In our crumbling world of today, where men seek God everywhere and rarely find him reflected in their fellow men, Madonna House is a special place. I would call it a healing place, an 'inn.' Maybe I should say it is a 'hospice,' from which we get the word 'hospital.' Whatever word you use, it is the place where God brings his tired ones, his bewildered ones, his believing ones, his unbelieving ones, his searching ones. He brings them to this hospice to be healed. How he chooses them no one can explain. But he knows!

All of us are in need of healing. So the first attitude we have to accept is that *Madonna House is built on the pain of Christ.* It is a healing place because we have

* One of Catherine's favorite sayings. She kept these words before her always, in the form of a wooden plaque on the wall of her cabin.

accepted his pain, because we follow a crucified Christ. Perhaps we have to approach this healing in a different way. We have to approach each other with that compassion, tenderness, understanding, forgiveness, and help which the Lord showed in his earthly life. Then we will communicate better, for we shall cease to be afraid of each other. As President Roosevelt* said, there is "nothing to fear but fear itself." We could say that, too.

Over and over, throughout the Gospel, we hear Christ saying, "Your faith has made you whole." And so, in faith, we must understand that Madonna House is an inn, a healing place, a place to which the Lord sends his Holy Spirit not only as a wind but as a veritable hurricane. It is a place of faith, a place where we take off our shoes because it is holy, a place where the bush that burned in the Old Testament has become a bonfire!

Madonna House has to have a little change of lifestyle. It should observe its priorities better. It should realize that its main 'work' is to be the icon of Christ. If we accept pain as Christ gives it to us for our purification, for our identification with him, Madonna House will become a resurrection place also. From being an inn, a hospice, a hospital in which the charity and goodness and love of Christ abide, it will become a fire – the fire of love that will give light to thousands – because those who have accepted to be kissed by Christ and have accepted his pain will know resurrection.

Our halt, our lame, our blind will change. And in each one, we will slowly see (as we are already beginning to see) this icon of Christ glowing with an inner fire that ever increases. As this continues to develop, the dimensions of Madonna House will grow to cosmic proportions – larger than anything we can understand or analyze. Because it beggars human understanding and human analysis, we must plunge into faith, totally and constantly. This also means plunging into his resurrection, for *Christ is in our midst!*

---

* In 1933, when the world was in the depths of an economic depression, Franklin Delano Roosevelt challenged the American people to put aside their fears and to work together to rebuild the structures of society.

In my sleepless nights, I kept imploring God to work his miracles on us – his miracles of love, of tenderness, of compassion, of understanding, but above all, his miracle of communication with him.

Lovingly yours in Mary,

SOBORNOST AND SELFLESSNESS

February 21, 1976

Dearly Beloved,

Sooner or later, people who go into the poustinia get a word or thought which they must share with others, for it comes from God for the sake of others. That is what people who go to, or live in, poustinia believe. Lately I have been constantly receiving the word *sobornost.**

I find that it is something exceedingly difficult to clarify. This concept has been more difficult than trying to explain to you what poustinia is.† I find that every time the thought of sobornost comes to me I 'tense up' as it were. I say to myself: "This is an impossible task! Americans and Canadians are brought up from their mother's milk on what they consider democracy. They are too literal about

---

* For a fuller explanation of the word `sobornost,' see Catherine's letter of August 29, 1972, *Dearly Beloved,* Volume Two, pages 296-299.
† For a fuller explanation of the word 'poustinia,' see Catherine's letter of July 8, 1972, *Dearly Beloved,* Volume Two, pages 287-290; and her letter of November 26, 1974, Volume Three, pages 32-36.

life." Sobornost and democracy are very far apart, as our Constitution tries to explain.

The word 'sobornost' does keeps recurring during my poustinia days, however, and it is evident that God wants me to share it with you. I constantly turn to him, as did the prophets of old, and say: "Lord, I cannot speak about this. I don't know where to begin!" But nothing happens; and this 'word from the poustinia' returns with more power every time, so I must try to share it.

Let me put it this way: one of the first signs of sobornost is spontaneity; a whole group, a whole community, a whole family, a whole nation *spontaneously* has the same thought and the same goal in mind. This happened at Madonna House in a special way when Father Briere was ill. First, he was quite open in revealing himself as he was; and he became totally vulnerable in this openness. What happened? The whole community of Madonna House rallied around him – the priests, the laymen, the women. Everyone converged in prayer and penance and in doing what they could. Everybody had a hand in his healing.

It was a healing through sobornost in the whole of Madonna House. There wasn't one person who didn't have this spontaneous, loving, eager desire to make Father Briere well (no matter what it cost) because all loved him, and because Madonna House was built on sobornost (whether or not it was realized). So, one aspect of sobornost is its 'spontaneity' in a manner of speaking.

But it is much more than that. Sobornost is 'born' deep in the hearts of people who are in love with God. And because they are in love with him, they are also servants of their brothers and sisters as well as lovers of all mankind. Yes, sobornost is first born in the depths of such hearts. When life presents situations that have to be decided upon, situations that demand the taking of responsibility, situations that demand specific actions, then people (in whose hearts sobornost was born out of love) allow this sobornost to come forth. It comes forth prayerfully and in abundance, pondering every step of its movement upward from the depth of the human heart to the mind and lips of each individual. As it travels upward, out of the depths of love, sobornost must move simply, directly, truthfully, without any but's or if's.

Ah, but here comes the rub! Since sobornost is born in the hearts of people who love God, and are following him totally and completely, each member of the group – whether a family, a community, or a nation – will, by the grace of the Holy Spirit, think alike. And this like-mindedness comes from deep prayer. *Where there is no prayer, there is no sobornost.*

Sobornost has one enemy and that enemy is 'self.' It is only by eliminating 'self' that sobornost can grow in the hearts of people, for this 'self' is also the enemy of God. I am talking about the 'self' that wants to manipulate others; that wants always to be right, no matter what; that tries to impose its own will, instead of praying for God's will to be done. I am talking about that egotistical self, that *I* which so dominates our spiritual landscape these days. Yes, sobornost is 'born' in the depths of people's hearts, in the hearts of those who love God and neighbor. And then it is wrapped up in the 'swaddling clothes' of trust.

For instance, as the Constitution states, we elect each Director General through the process of sobornost. After that, we gather up our sobornost and lay it in the hands of those three Directors whom it has elected. It is their concern, therefore, to express in daily living the consensus of everyone, the consensus of the group. They can do so because we leave such matters entirely up to them. Our mutual love, and mutual trust, make this so easily possible. In grave and deep problems, however, ones which require solutions of all and each (as in the case of Father Briere's health), the matter-at-hand is presented to everyone for an expression of sobornost.

This is very important to understand this aspect of our life. Unless we remember that we have elected people through sobornost and that we trust them to deal with the obvious needs of the community, the family, (or whatever the group), we will go back to the 'democratic' attitudes that will kill sobornost. This will happen because the *I* becomes very pronounced in the struggle for democracy.

So then, it is 'in God' and 'with God' that we are going to gather together in sobornost (which means 'gathering' in Russian). Our sobornost should be so filled with faith, and love, and hope, that it literally oozes out of our bones ... out of our heart, mind, speech, and conduct. Then we shall arrive at the God-desired solution of whatever problem or difficulty has arisen in the course of our apostolic life. We must keep in our hearts that strange and incredible 'faithfulness' and 'understanding of the Church' which (through Baptism) is our inheritance, a gift from God. We must stand witness to this truth, which is often hidden in our hearts.

If we pray and fast, if we prepare ourselves in prayer and fasting to come to this sobornost, to make decisions that may affect our very existence and make them in total faith, total love, and total hope (the three being the truth of the Lord), then Madonna House will survive to the end of time.

This is what I have been thinking about, in regard to sobornost. As you see, I find myself straining for words because, as I explained before, it is so difficult for me to write on this subject. I will write about it again, however, God willing and Our Lady helping.

Lovingly yours in Mary,

CELEBRATION

March 5, 1976

Dearly Beloved,

Perhaps I have not written enough in my letters about celebration, so I shall direct this letter to a member of Madonna House who asked me to do this.

Approaching this subject, one must really walk on

quiet feet, for celebration doesn't mean a big New Year's Eve party with balloons, drinking, carousing, and in general creating a lot of noise to assure oneself that one is celebrating. It isn't 'painting the town red,' a strange expression which doesn't easily fit into the context of religious celebration. Yes, we must plunge deeply into that word celebration for it contains so much more than we attribute to it.

Celebration is the song of praise coming from the heart of a human being and going to the heart of God. It is a song, a dance, a light that comes forth from a human heart that is totally ready to surrender to God's will, a heart that has begun to regard each new surrender as a cause for greater celebration (even though this surrender may lead to pain, sorrow, sickness, loss, as well as to joy and gladness).

Celebration is a joy. But it is a type of joy that comes to you from passing through the archway of God's pain into the joy of his heart. Factually, to celebrate means to bring this joy and gladness into every step of our lives. Once this new dimension of celebration opens before our eyes, life changes completely! Now we can bring to it, and into it, new ways of helping and serving our brethren in the Lord. By our own celebration *of all the events* which the Will of the Lord brings to us, we give courage and benediction to everyone we meet.

Celebration is a return to childhood. It is not the return of a regressive psychiatric patient (there is nothing psychiatric about it); it is simply *the ability to wonder again*. So many times have I watched our young members or visitors walk from the dining room over to St. Germaine's dormitory, or the gift shop, or the handicraft building, or the office. They never notice the beautiful blending of colors on the rocks that are covered with raspberries in the summer. Nor have they observed the soft and tender needles of the tamarack tree, near the statue of Our Lady of the Snows. Eddie and I planted that tree, you know. It is a great contrast to the pine trees beyond it, which shelter St. Martin de Porres cabin.

Some exclaim over the beauty of the rose bushes as they walk to St. Martha's office; but few have noticed the devil's paintbrush, the yellow dandelions, or the little violets that lie by the edge of the road they must cross to get to their destination. It takes the eyes of a child to see all of this, the eyes of an adult-child to wonder at the sight, and to hear in the depths of one's heart the music of celebration. It takes an 'innocent' eye to catch the sparkle of sunlight on the waves of the river, to notice the violets in their grass cushion, to see the beauty of the tamarack tree ... to look at oneself, and realize that one's soul is part of all creation ... *because everything is God's unrehearsed celebration.*

All the 'voices' of the various musical instruments of the world sing in tune with one's heart. They sing the testament of love, given to us by God through all of creation. It is a testament to read and hear every day (if we but learn how to do so); it is best learned 'on our knees' or 'on tiptoe.'

Celebration is the dance of faith that man dances throughout his whole life, from birth to death. It is a beautiful dance with an ever-changing pattern of notes, now intricate, now simple. Celebration is the expression of hope when man walks in darkness, seemingly without anything feeding that hope, except his dance of faith. Celebration is love that brings to earth the song of praise, the sound of dancing feet. It is a light, which hope sheds in a total darkness.

It is imperative, then, that we learn to *extend our hearts* to embrace new dimensions of celebration. Usually we think of it as song, or as dance, or as light; we have many ways of thinking about it. As with all spiritual depths, though, we must not pause before one of its sunlit or shadowed landscapes and become overly entranced with the view. We must continue on, always going upwards unto the mountain of the Lord. With every step of the way, the 'life of the spirit' will embrace wider horizons and acquire new dimensions that we never suspected were there. This pilgrimage up the holy mountain of the Lord is what our real spiritual life is all about – climbing to the heights of an untouchable mountain and, like Moses on Mount Sinai, meeting God there, face to face, in truth.

Yes, the heart of those who celebrate constantly will

be able to celebrate the Will of God in *every* event of life. We have come to sick beds where people give out the clear notes of joyous song praising God; it may sometimes be people with terminal diseases who sing these Glorias and Alleluias. They cannot walk but they have 'dancing feet,' it seems. They radiate a light that comes from the 'candle of hope' dwelling in their hearts.

Visitors who come to see these sick or dying patients are reminded of pictures they have seen before, of Oriental women who carry water jugs on their heads as they walk toward the well. Visitors enter the sick room, filled with a sense of despair and sorrow; they leave the sick room, their hearts flooded with joy and hope, even though they may have abandoned all hope for physical recovery of the patient. The person who is always of joyous heart, who celebrates the will of God in everything, is equal to a choir of angels singing their Gloria in Excelsis. "Come to the stable. Come and witness the birth of Hope in human flesh." It is a clarion call, sent out all who are seeking and not finding.

There are the great celebrations of the liturgical year: Christmas, Easter, Pentecost. Liturgy makes music in the heart, as memories are aroused of these wonderful deeds of the Triune God, Father, Son, and Holy Spirit. *Liturgy is one great cry of celebration,* so immense, so incredible, so ineffable. So much so that, when you want to capture it in words, it passes through your fingers like molten gold and silver. The glowing metal doesn't burn you, but it re-creates you anew; and brings music and dance into your life. Whoever celebrates the liturgy, and fully and actively participates in it, has never a drab life. Life goes from celebration to celebration, moving to a music in which heaven and earth blend their voices.

For human beings, celebration must always be a part of the great festival days of life. The Christian soul always moves in a rhythm of celebration, a beautiful rhythm of birth, baptism, communion, confirmation, marriage, priesthood, religious life, single life in the world, widowhood. These are major signposts in life; they call, cry out for, demand celebration. In our prayers, we commemorate the holy men and women who trod this earth before us. We remember their lives from birth to death, and everything in between.

Death, too, is a cause for celebration. Let it be celebrated with tambourines and drums, with bells and stringed instruments. For death is the greatest celebration of all. All of the other events of life lead up to it. Now the doors of the Kingdom are fully opened. The soul stands upon the threshold, surrounded by angels and archangels, by saints and all those whom the soul has served and helped throughout its life. The soul listens to a music that few can hear yet; but eventually all will hear the same music. So death is a time of celebration too.

Yes, all of life's great events are celebrated with him who has counted each of our days; and we celebrate in him. Those who fall in love with God have a happy heart and they walk in music that is both earthly and heavenly. They are the ones whose hands are always filled by God to help them celebrate with all the rest of humanity. They celebrate sickness and health, pain and joy; for all the events of life are like harp-strings in their hands. Out of everything, they fashion a song to the Lord. Because it is so deep and profound, it always comes out the same: *Alleluia! Alleluia! Alleluia!*

When all is said and done, celebration is simply love bursting open like a new apple blossom, and spreading its perfume across the world in which it lives. Come, then. Let us together, hand in hand, climb the mountain of the Lord so that we might understand better what celebration means. (And let us start celebrating in earnest.)

Lovingly yours in Mary,

WITH AN EVERLASTING LOVE

March 13, 1976

Dearly Beloved,

"I have loved you with an everlasting love ..." These words kept singing themselves in my heart, and I didn't seem to be able to stop them. So, as I usually do, I began to 'listen with my heart.' Suddenly it was as though the song ceased to exist. Instead, I saw the Gospel before me, and it was opened to one sentence: "Greater love hath no man than he who lays down his life for his fellowmen" (John 15:13).

Since this is Lent, I suddenly and very clearly saw Golgotha and Christ crucified, but somehow the cross and his pain changed. They were a door to the resurrection. Again from afar a new song was coming to me. Oh, I could barely hear it, and it seemed to be composed of nothing but alleluias. I realized that this was love. It was a love that no human mind could absorb, but a human heart could encompass. Did I kneel? Did I stand? Or did I sit before this inner vision of mine? I cannot tell you because I don't remember.

I saw this incredible love of Jesus Christ embracing all of us at Madonna House, no matter who we were. It didn't have anything to do with education, knowledge, any kind of superiority or inferiority. It was the immense, fantastic, incomprehensible love of a crucified God who through that crucifixion led us to the resurrection, led us into the heart of the Father, there to sing thousands of alleluias because he loved you and me. This is what I understood, and this is what I want *you* to understand.

How wonderful it is to wake up in the morning and to have as a first thought: "God loves me!" How healing to let that beautiful thought be absorbed through our spiritual pores, as a sponge absorbs water! Yes, God loves me. We are 'saved' sinners. Oh, we know that we will probably continue to sin in one way or another; but here is this beautiful thought that, sinner or saint, I am loved by God!

In our various houses, there are showers and baths and basins to wash in, and soap to wash with. But we forget that as we wake up in the morning there is a whole sea of God's mercy, warm and pleasant, waiting for us to plunge into it so that we can be cleansed for the day ahead. God's mercy is such that it takes away *every* kind of stain. I am not denying that there will be times when we will have to go to confession (which is another way that this sea of mercy washes over us). But we should wake up each morning, knowing that God is in our midst, loving us! Knowing that he has loved us enough to die for us.

We will have good days and bad days, peaceful days and unpeaceful ones. But the majority of them should be peaceful because we remember that *God loves us*. Do you know what his love does? His love binds us together in so many beautiful ways. He loves children, and he wants us to be childlike. I think he desires that we should 'hold hands and dance' sometime during the day, at least in our hearts, so that the joy of his heart may enter into ours.

He is so open. What is more open than a naked man, pierced with nails, hanging high on a cross? Naked he came out of his mother's womb; naked he died. Do you ever think about that? Nakedness is revelation. In his case, it is the revelation of love; for he showed us what poverty is, as no one else could do. And looking upon him, we see this poverty resplendently blended into love. Somehow, without our understanding it, this blending shows us the beautiful face of hope. It shows us the love, poverty, and hope that should flow through our days. Fear can have no place, for perfect love banishes away fear ... far far away!

This is the time, dearly beloved, to understand how much you are beloved by God. And, since you are beloved by God, *YOU ARE LOVABLE!* Never mind how you 'feel' about yourself. Emotions aren't too important when you are beloved by God so deeply, so profoundly, so totally.

Now, having understood this, we feel his fingers covered with clay and spittle, touching the eyes of our hearts and revealing to us that we are able to love one another ... we can really, deeply, beautifully, love one another. We can accept peacefully all of the little difficulties with one another (they are present in any family!), for 'nothing matters very much' as long as we love one another.

I think we should devote this Lent to prayer, so that we will absorb into our deepest heart the fact that *we are beloved by God!* And hence we will gain that immense grace – charism, if you want – to love one another as the Gospel calls us to do. Why not start now? Why not let go of all the inhibitions, the anger towards ourself and one another, the feeling of self-pity and loneliness? Throw them all out ... and allow our tired souls, and tired hearts, to expand.

Let us hold hands. Let us be childlike. Let us love one another. Let us sing an *alleluia* 'in our hearts' throughout Lent.*

Lovingly yours in Mary,

FAILURE

March 13, 1976

Dearly Beloved,

How often do we look at ourselves and feel that we are a total failure? We grow older, we look at our lives, and we don't feel there is anything in them worth recording. We feel we have been utter failures. That is the moment when we should go to Golgotha and look at Jesus on the Cross. There is no greater failure than Jesus Christ. In fact, he was the 'perfect' failure.

---

* In Lent, the word *alleluia* is not sung during Roman Catholic worship services. But it remains alive, just under the surface, ready to break forth in praise at Eastertime (like Handel's Hallelujah Chorus).

Someone has published a Christmas card that is entitled *One Solitary Life*. Its message tells us what a great failure Jesus appeared to be, as far as human eyes can see. He was born in an obscure village of poor parents, and grew up in a village just as obscure. He worked at manual labor in a carpenter's shop until he was thirty years of age. Then for three years he was an itinerant preacher, although he never traveled more than 200 miles from his birthplace. He had no credentials but himself. When he was thirty-three, public opinion turned against him. His friends ran away, and he was delivered into the hands of his enemies. They mocked him, scourged him, and crucified him between two thieves. While he was dying, his executioners gambled for his clothing, the only property he had. When he was dead, he was laid in a tomb donated by a friend. Yet, nineteen centuries later, he is the central figure of the human race and the leader of mankind's progress. All of the armies that ever marched, all of the navies that ever sailed, all of the parliaments that ever sat, all of the kings who ever reigned have not affected the life of man on this earth as much as that One Solitary Life has done.

Yes, let us face that word *failure* head-on, mind-on, heart-on, because it is a devastating word in our vocabulary. It doesn't lead us anywhere except to various doctors, either of body or of mind. Let us get away from that soul-searing word and understand that, within its letters, it holds fantastic deeds of valor, and extraordinary acts of holiness, and depths of love that are unprobed by human hearts and unheard by human ears. So let's ask ourselves what failure is, really!

What is this strange word that everybody in Madonna House is so worried about? What is this word which we equate with a loss of 'face' as the Chinese would say? What is this word that says that we don't amount to much; that we don't live up to that strange yardstick which the devil has fashioned for us on this continent – the yardstick of production* and being measured by it?

None of us are failures, dearly beloved, *unless we make ourselves so*. What we call 'failure' in ordinary life is

---

* See the Staff Letter of August 20, 1965, in *Dearly Beloved*, Volume Two, pages 154-160.

actually a 'stepping stone' to success. You can't become proficient in anything unless you fail in it again and again and again. You just can't! It takes a lot of clay to make a pot. It takes many a thread to make beautiful embroidery. Failure and time are married to each other; the offspring they produce are beauty and joy.

I knew a Negro woman in Harlem who was totally paralyzed, yet she helped more people than Friendship House did, and in greater depth. I knew Gertsky, a little Polish girl whose heart was greatly enlarged. She was in terrible pain most of the time, and eventually died a very holy death. Father Eddie wrote about her. Bishops, cardinals, priests, nuns – even politicians – came to talk to her, although she had barely finished grade school. She would seem to be a failure as the world would reckon it, but she certainly wasn't a failure. As God sees things, she was just the opposite!

I could go on endlessly, but what I want to say is this: Don't be afraid to fail, for *failure is but a stepping-stone to success*. Failure is painful; but without pain there is no living in love. So then, go through the arches of Christ's pain and enter into the joy of his heart. In the process, there will be many times when you will fail. You will fall flat on your face, even as he did on the way of the cross ... Alleluia!

Lovingly yours in Mary,

THOUGHTS ABOUT COMBERMERE

March 29, 1976

Dearly Beloved,

In a sense this is a 'special' letter, for I have prayed and thought a lot about it. I visualize all of you right here with me, talking all of this over with a deep peace and with a prayer of gratitude to the Lord.

The words of President Kennedy come to my mind: "Ask not what your country can do for you, but what you can do for your country." These memorable words can be applied to many things besides countries. They can be applied to our Apostolate!

Lately, I have been pondering in the depths of my heart a very strange manner of thinking which I find occurring among some members of Madonna House. I think it is really an attempt to clarify our values. The training center at Combermere should be for all of you a place of joy, of rest, of 'coming home'... for Combermere has given you a special birth, and from this place you will receive life as long as the Madonna House Apostolate exists.

It seems that many of you think of the headquarters here as 'too big,' a place where one can 'get lost,' a place where a person sort of 'merges' into the collective. Oh, you have many thoughts about all of this. Some of you (I don't mean to say all of you) wouldn't like it if you were reappointed to Combermere.

On the other hand, some of you have often dreamt about being stationed in a small fieldhouse. But, having gone out to such a mission, you very quickly find that living with only a director, and one or two other staff, is not all that you thought it would be. The confined atmosphere of a small house sometimes causes inimical relations between staff workers.

Some say that the headquarters of Madonna House is *too big*. Some say that a small house is *too tense*. Here we are faced with our own (shall we say?) 'perverse' nature. For we are sort of perverse at times, aren't we? So I am faced with the fact that some members desire to come back, to escape the pressures of a small house; other members do not desire to be reappointed here, for fear of being overwhelmed by people.

Therefore, I stand before the Lord – not in personal hurt (because Madonna House is not my own creation, but his) – and I pray to him. I tell him that I am a bit bewildered by the kinds of thoughts which come to me; and I want to cry out to him: "Lord, give me an answer. Please!" (You may think that I exaggerate here, but my heart tells me that I do not.)

My heart tells me many things. As I stand before God, I think of the fact that quite a few people may have 'left home' when they were quite young, and that the concept of Father and Mother has changed over a period of years. So it could be that, because of one's previous experiences, the spirit of Madonna House hasn't penetrated the hearts of everyone as deeply as it should.

I find this a very hard letter to write. With all my heart, with all my mind, with all of my soul, I see Combermere as our 'birthplace' in a sense. I think of it as a 'Bethlehem' and of each of you as being placed into the 'crib' of God's heart, and being mothered there by Our Lady's special care, so that you grow and are shaped according to the Will of the Lord.

Combermere is a training center; but whatever 'training' goes on here comes from God and Our Lady, through us human instruments, as we interact with each other. Combermere should also be a place of rest, of vacation; an oasis where those who have been away would want to return with eager feet to share their lives with us, and so we could share our lives with them. (Right now, though, I don't want to speak about vacations or short-term visits.)

I'm speaking of this strange trend of thought that exists among a few of you when confronted with the possibility of being reassigned here. I don't think it exists among all of you, of course; but even *one* person thinking this way could be disastrous. It bites deeply into the spirit of Madonna

House, into its Bethlehem and its Nazareth. Scripture speaks of the youth of Jesus, telling us that "he was obedient to them." Gently, Our Lord seeks those whom he wants. He brings them to the creche of Madonna House, to train them in the spirit of Nazareth as he had been trained by Joseph and Mary. (Do you follow what I am saying?)

It is said that Madonna House is too big. Is that true? Physically speaking, we are not overly large because we are divided between here and St. Benedict's farm and St. Joseph's Rural Apostolate. We do have many people passing through here, however. I think the idea of bigness comes to some of the staff because they 'get lost' here; whereas in a small house they are constantly faced with the other staff and no one is 'overlooked.'

Here, I think, I am coming to the essence ... to the very heart of this letter. If you consider this place so big that you feel overlooked, just 'one of the crowd,' or what-have-you, then you are grappling with the psychological problem of *depersonalization.** The words of President Kennedy should strike like arrows into the hearts of those who think this way.

If the place is too big, it is the duty of each one of us to make it 'small' by paying attention to each other, by being friends with one another, by all the ways we can find to reduce 'bigness' to coziness and simplicity. It is the duty of each one of us, and we can't just pass it on to others. Let's not wait for others to 'make us welcome'; let's reach out and care about the others! If the place is depersonalized, then let us each put our 'person' into it. Let us 'personalize' the atmosphere so that each one of us cares for the other. Let us love one another *so deeply* that no one feels depersonalized. If someone nearby seems to be overlooked, then let us open our eyes and our hearts to him or her. Let us all move right into the family so that we stop feeling overlooked. Again it is up to us: "... not what my country can do for me, but what I can do for my country."

I stood before God with all of these things that I have tried to explain. I felt sad and a bit bewildered; but I feel

---

* To feel deprived of one's personal identity (Joe, Mary, Fred, Sarah, Catherine) and to be regarded as a 'thing,' a tool, or a stereotyped category (nurse, cook, teacher, chauffeur, maid, handyman, janitor, kids, teenagers, they, them.)

these questions have to be answered by each one of us. Let us start with ourselves and put into Madonna House that which we want it to be, that which is the very essence of Our Lord's and Our Lady's training in Bethlehem and Nazareth. It's what he died for – *that we should love one another.* Yes, Madonna House is his place; and he wants us to love one another here. And in that loving lies the secret of these questions about bigness, and smallness, and 'interpersonal relationships.'

Forgive this meandering letter, but I think I've touched on something simply because I have prayed so much about it during my poustinia time. This is, my beloved ones, what love has dictated; I hope you will see that love 'between the lines' of this letter.

Lovingly yours in Mary,

GENTLENESS TO YOURSELF

April 21, 1976

Dearly Beloved,

On Holy Saturday, while I was in the poustinia, a strange word came to me. And since the word that one receives in the poustinia is sometimes meant for everybody, I bring it to you. The word was *gentleness*.

I thought about it a lot. I prayed about it as I sorted the bits and pieces of donated jewelry, trying to match them by color and size and function. It came to me that gentleness primarily meant being *gentle with yourself.* Christ said to love our neighbor as ourselves; and our first neighbor is ourselves. That is the person whom we must first love, if we're to set about loving anybody else.

How important it is to be gentle with ourselves! And how often we swing in the opposite direction, getting angry with ourselves, or even angry at God! I thought of how we flagellate ourselves, mentally speaking. We dwell upon our sins and think of ourselves as horrible people. Or we harass ourselves with the 'wrong decisions' we have made or with 'indecisions' ... especially in regard to sin. We become exhausted.

We forget that the mercy of God is part of his gentleness. We forget that if we but turn to him when we have sinned and say "I'm sorry," the sin is erased completely. He does not remember, because *he does not want to.* His mercy overshadows all. And if we are indecisive about inspirations that we may think are from the Holy Spirit, something God wants us to do, we should 'check it out' with a priest. Then we can be gentle with ourselves, because gentleness comes from faith and trust. God will show the way so that we do not need to be always in a state of flux.

We need to check out things because we all can walk through periods of darkness where things get all out of proportion and we can't distinguish anything. In the 1960s everybody was trying to be *relevant.* You wore long hair if everybody else did. You went to the inner city or to the Negro and so on, because it was 'relevant' to do so. But the work often was not beneficial because people weren't loving one another first.

We have to be gentle with ourselves, so that we can be gentle with God and with our neighbor. Then – whether we are washing dishes, sweeping a floor, or doing carpentry – *we can be deeply united with Christ in prayer.* In the 1970s there is so much talk about prayer. Now, *how* you pray and *why* you pray is another story, but prayer resides first and foremost in the service of our fellowmen. Prayer time must be interrupted whenever you are called to help others who are in need, to 'wash their feet.' Our gentleness will be expressed in the way we serve them.

This applies to everyone, even those who live a solitary life. There is no hermit who is completely aloof from this. Those who dwell in the poustinias at Combermere are ready to serve the community whenever needed. Prayer walks hand-in-hand with charity. It is always gentle and merciful. It is always forgetful of self; forgetful of time, place, and so forth. While Jesus was working with St. Joseph polishing wood, where was he? He was in union with his Father. So *whatever we are doing* is an opportunity to be gentle with ourselves, with our neighbor, and with God.

This meditation on the mercy and gentleness of God kept me awake at night, and an infinite compassion came out of my heart. I thought of how often we are 'un-gentle' with ourselves. We can inflict so many wounds on ourselves. I can almost take you in my arms and say: "Rest now. Be gentle with yourselves. Be gentle."

Where do you learn how to be gentle? St. John used to recline on the breast of Christ. I think we will become gentle toward ourselves, and toward others, if we go and do likewise. Then we will hear the heartbeats of God, and we will be able to let others hear them. Then we will be gentle to ourselves and to everybody else.

Lovingly yours in Mary,

THE FEAR OF RISK AND RIDICULE

April 27, 1976

Dearly Beloved,

Recently I was meditating on fear and asking myself, "Why are Christians fearful, for perfect love casts out fear?" I tried to find out why we are afraid, what we are afraid of; and a strange word came to me. It was *ridicule*.

Most people are terribly afraid to express themselves lest they be ridiculed. So that makes them keep silent and retreat into themselves. Or else, if they speak at all, they look to the right and to the left and wonder what others are thinking about what they have said. Why are we so afraid of being ridiculed?

I thought about this, these past two weeks of Lent, as I sorted the holy cards which had come in donation. I thought of how Christ was buffeted, hit on the face, tortured ... and especially, how he was ridiculed. When he was given over to the Roman soldiers, they bowed to him and mocked: "So you're the King of the Jews?" They ridiculed him; they ridiculed his Kingship. (And he, the King of Kings, allowed it.) So, if we are really in love with God, why should we be afraid of ridicule?

As one of the staff wrote me: "It's like we have to take fumbling baby steps because we're so afraid to 'walk in faith' ... we're so afraid. Afraid of what? Oh, the usual stuff: rejection, disapproval. But more than that, I think that we are really *afraid of risk!*"

This is why the world today shies away from any sort of commitment – especially a commitment to authority, even God's authority. Marriage, religious life, all these things are viewed as only temporary. *But with God there is nothing 'temporary'; with God it is 'all or nothing'!* He said: "If you acknowledge Me before men, I shall acknowledge you before My Father."

There was Brother Juniper, a friend of St. Francis. He

used to ride a seesaw and let the children laugh at him for doing so. Even the adults laughed to see a grown man going up and down on a seesaw. Brother Juniper tried to 'act foolish' for Christ's sake because Christ had said to St. Francis: "Be a fool the like of which nobody ever saw." To be a fool for Christ's sake is to *expect* to expose yourself to ridicule. I said to myself, "If you are a Christian, you don't go to a psychiatrist just because you are afraid of ridicule."

St. Francis prayed not to be consoled but to console, not to be loved, but to love. If he could have used the word *approve,* he would probably have said also, "not to be approved, but to approve." He certainly was not approved of by many of his 'staff' ... his brethren in the Friars Minor. But he became a great saint. It seems that those who are willing to be ridiculed and disapproved of become saints, while the rest of us do not.

So we are afraid of being ridiculed. Our emotions cause us to need approval as we need air. We must have the approval of our fellowmen. We have such a wrong image of ourselves, which adds to all our misery and need for approval. We have such a wrong yardstick to measure ourselves by – the yardstick of production. We are afraid of not following what everyone else is doing. If people wear miniskirts, we will wear miniskirts. If others wear beards, we must wear beards. If others wear long hair, we must wear long hair. Why do we always do what others do? We are afraid to 'stand out from the crowd' ... but that is what God wants us to do!

To be a Christian is to risk *everything,* including your life! There is nothing that can be held back. You are entering into no-man's-land. On one side, you will be laughed out of house and home, ridiculed and rejected. On the other side, you will be maligned, persecuted, misunderstood, gossiped about. And you have to walk in that no-man's-land, following Christ's footsteps because you love him. And nothing – *but nothing!* – should be allowed to make you deviate from those footsteps.

Yes, there is risk in opening your heart to your fellowmen, and to God; but it has to be done. Otherwise, one is a sort of half-Christian. Do you expect God to accept that? I don't think he will. He will accept the atheist. He will accept one who seeks deeply. But to the one who tries to hide behind a thousand screens, he will turn his face and say: "Break down the screens, and you will find me."

How many approved of Christ in his lifetime? All over the world there are people the world doesn't approve of; but they carry on, because they have put their roots in Christ. We are Christians, so we must measure ourselves by the example of Christ – by his incarnation, his life, his death, and resurrection. Think for a while at what price he has purchased us. We must not be lured into thinking that Christ died only for 'mankind.' That is an amorphous word. If you or I were all alone on earth, he would have died for you and me, because he loves us individually. When we consider the price that he paid, what a prostitution of ourselves it is to measure our worth by production. We are not meant to be production-minded robots, but God-minded, God-rescued people.

When are we going to live the Gospel without compromise? For that is what Christ has asked us to do when he said: "Who is not with me is against me." To be 'with him' is to stand apart from the crowd. If we had this attitude toward the price that we are worth, if we really understood this Gospel message, then life would be much easier for us.

I was thinking of all of these things yesterday; and it was impossible to do anything but kneel down and pray for those who are afraid, for those whose fears take them away from God, ruin their health, and create tragedy. Jesus has told us: "Whatsoever you ask in my name from the Father, he will grant you." I am not ashamed to say that I cry out to the Father to take those fears away from us – especially from you, the younger ones, who struggle so much to live the Christian life; to live the Gospel without compromise.

I felt so compassionate, so tender toward you, as I was reading this book about the healing of memories. I was thinking that the memories which most often needs healing are the ones of 'not being approved of' by our fathers or mothers, or 'not being loved enough.' If we brought forth all these memories and faced them without fear, they would soon evaporate.

Fear is certainly a weapon of the devil, and it is

exorcised by two things – one is prayer; the other is forgiveness of those who have done us harm. Surprisingly, the first person whom we must forgive is *ourselves*. That is where we have to start! Then we can forgive our parents or relatives who have hurt us. So start with forgiving yourselves. And I think that, if you really *do* forgive yourselves, you will have peace – the peace that surpasseth all understanding.

Lovingly yours in Mary,

(signature)

HOPE IS THE ANTIDOTE TO FEAR

April 28, 1976

Dearly Beloved,

As I was meditating on fear last night, I began to think about the virtue of hope. I asked myself what was the connection between them. It took me quite a while to really focus on this, and understanding came when I thought of the old saying: *With God, every moment is the moment of beginning again!*

That is when I saw the connection between fear and hope. Hope should allay fear; it should kill fear. There has always been evil in the world, but each human being is free to choose good or evil, and that is why the Gospel is not fully lived out. It is because we say *no* to the Holy Spirit. We tell ourselves that nothing has come together; every moment we hear news of everything falling apart. But

Christ has risen; and every moment can become the moment of beginning again.

For some unaccountable reason, I thought of Saint Joseph. There was Joseph, facing a pregnant wife; and he had not touched her. Then he had a dream, which he had to act upon in faith. I thought of his response to this dream, how he must have wondered about it – "Was it really true?" – and I realized that, in a sense, he personified (in the nitty-gritty) what it is like to hope before some very tangible problem. I wondered how much hope Saint Joseph had during those nine months. He must have been tempted to wonder at times, because he was human.

In our search for reality, in our running from fear, in all of those emotional problems, there is hope. Stretch out your hand and hope will come to you, and whatever seems hopeless will be filled with light. Saint Catherine of Siena (who is my patron saint) was praying for a man who was condemned to death; and just before he was beheaded, he returned to the Church. The trip between the prison and the scaffold was his 'moment of beginning again.'

A man who was crucified next to Christ rebuked the other one, and asked God to take care of him. Christ said to this 'good' thief: "This very day you will be with me in my Kingdom." This, too, was a moment of new beginnings. Between the speech of the thief and the speech of Christ, hope surged forth, immense and all-embracing.

We say that "perfect love casts out all fear." But do we believe it? It is a very good intellectual exercise to repeat that sentence to ourselves, or to write it out on paper. Then, perhaps, it will sink into our hearts. If we turn our faces to hope, and look hope 'in the eye' as it were, then it becomes very simple; for hope holds love in the hollow of its hand. Faith, while we live, also holds love.

Hope makes us see that our price has been the incarnation, life, death and resurrection of Christ. Hope is like an avalanche of sorts, or like a fire that enters into you and renews you. Hope is the 'sauna' of the Holy Spirit; he uses it to cleanse us from all of our emotions, and from whatever else weighs us down. Faith whispers: "Look! It's not so tragic! Nothing is tragic in the Lord. Every moment is the moment of beginning again."

So you have sinned. Guilt holds you in its claws and throws you around like a hockey puck. You look at it and say, "Out! Out! Out!" And all that guilt just shrivels (or should) and crawls right out of the door. For if you really put hope into action, this will work out. With God, *every moment* is the moment of beginning again. And that really cheers you up, doesn't it? It cheers me.

So you see how utterly useless it is to indulge in guilt. So you're guilty! So I'm guilty! So we're all guilty! If we apologize to God via confession, then every moment becomes the moment of beginning again. *Every moment holds hope for us!*

You remember the story of how Eddie and I struggled to stay in Combermere in the early days. We had arrived from Chicago, and this was 'the end of the road' for us. Buses didn't travel Highway 62; trains came to Barry's Bay only three times a week; nobody came here! We struggled mightily. What would have happened if we had finally given in to hopelessness? You all know of moments when I said, "This is impossible!" But I remembered about hope coming with every moment.

There is only one thing which can stop hope. It is desiring to do *our* will and not God's. That is very dangerous. That is what's been happening in the Church for the past ten or twelve years – people are saying, "I want to do *my* thing!" That expression goes directly against the virtue of hope; it is the door to hopelessness.

So cheer up, truly cheer up, my dear friends. God is love; and with him, every moment is the moment of beginning again. This means that every moment is the moment of joy and hope. Christ is risen; verily, he is risen. Alleluia!

Lovingly yours in Mary,

MARY AND FAITH

April 30, 1976

Dearly Beloved,

Some members of Madonna House were visiting me the other day, and I was showing them my 'intention book.' I have had it since about 1952, so it is quite old. In this book I write the intentions for which people ask me to pray. And I have a funny idea about it: I think that, because the book is kept beneath her picture, Our Lady gets up at night and reads all the intentions to Jesus, as I always remind her to do.

Talking about this 'intention book' started me thinking about Our Lady. I said to myself, "We don't talk much about Our Lady." (Most of us – the seniors, anyway – already know quite a bit about her and are dedicated to her through Saint Louis de Montfort's *Act of Consecration;* read Eddie's book* sometime about that.) I asked myself, "What do people think about Mary in the year of 1976?" I can't tell, of course, but so often she seems to be neglected.

The first image of her that comes to my mind is that of a very young girl. She comes from a small town or village, and her parents are bringing her to the Temple where she can learn to read and to do many things. (I love to meditate on Our Lady; I have written a lot of poems about her.) I see her little hands as they become accustomed to labor. She learns to weave, cook, sweep, spin. She does so many things that fourteen-year-old girls of today cannot do. I see her as being very simple and unobtrusive, melting into the group to which she belongs, unobserved – she who was to become the Mother of God, to hold Jesus in her motherly arms, to hold my own heart in her delicate hands.

Then I think of how she must have played as all children played: jumping, dancing, running through the

---

* *True Devotion to Mary,* by de Monfort, (as adapted by Eddie Doherty), Montfort Publications, Bay Shore, New York, 1956.

fields; and I feel as if I could celebrate with her. She was attentive to all the feasts of the synagogue, to the Psalms, to all the things of God. I asked myself, "How attentive?" And it came to me that her attentiveness was probably fantastic, because it was an all-absorbing activity. She drank deeply of the Psalms. She was enraptured of the Scriptures, reading the ones that we now know refer to her. She did not know that they were going to be applied to her; yet in some way she must have absorbed them deeply, and "kept them all in her heart." I like to meditate on all of this.

Then came that strange event: just imagine a fourteen or fifteen-year-old girl having an angel stand before her and say: "Hail, full of grace, the Lord is with thee." How does it feel to be addressed by an angel? But she answered simply, directly, regally, without any false modesty. She said: "How can this happen to me, for I do not know a man?" Then she was told that the Holy Spirit would overshadow her and ... (But I am sure that you all have read *The Reed of God,* by Caryll Houselander.* Read it again, line by line, slowly. The opening chapters are beautiful.)

When it was explained, Mary said: "Let it be done unto me according to his will." Incredible! Now that's something that should penetrate our hearts. Do you feel it penetrating your heart?

We say that our whole existence depends on whether we do *his* will or our own will. Here is this little girl offering up her own will and accepting God's will. The *world's* existence depends upon it. I think of how she was betrothed to Joseph and his wonder at it all. Did *she* question it? As her pregnancy became more and more obvious, and she felt the Child's movement within herself, what did she think? Time of pregnancy. Time of mystery.

It is almost incredible because, you see, she was just like you and me! She was a person, a human being; she had certain graces given to her; but she wasn't God. And she didn't understand many things. Later, when she found Jesus teaching in the Temple, she didn't understand it all, but she put into her heart what she did not understand. It was not understanding, but *a plunge into faith,* my dear friends!

* Published by Sheed and Ward, New York, 1944.

With our overactive minds, we want to probe everything in this technological society; we want to probe everything, no matter what. Nothing is sacrosanct to us these days. But this little girl took a plunge into such faith that it brings gooseflesh to anyone of inquiring mind. And when *we* have difficulties in faith, we should turn to her who said: "Let it be done according to his will." Joseph, too, had to take a deep plunge into faith. And so do we.

I stop here for a moment to bow low before this little girl-woman. She is truly 'the Mother of all those who believe.' She has shown a faith beyond our understanding. Right now, this very moment, I invite you to enter into that solitude of faith, as Mary did. Cast your minds inward, and open your hearts. Do you really believe? All you have to do is to enter this solitude of faith, as Mary did, and say *yes!* That's all.

Mary traveled the dusty roads to Bethlehem on the back of a donkey. That is not exactly a good way to prepare for the birth of one's child. Then there was the cave in which Mary and Joseph had to stay. Sometimes these caves are fairly pleasant; they are used for storage spaces or for animals in the Holy Land. Mary said *yes* to all of this.

Just as the Risen Christ came through doors that were closed, so the Infant Jesus came into the world without doing any harm to Mary's virginity, so we are told. Then she was washing her newborn son, dressing him – 'putting diapers on God.' Can you imagine this? *Looking after God, not understanding everything?* Here, too, one must move in faith.

When my husband, Eddie, was writing an article, he was wondering what color the eyes of Jesus were. He said that Joseph must know because he had the greatest opportunity to see them. One night, Eddie woke me up and said: "Catherine, I just received an answer from Saint Joseph." I was as sleepy as I could only be around 2 a.m., and I just said, "Uh huh?"

"Yes," said Eddie. "St. Joseph looked me straight in the face and said: *What color is the Glory of God? ...* Now I can get up and write."

What color is God's glory? These two quiet Jewish people, an artisan and his wife, must have seen that glory. It must have been revealed to them in many ways. They had faith in it, whether or not they understood everything.

I believe that Mary did understand some things (this is all speculation, you understand) because she was to become the Mother of men, the Queen of Martyrs. I believe that she understood when she came to that place where Jesus was preaching, and somebody went to him and said, "Look, your mother and brother and sisters are outside asking for you." Scripture tells us that he looked around at all the people and asked, "Who are my mother and my brothers?" And turning back to those he had been talking with, he said: "Here is my mother and my brothers. *Anyone who does the will of God* is my brother and sister and mother." It seemed as if he didn't want to see her, that he had rejected her. But she understood.

We have a Mother who understands because, before he died, Jesus handed her over to John, the well-beloved disciple, to become his Mother – and ours. She not only understands, but she loves both sinners and saints, and holds them in her arms and makes saints out of sinners.

I just received a letter from a woman who had gotten herself deeply into the occult. She asked for my help; but what can I do? I can only pray for her. But I also sent her a picture of Our Lady. In Genesis, there is the prediction that a woman will arise who will crush the head of the serpent. Mary will do this. Her heel is ready to do so, provided we pray at her feet. She will crush the serpent that is slithering around in our hearts. We hear that serpent voice whispering to us: "Don't be a 'sap.' All that religious stuff is for nothing. There is no God." It whispers so many things, half-truths and quarter-truths and downright lies. If we pray to Mary, *she becomes powerful and immense.* And the devil is exceedingly afraid of her; for he knows when he has met the one who can crush his head.

To go to Mary is to be near Jesus. He chose to come through her. The Holy Spirit overshadowed her. It should be very easy for us to go to her when we are full of tears, of loneliness, of slithering serpents, because she has the answers.

These were my thoughts when the staff left the island, and I picked up my little intention book and said, "How beautiful that the Lord gave us a Mother!" Amen.

Lovingly yours in Mary,

THE PITY OF GOD

May 11, 1976

Dearly Beloved,

Yesterday I was meditating on the pity of God, and I wondered if any of us realize how it constantly envelops us with its gentleness, its kindness, its warmth.

Because of Father Pelton's seminar, everybody is talking about 'opening up' and sharing themselves, saying just what is 'on their minds.' It is beautiful and wonderful to observe this new trend. But many of our inner hurts could be alleviated *without* speech if we would only allow them to disappear into the furnace of God's pity. His pity is so profound and so immense. Sin can be burned up in this pity simply by approaching it, because God loves a sinner. He said that he came not for the healthy but for the sick, for the sinner.

God's pity is visible in people like Saint Francis of Assisi who kissed a leper. That was pity. Pity is *not* the condescension of one person toward another. "Oh, those poor Negroes in Harlem! Isn't it terrible? How I pity them!" No, that is not the kind of pity I am talking about. God's pity is strong; it is *very* strong. It lifts up a completely discouraged person, but it is not condescending. Having lifted up the bruised and crushed soul, God embraces the whole person and speaks words of tender affection – 'brother,' 'sister,' 'friend.'

God's pity is like a fresh wind that suddenly comes on a torrid day. His pity is like a cool evening when the sky is pink and blue and red, and beautiful to behold. That is how God's pity is.

It is something that we should desire to hold on to, something that we should want to delight in, to 'wallow in' as it were. The pity of God is so gentle that it is like a cradle rocked by a loving mother. It puts us to sleep ... that is to say, not us but rather our fears and negative emotions. The pity of God is like oil that makes the skin soft; it makes the heart soft.

The pity of God is 'catching.' If we 'let ourselves go' and enter into this divine pity, we will be able to pity others with the same strength, with the same ability to lift the other one (if we need to carry him on our back) ... but certainly to embrace him, to hold him tight and call him brother or sister.

But first, we must allow ourselves to relax and let God's pity (which is another facet of his love) penetrate the deepest levels of our hearts. *To accept the pity of God ourselves is to start on the road to sanctity.* Sanctity, you know, is simply loving God. A saint is a lover of Christ. It is as simple as that.

Let us go without fear into that pity, which he offers us with such great tenderness and gentleness. Let us enter into that 'brotherhood' with himself to which he calls us. If we do this, so many of our tensions will disappear. Our loneliness will cease, because we will have found a 'brother' who looks after us. So much depends upon our *allowing* his pity to enter the very depths of our souls. If we do so, we will no longer have a sense of inner 'depression' because Christ will descend into the depths of it and will lift it up. So many painful things will vanish, if only we allow the gentle pity of Christ to take hold of us and to remember, each moment of our lives, that *God truly is with us.*

During this Eastertime, we find ourselves saying: "Christ is risen!" Do we realize what it is we are

94

proclaiming? *My Lover is risen!* He who showers upon me gentleness, kindness, pity, understanding, help, compassion, has arisen! Alleluia! Let us incarnate in our daily tasks what the words "Christ is risen" mean to us. Otherwise, they will just be sounds in the air; they will not be real. We cannot allow the meaning of them to vanish like this. The reality of those words must penetrate the depths of our hearts; and then we must turn around and give it to others.

The gentle, unassuming, yet infinitely strong and loving pity of God is ours for the asking. Let us ask.

Lovingly yours in Mary,

PROCLAIM HIS GLORY

May 26, 1976

Dearly Beloved,

As you all know, I recently gave a lecture in Albany, New York. I drove there with one of our Madonna House priests, Father Wild. The trip was pleasant, and we stopped over in various places where Father Wild could say Mass, just as Father Briere used to do.

At one place where we stopped for Mass, I really *listened* with my whole heart, my whole mind, my whole body; and I was astounded at the content of the Mass. It seemed to come right to me from the Lord, just before I was going to lecture. Listen:

Proclaim his glory among the nations, his marvelous deeds to the people. Great is the Lord and worthy of all praise. (Psalm 95:3-4).

I was really struck by this passage, for there was God telling me to proclaim his glory to all the nations. Do you understand, dearly beloved, what it means to proclaim the glory of God? It means that one must come close to 'the glory of God' again and again and again. And, as has happened a thousand times before, we hear the voice of God saying to us, "Friend, come up higher."

Yes, that is what he wants us to do; to proclaim his glory. Thus we must touch it. But how does one touch the glory of God? How does one come close to him? There I was, kneeling at Mass, wondering about it. Then I knew that it was very simple – I had to touch my neighbor.

The words of my mother came back to me. As a child, I said to her: "Mother, I want to touch Jesus Christ." She said to me, "Then touch me." Tears came to my eyes as I thought of the simplicity of God, and I knew that indeed I could proclaim his glory because, sinner that I am, I touched him for many years – practically my whole life – in others. So I caught a glimpse of his glory and I could pass it on with his help. The Mass continued:

The Lord sent disciples to proclaim to all the towns: *"The kingdom of God is very near to you."* (Luke 10:1-9)

I knew that the kingdom of God was 'very near' to me, to all of us at Madonna House. We were chosen by God, it seems to me, to be close to him because so few would be with him there, in the 'marketplaces' of this world. The time will come when those who are close to him will be martyrs. They will be shot, tortured, killed in various ways. They will be martyred, and Christ will stand 'in the marketplace' very much alone. But the Kingdom of God will be very close to those who stand with him, because he said: *Whoever is not with me is against me.*

And it has come to pass. Here is a letter which I received from a priest:

> Most of the missionaries are being expelled by governments now whose officials are not simply people who represent the popular will in a country, or the legitimate nationalistic aspirations of a colonized people. The groups taking over these governments are 'communistic' – not in any ideological sense of desiring a more just distribution of wealth or making more intelligent use of the resources of the nation than colonial capitalism can provide. They are godless people, very often explicitly or implicitly moved by demonic forces ... .

I believe this priest completely. I have experienced these demonic forces. I think the time for prayer, deep prayer, is at hand. In a little while, we shall see God's anger (which is his mercy) spilling over the earth, greater than an earthquake, greater than a flood, greater than all of the signs of nature. But the Kingdom of God is close at hand. That is very true if we but only open our eyes to what is *really* happening, and not just what we think is happening.

In order to touch God, in order to be close to him and to tell about the Kingdom which is nigh, as present circumstances show us, *we must forgive*. We must forgive ourselves. We must forgive our brethren. We must become humble, submissive, moved only by the will of God, not by our intellects. Soon, very soon, an intellect which is demonic is going to take over; and against it our intellect will be as nothing. But our hearts, our cruciform hearts, can stop all demons, for we are Mary's children and she will help us.

Father Wild went on to read the Gospel of the Mass:

> As the Father has loved me, so I have loved you. Remain in my love. If you keep my commandments you will remain in my love, just as I have kept my Father's commandments and remain in his love. I have told you this so that my joy may be in you and your joy be complete. This is my commandment: love one another as I have loved you! A man can have no greater love than to lay down his life for his friends. You are my friends if you do what I command you. I

shall not call you servants any more because a servant does not know his master's business; I call you friends because I have made known to you everything I have learned from the Father.

You did not choose me; no, I chose you! And I commissioned you to *go out and bear fruit,* fruit that will last. And then the Father will give you anything you ask in my name. What I command you is to *love* one another. (Luke 15: 9-17).

When I heard this, my faith was not shaken; but *I* was! It is so clear, so obvious, that the Lord is writing out for us our whole life, our whole mode of conduct, our whole 'existence' as it were. He commissioned us to bear fruit and we *are* bearing fruit. He commissioned us to love one another, and we *are* loving one another. But love has no limits, and we must love one another *more*.

This is a strange letter, but I share it with you to show how deeply shaken I was at that Mass on my way to Albany. Because of these readings, I gave (I think) a good lecture.

During the return trip, while I was in my motel room, I felt such an immense surge of love for all of you that once more I was shaken. I fell prostrate, as we Russians do, and for once I cried. I don't cry much, but this time I cried with joy. I knew the 'gift of tears' had been given to me at that moment to encompass all of you. It is said that Our Lady collects such tears to bring them to her Son. (What he does with them, I do not know; but I thought I would share this with you.)

When I got back to Combermere, I learned that my brother Serge – who lives in Belgium – had died during the night of my return. I sent his wife this cablegram:

There are no words. So I will not say anything. Pain and joy live in silence. I am silent with you in prayer.

Lovingly yours in Mary,

TWO WHITE CANDLES

June 14, 1976

Dearly Beloved,

Two little white tapers, one somewhat broken ... That is all that I have in my hands from the funeral of my brother Serge. A friend brought these to me. *Two little tapers, one a little broken in the middle* ... I keep them on my table and often hold them in my hands, for somehow they make the presence of my brother seem very near. They make me think of his life, for he was like these tapers, clean and white. And he burned before God as they do, but in a hidden and humble way. He was broken in the middle, too! During his teenage years the Russian Revolution happened, and his life was 'shattered' in a manner of speaking.

Two little tapers, one broken in the middle ... I thought of our childhood. He was born in Egypt and he was younger than I, so I was very interested in him.* Ever since he was a baby I loved to look at him, to hold him on my lap. I liked the feel of his little fingers around my own. He had a beautiful laughter. As I hold the little white tapers, I can still hear it. It is as if the tapers laugh and tell me, gently and hiddenly, that even as he burns before God, he is quite close in the Communion of Saints. And I realize more what that means. They seem to tell me he is joyful before the Lord.

Two little tapers, one broken in the middle ... How close we were as we grew up together! If one of us received a piece of candy, we always cut it in two so that the other had his share. Our motto, childish as it was, grew into an adult one: "Share and share alike."

Just before he died, he wrote me two letters and sent me a postcard of the boat on which my first husband, Boris,

---

* Catherine was born in Russia on August 15, 1896. Serge was born eight years later, on August 30, 1904. At the time of the Russian Revolution, Catherine had just turned 21 years old, Serge was barely 13 years old.

and I had come to Canada. I had written him that card while I was on this ship, which was called the *Minnedosa*. (It was part of the Canadian Pacific Line.) On the top he had written, "This was sent to me fifty years ago." We didn't write to each other very much, for as he used to say, "When one loves very much, space and time don't exist." It is true. He was always present to me, and I think I was always present to him.

Two little tapers, one broken in the middle ... He died in peacefully, in his sleep. I couldn't go to Belgium, but the Lord sent Archbishop Joseph Raya* of the Melkite Rite, who gave homilies both at the church and the cemetery.

Two little white tapers, one broken in the middle ... That's all I have now; yet I have a tremendous store of fantastic memories of his life. He enlisted in the English army during the Second World War, for he was married to an English girl. He was part of the D-Day invasion of Europe. He saw the camps of Auschwitz, and was used sometimes as a translator between the English and the Russians whom he met in Berlin. He talked to me about those memories.

Thanks be to God, he came to Madonna House once, bringing his wife. After he had looked the whole place over, he turned to me and said: "Katia, my darling, you have reproduced our childhood here. This is just like a Russian estate or farm. God bless you for bringing a bit of Russia to a foreign land."

Yes, all I have are *two little tapers ... one broken in the middle ...* but I have fantastic memories of a man who was 'a gentleman of the old school.' He was exceedingly gentle, loving, patient. A son of his had predeceased him by nine years. (I thought that was probably another reason why one taper was broken in the middle. The revolution and the death of his son had, in a way, dented that hidden courage and that strong will.)

Serge didn't talk a lot, but the words that were always on his lips were the words of our father, Theodore, who – when he had lost all of his possessions – said: "God has given. God has taken away. Let the will of the Lord be done."

* An associate member of Madonna House who was visiting Belgium at the time.

Two little white tapers ... one broken in the middle!
Yes, I hold in my hand 'light' and I know that the light of
Serge is illuminating my life. Thank you, Serge.

Lovingly yours in Mary,

THE SIMPLICITY OF GOD

July 26, 1976

Dearly Beloved,

Last Saturday, in the poustinia, the word that came to
me was *simplicity*. I paused and meditated upon it for the
rest of my poustinia, and for some time afterwards. When
you apply this word to God, it really becomes incredible.

We are not wrong when we think of God as being the
very essence of simplicity. Yet the more I think of God's
simplicity, the more I realize (by contrast) there's no
denying that we cannot understand the mystery and depth
of that simplicity! At the same time, how very many
wounds of ours would be healed if we approached him
humbly and *simply,* and asked him to allow us to become as
simple as he was when he took on our daily, nitty-gritty,
uneventful existence.

Consider, dearly beloved, how simply he entered the
womb of a woman. It is true that an angel announced his
coming to her; but in a physical sense (in the sense that we
understand pregnancy) he lay in the womb of that woman
nine months, just as all of us have done. He simply 'existed

through her existence' as it were. This was a time of total dependency. Here you find an incredible condition – God *depending on* his creature!

So simplicity is also dependency. As the Lord depended upon his creature, so we creatures should depend upon him. As he lay in the womb of a woman, so our life should consist in lying in his heart. After all, baptism is the beginning of that union of man with God, and somehow it brings forth the incredibly personal union of God with a woman, the fantastic oneness that a child has with his mother.

Then let us deeply, reverently, prayerfully, consider his birth. Here, stark simplicity reigned. Was it meant as a precursor to his meeting later with the rich young man? When Christ looked at him lovingly and suggested that he give up everything and follow him, the rich young man would have had to become very simple and uncomplicated. All the worries about his wealth should have fallen away from him like an old and worn-out mantle, and he should have followed Christ. Then Christ would have imparted to him *the naked simplicity of his birth,* and would have enabled him to speak about poverty the only way he could have spoken after that.

Simplicity followed Jesus wherever he went, from childhood on. What is more simple than the life of a carpenter in a small village where everybody knows one another? The very simplicity of his occupation must have been monotonous, and very hard on his muscles. Even tedious, perhaps, for simplicity is like that. Simplicity accepts the nitty-gritty aspect of life – its sameness, its monotony. Once we understand this, however, we find that simplicity is shot through with great joy, for it holds within itself a fantastic joy.

At some point in his simple life, Jesus must have been confronted with a choice. He was sent to redeem the human race by preaching the Good News of the love that God, the Triune God, had for all humanity. Without hesitation, he left his mother, his familiar village, the occupation which must have become pleasant and dear to him. *He left everything!* He started going across Palestine on foot, preaching and performing miracles. He also prayed unceasingly, as he has told us to do. Again, the simplicity of the choice and the means staggers me.

He did not hesitate to antagonize the ruling powers, because he had to do so. They did not accept truth; and he was Truth itself. He came to make that truth available to everyone, at all times, in all conditions. And he is available to all of us now, even as he was back then when he walked the paths of Palestine, because he is *still* in our midst.

Yes, simplicity walked with him throughout all of his journeying, for simplicity is fearless. True, he was God. He did the will of his Father. He made us 'gods' too; for he made us brothers and sisters of him, and heirs of the Father. Because he loved us, he preached and taught us to *love God back* in a simple and childlike way – a way in which we would not be afraid to preach and teach the truth because, if we accept his simplicity, we will never imagine that *we* are doing the preaching. We will truly know that it is he who preaches in us. Yes, that will happen, if our hearts are simple.

Then he was crucified. Here, we enter into our identification with him and allow ourselves to be crucified on the other side of his cross. It will be a very simple act. It will not require a cross of wood, nor will the nails be of iron. This 'crucifixion' will be a slow, powerful 'emptying of self' so that our outstretched arms will be – very simply – 'nailed' in an embrace of the whole world.

I wrote a little poem about simplicity once:

You speak so easily of her
They call Simplicity ...
But do you know the way
To her?

It, too, is simple – like Herself!
Two beams that make a cross
Are simple, homey things ...
Formed from trees
That grow abundantly.

Three nails ... so easily come by ...
So cheap, 'so simple' ...

A hammer – old, familiar tool –
Will do nicely too!

Now ... your hands and feet –
Simple, familiar parts of
YOU!

You will find Simplicity.
The way will be quite simple,
Straight and clear ...
When "wood and nails and YOU"
are One!

Then she is yours!

As I meditated on all the things I've tried to put down on paper for you, my dearly beloved, I began to realize that the word *simplicity* applies to all of us across the whole Apostolate. If we really embrace it, we will become childlike – just as he asks us to do. Our wounds, especially the memory of wrongs inflicted upon us in our youth, would disappear. For simplicity is a marvelous God-given medicine. It does more than comfort; it *heals*. The nitty-gritty 'sameness' of our everyday lives would be shot through with songs of joy, because our lives would be very much like the life of the Holy Family.

The more we grow in simplicity, the more joyous we would become. The more joyous we become, the more we will sing and dance before the Lord ... if not with our feet and voice, at least with our hearts. The music of simplicity will become a constant beat in our hearts.

Yes, on July 24th, 1976, I clearly heard the one word which God gave to us: *simplicity.*

Lovingly yours in Mary,

TIME TO SURRENDER

August 10, 1976

Dearly Beloved,

Last Saturday I went to the poustinia, and the word that came to me was *surrender*. As I pondered that word, I found that it is a very mysterious one. It pertains to the immense 'mystery of the incarnation'; and before its depths I stood as one transfigured.

Truth and love brought the Second Person of the Most Holy Trinity into our midst. First, the love of his Father; for when one loves, one surrenders to the will of the beloved. But this part of the mystery was beyond me. I just prostrated myself before it because that was all that I could do.

It was the second part of that 'mystery' which gripped my whole being in its immensity, for by his incarnation the Lord surrendered himself to human beings. He did so out of love – a totality of love which stretched itself out before me as another mystery. It is awesome to be led to behold the mysteries of God. They are the expression of his love. Yes, trembling with awe I beheld *the surrender of God to man!*

Mary carried the Divine Infant wherever she went, and he let himself be carried. This brought me to consider the Eucharist, in which the Lord, in the shape of bread, allows himself to be carried wherever a priest (or anyone appointed to do so) wants to carry him.

Images of the word *surrender* began to enter my heart. I saw the deep surrender of Jesus to the kiss of Judas, his surrender to the soldiers of the Sanhedrin, his surrender to the Romans, to the soldiers of Pontius Pilate, to crucifixion. And finally, his surrender to death and the tomb.

Then, as if a strange explosion occurred in my heart, I knew that this surrender of God to man through his incarnation was his way of showing us that *HE WAS THE WAY*. He was the exemplar; he was the leader in that strange game of love which God has played from the beginning, when he created us; for he loved us first.

Now it is my time, now it is your time – the time of all Christians – to, surrender to God ... and to do so as totally, as irrevocably, as he has surrendered to us! Only love can do that sort of surrendering. Only love can enter into that 'self-surrender' and make it its lifestyle. *For surrender is another way of saying commitment.* When a man and a woman love each other, they 'surrender' to each other because they love. After such a commitment, there will be 'no one else' because self-surrender means complete loyalty and faithfulness toward the other.

Slowly, I began to see that the word which Our Lord placed in my heart, that Saturday in poustinia, was indeed a mysterious word. It was profound, immense; yet, at the same time, it was simple and direct and childlike. A child 'surrenders' to its parents quite easily. All I really have to do is to pray to God to give me 'the heart of a child' and 'the awesome courage to live it out as an adult.'

This is the time of surrender, dearly beloved. This is the time of laying aside 'concern for self' – all the worries and angers and emotional 'claptrap' which seem to follow us eternally, wherever we go, and which make us blind and deaf to the voice of God speaking within us. Yes, it is time to surrender.

It is natural for us to consider the cost of that surrender; but then, supernaturally, such considerations will disappear from our consciousness. It will be as it was when Eddie and I were approached by the bishop, who asked us if we would take the promise of chastity, the same as unmarried Staff Workers. Eddie replied very simply: "Of course, Your Excellency, we will do this. *It is so little to give God, who gave us so much!*" I remember well how Eddie then turned to me and said: "Don't you agree, Catherine?" Of course I agreed. What else could I do?

Unless surrender is *total*, it is not surrender at all because I am keeping something to myself. I should give God *all* of myself for I belong to him. No matter who I am – priest, nun, married or single – I *belong* to him because he created me. I rest on the 'palm of his hand' as it were. He has full dominion over me; over my life, and over my death!

106

But it is not out of 'fear' that I should surrender, dearly beloved. Oh, no! I should surrender out of a 'passionate love' of him who surrendered himself so passionately for me. Then, indeed, I will enter into the resurrection of the Lord; and he will continue to 'unroll the parchment' of his mysteries to me, slowly and gently, while the Holy Spirit will reveal to me anything that I do not understand.

God the Father will bend benevolently and lovingly over those 'lessons' (if I may call them that), all those lessons of theology given by Jesus Christ to the learned and unlearned, to those who love him.

Yes, *surrender* is the gentle song of love.

Lovingly yours in Mary,

STABILITY

September 30, 1976

Dearly Beloved,

I have been praying and thinking much about the word stability. As you know. We used to have a tape-recording called "Loyalty, Stability, and Dedication." Perhaps we should listen to it again. I thought of the related words: permanency, dedication, and immobility.

Then a strange thought filtered in: we call the place where the animals are kept a stable. Is that perhaps because a farmer is bound by the stable? He cannot leave a stable for any length of time because cows have to be milked and all the animals fed. So maybe stability originated from a rural way of life.*

Then my fertile mind went further, and I asked myself why God was born in a stable. Maybe he wanted to be born in a place to which people are attached by so many strands of their lives. I don't think it is wrong to say that *stable* and *stability* are not only a play on words; they have a big spiritual significance. These were the thoughts which have been passing through my mind during the local directors' meetings and at night when I prayed.

Today we are subjected to a tremendous pressure to change. One of our priests clearly explained to me the immense changes which are overtaking us. His own parents were born and raised in the horse-and-buggy age, and suddenly were propelled into the age of automobiles. When they had barely become accustomed to that, there was the age of small airplanes and fast railroad trains. After that came jet-planes. Then there was the atomic age. How easy was that adaptation?

But that is older people. Younger people now feel this intolerable pressure from their elders, as well as their own memories of the past, and the fast-moving pace of today's educational changes. It is difficult to know *how* to learn, or *what* to learn, because the yesterday's system of teaching is already changed today. Nothing is the same; not even physics or mathematics.

Bewildered and miserable, people of all ages are seeking stability as human beings have never sought it before. All around us, people are unmoored; but the Lord will not leave us 'alone' ... shepherdless, fatherless, brotherless. No! He comes, softly, and calls us to this stability of the 'stable' in which he was born, of a way of life that is different from that around us. He calls us to permanency. He calls us to the acceptance of our lot in Madonna House, because Madonna House needs us, and because it is the house of his mother. Yes, let us squarely face the fact that God created this house in which we live;

* The Latin root *sta* means to be 'motionless, still, in one location.' Stable and stability come from this ancient source, as do English words like stall, stand, status, statue, establishment.

108

in a manner of speaking, he 'handed it over' to his mother. Nevertheless, his hand is over it at all times.

How does he call certain people to Madonna House? There is something that happens between a human being and God. It is as if he were walking, as he passed by the apostles, and the swish of his garment is heard, and the wind blows his word toward whoever it is that he is calling. The wind softly brings the words: "Come, follow Me." He calls people to Madonna House because *he has a plan in mind for them.* We should be 'on our knees' as it were, listening to the evolvement of this plan. It will come to us *through things and events and people* (and occasionally through myself), because that is the way God usually speaks.

We must make up our minds that we have come to the Apostolate to serve it, and that it does not 'exist' to serve us. *Yes, we are here to serve others!* At the same time, however, the Apostolate does tend to fulfill our individual needs in some respects. It does so through our mutual love, through our mutual friendship, through support, through making us a real Christian family.

Each of us are 'at the disposal of' the Apostolate, as far as work is concerned. We go where we are needed, and stay there as long as we are asked to. *This is stability.* We do not wish to change for the sake of change. We should be perfectly content to spend our lives in the kitchen, in the laundry, in the office, or wherever we are placed. If change comes to us, it is to meet a need of the Apostolate ... and only that.

The preceding paragraph, however, does *not* apply to the young members. As soon as they receive the Cross,* they should expect to be moved to different places in the Apostolate. They need to confront the realities of life, and to understand how our God-given vocation is to be 'lived out' in various departments and mission houses, in the face of those urgent realities. But once this stage is over, they too must make up their minds to remain where the Apostolate needs them and not to desire 'change for the sake of a change.' *That is stability.* That leads to fidelity,

* A stainless-steel cross, with *Pax* and *Caritas* inscribed on it, is given to each person who becomes a member of Madonna House.

and it is crowned at the end by perseverance.

I haven't really begun to share my ideas on stability. I have to pray more, and then I will write more to you. In this 'un-stable' world that has "no cows, no ox, no ass to witness the eternal birth of the King" in people's lives, someone has to clarify stability in a big way. I do not know whether I am that person, but stability is a word that I hear in the deep of the night, and it won't let me sleep. It keeps hammering at my heart like a thousand little hammers, so you will hear more about it.

Lovingly yours in Mary,

DUTY OF THE MOMENT – DUTY OF GOD

October 16, 1976

Dearly Beloved,

I have been praying very much for our enlightenment. Recently, my prayer has been spearheaded by a remark of one of our members who said that she wished that she had something 'to sink her teeth into.' Upon discussion, I found that this was a general feeling in the particular group of people who were having tea together. They felt that Madonna House life, or part of it, had become unchallenging and monotonous.

They spoke of the office and its constant routine: bundling up and sending out the *Restoration* newspaper each month; thanking the donors for things received;

endlessly entering names, changing addresses, renewing subscriptions to the paper; answering the telephone (which never stops ringing!); doing the bookkeeping; and so forth. Then they spoke of the 'sameness' of the kitchen: preparing endless meals and getting them onto the table; washing dishes that seem to pile up like an enormous fortress to which there is no entrance.

On Monday, our usual day for sorting donations, there are literally tons of clothing to sort, plus other items. Then there is the sorting of books. Between the person responsible for the bookstore, the staff who run our library, and myself, we figured out that we handle about a thousand books each time we sort.

Then there is the jewelry, and the holy cards, and many other items to send out to the missions or to keep for the religious museum. What a dull (seemingly dull) and unchallenging routine it is. After that, the handicraft department endlessly re-sorts whatever is left behind and puts them into finer divisions, sending items to a particular mission or having things repaired so they that can be sold in our gift shop to help the poor. (I don't even mention the laundry, or the work of the men at the farm, and the constant repetitive 'chores' which must be done in those occupations!)

Yes, we are forever surrounded by tasks that appear to be dull, monotonous, routine, unchallenging. I listened to all of this chitchat around the tea table, and to the tremendous desires which seemed to animate the members of this particular group. They were not just idly talking. They were not at all upset, but were 'presenting their ideas.' But as they continued to talk, their voices suddenly did not reach me any more. Somehow I was lost in Palestine. I saw a hammer, a chisel, a hand-plane. Somehow I was utterly astounded – as if I had never thought of it before – a carpenter's shop!

The challenge that it presented was beyond my ability to absorb. The Second Person of the Most Holy Trinity – someone who could have been a rabbi, a king, an emperor, a man of tremendous renown, a philosopher; someone at whose feet the whole world would come to sit and listen – this awesome Person was right there, bent over a workbench in that shop, chiseling and planing pieces of wood, doing little 'unimportant' tasks: building a table for someone, making a cradle for somebody else, crafting a chair for another.

I saw his calloused hands (for he did have calloused hands!) and I asked myself: Why did he choose such humble, uninspiring, unchallenging tasks? Once you knew how to do them, they could never be called things 'to sink your teeth into.' On some side street in an unimportant village, he worked as an ordinary carpenter, just as his foster father did. And what did his mother do? She washed and scrubbed, and took the laundry to the river, and milled the kernels of wheat manually between two stones. She wove cloth; it is said that she wove the cloak that the Romans threw dice for because it was so beautiful.

I began to hear again the teatime discussion about the mounds of dishes, the eternal sorting of donations, the answering of phones, the filing of cards ... the dulling rhythm of seemingly unimportant tasks. It all became filled with a strange glow and I understood the fantastic, incredible, holy words contained in that sentence: *The duty of the moment is the duty of God.* I understood also that *anything* done for him is glamorous, exciting, wondrous – if only we can see it for what it truly is!

But we are human. And it takes a long time, my dearly beloved ones, to see reality through God's eyes. Unless we pray exceedingly hard, it takes a long time to 'make straight the paths of the Lord' in our souls. We can get into a depression for many reasons. We even become sick for what might be called 'environmental' reasons. But oh, dearly beloved, let me ask you one thing: What would you do *outside* of Madonna House, if you were to leave it? Perhaps it would be office work with nothing 'to bite deeply into.' Of course, you would receive money for it. But the money would be very dull after having experienced the joy of working for Christ, and of doing little things for him. You could become a salesclerk, but it would be the same thing. True, you would be free from 5 p.m. onwards (or whatever the quitting time it might be), but what are you going to *do* with your freedom?

When we experience the depths of pain in our lives –

the pain of 'making straight the paths of the Lord' in our hearts – it would be a very good idea to remind ourselves that such pain is not confined to Madonna House. It is found everywhere; it is part of the human condition. *And the pain will be with us until we die.* The answer to that strange and mysterious pain, in Madonna House or anywhere else, is prayer. Nothing else will do it, my dearly beloved; nothing else.

But – *with prayer!* – we see an entirely different world about us. Sorting clothes becomes a joy. Washing dishes becomes an exciting challenge. The careful repetitious tasks of creating beauty (as in embroidery work, weaving, painting, pottery, carpentry, etc.) take on a new meaning.

Yes, I came back from wherever I was, watching Jesus doing carpenter work; and I thanked God that he became a manual laborer to show us the way to the Father. There is more that I want to write to you, but this will suffice for today. Send me your feedback, dearly beloved.

Lovingly yours in Mary,

THE HOUR OF KENOSIS

November 23, 1976

Dearly Beloved,

We are on the threshold of Advent, and Christmas is approaching. I have been thinking that this is *the moment of stripping*. God stripped himself of everything. He was the Son of God; and he became the Son of Man, taking upon himself our humanity,

Surely the spirit of Advent must fill you with tremendous awe. As you live the weeks of it, you feel this kenosis, this 'stripping,' as it works in your heart, mind, and body! This is the moment of 'giving up.' This is the moment, the small tiny moment, when you give up your father, mother, sister, brother, your relatives, for whom you are accustomed to making gifts. Let your gift this year be a prayer at the creche.* That is the greatest gift you can give your friends and relatives. By the time you kneel before the Christ Child in the manger, your hands will be filled with gifts – the ones you give up for his sake.

It is a strange thing that you see happening there. Call it whatever you will (your imagination or whatever), but each time you 'give it up' the angels pick up what you gave and bring your gifts to the stable in preparation for his coming.

If your parents are poor, if your relatives lack what is necessary, come and ask me; and for them, as an exception, you and I will kneel together before Christ in the chapel, and we will find out what it is that he wants you to give them.

Yes, this is the hour of kenosis. This is the hour of stripping. This is the hour of 'giving up' as he gave up so much for love of you. This is a love affair with a baby in a creche. Tomorrow it will be a love affair with a man on a cross.

Lovingly yours in Mary,

* A crib scene of the Nativity, displayed at Christmas time.

114

DOUBT AND TRUST

December 2, 1976

Dearly Beloved,

Having the sniffles and being in bed have given me much time to think and pray about two words which have recently entered deeply into my consciousness. They are the words *doubt* and *trust*.

Did you know, dear ones, that words are things that can be looked at from many angles? Sometimes God gives us special help to do this. Yes, I looked at those two words, turning them around and around, allowing them to catch the morning light, the sunlight, the evening light. I saw them most clearly at night, for that is the time when they could be placed upon the heart of God and there reflect their true meaning.

Doubt

Who among us does not doubt? Right now, many of you doubt your vocation. You are reaching the thirties, the forties; and your life, at times, appears to be almost meaningless. What is it that you have to show for it? This is an important question to you, especially so because the North American culture is one of self-analysis. You measure yourself against the yardstick of success; you dream of being a person who 'comes home in glory.' In a word, you desire to be the man or woman who has 'made good' somehow!

Because you have been constantly exposed to this type of thinking so prevalent in modern society, your life now appears almost useless. You look around, and what do you see? Mounds of clothing that you have sorted. Mounds of dishes that you have washed. Endless stenography books, full of little squiggles that you typed and typed and typed, until your back ached and you felt totally 'fed up' with your work.

Or maybe your nose was all day long in bookkeeping, your ears constantly answering the phone. Maybe you were working on our newspaper, and dealt constantly with 2 x 4 Elliott stencils and 3 x 5 file cards, shuffling them and reshuffling them, eternally putting down names and addresses, correcting and recorrecting them. Perhaps you have been in the kitchen or laundry, doing work that you didn't feel you could really 'do well.'

Yes, looking back, you see all of these things; and they look like gray pebbles along your road. They make your life seem like a dreary highway, empty of anyone passing by. Your thoughts take a thousand shapes, all of them negative, and you begin to doubt. You doubt the wisdom of God who brought you here. You doubt your own wisdom in staying. You question various spiritual directors, and you change from one to another to a third because they never quite agree with you. At times, doubt surrounds you like a London fog. You are blanketed with a dank, chilly, penetrating fog that blinds you to where you are going.

Trust

Then there is the question of trust. Why are you so afraid of trusting God, or the priests, or your brothers and sisters in the Apostolate? You seem so very afraid of others, and deeply protective of your own being. Why is this? What do you have to hide? None of us at Madonna House are a bunch of criminals, after all. And as for 'sin' ... well, other people aren't much interested in dwelling on your personal sins, probably because they already have committed these sins (or most of them) themselves.

So then, where does this terrible mistrust of priests or of each another come from? How can we build even a semblance of sobornost if we don't trust one another? The only answer that I can give is *fear:* Fear of pain; fear of ridicule; fear of rejection; fear of non-acceptance (which is the same as 'rejection' but a bit more profound).

Why do any of us have such fears? We are all God's children. We came into a family which God has created so that we could belong to one another. Can't you see – really see with the eyes of your soul, your heart – what kind of life you have led at Madonna House in the last twenty-five, fifteen, ten, or five years? Is it true that your life has been just a lot of bookkeeping, kitchen work, laundry, and so forth?

Do you realize how many people your life has touched? You have been called by God to witness *by your presence,* wherever you might be, whatever task you might be doing! If your job, your department, your workplace seems humble to you, remember that it is as humble as the carpenter's shop in which the God-Man worked with his hands – those hands which were later pierced by nails, on wood such as he had handled daily. Your work certainly won't lead you to getting a Ph.D., or to being a man or woman who 'made good' in the eyes of the world. (But in God's eyes ... ah, that's different!)

When I first came to Canada, I remember being at a railway station where there was a lot of music and excitement. I asked what had happened, and the people said, "A tycoon who made good was here." I didn't know what a tycoon was or what 'made good' meant, so I asked them. I was told that he had made a million dollars. They were equating money with 'good.'

Here at Madonna House, we live a life of poverty just as Christ himself lived. We do the same monotonous jobs that ordinary folks do. We should never be afraid of ridicule in this regard. We should never mistrust what life will bring us in the way of work or jobs or tasks to be done. We should simply offer our hands to the nails of pain or ridicule (or whatever else there might be) because Christ did so, and we have chosen to follow him. How can we doubt that our lives are glorious, shining like the sun, when He-who-is-God has called us to live that life?

Yes, last night I was holding these words – doubt and trust (and lack of trust) – in my hands. And as I told you, I see them best in darkness, illuminated by his light and his heart. I pass on to you what I saw in that dark night.

Lovingly yours in Mary,

THE WORLD OF SILENCE

Christmas 1976

Dearly Beloved,

It seems to me that, as time goes on, I come closer and closer to the world of silence. It is a strange world. I have described it somewhat in my book, *Poustinia*,* for to go into the desert, one perforce enters silence.

At first, silence is a hard taskmaster. But then, slowly, it ceases to press you down, to make you face yourself, to cause you to have strange and unaccountable fits of anger against yourself and everybody else. (Yes, silence often brings these things about.)

After a time, silence becomes a mirror. In the heat of the desert, distorted images often arise to confuse the traveler. For example, a person who is very thirsty may suddenly see a lake where there is actually none. That is called a *mirage*. The word, I imagine, stems from the word *mirror*, which is a word much like the French word *miroir*.† Mirage has something to do with 'mirrors that are not there'; but the silence of which I speak is a true mirror.

At first, the mirror of silence is a bit blurred. But if we stand before it long enough, in some sort of way we begin to realize that we are standing before the face of God, and that we are really created in his image. So that looking into the mirror of the desert, the mirror of silence, simply means that I am looking at the face of God and seeing my own face reflected there.

True, Christ said that no one can come to the Father except through him, and the Scriptures are full of the fact that one cannot see God without dying. But in my strange

---

* Published in 1974 by Ave Maria Press, Notre Dame, Indiana. In 1982, Crossroad Publishing, New York City, came out with Catherine's book on 'The Silence of God' under the title of *Molchanie*.
† Catherine is correct. The Latin verb *mirari* means 'to admire, wonder, be astonished.' From it are derived mirror, mirage, and miracle in English, and the equivalent words in French.

silence I see God very well. I can see myself very well in this silence, to which God leads me in that desert; and if I see myself, then in a manner of speaking, in almost incredible depths, I see God present within me.

These days, I am sort of hovering on the edge of a deep silence. You know something about silence, dear ones? Silence is not the absence of sound. In fact, *it is in silence that every noise can be clearly heard.* In my new-found silence, I hear the noise of many feet. Some come slowly, some come hurriedly, some reluctantly, some haltingly; but they come. It doesn't disturb my silence. On the contrary, it deepens it in some strange manner. Somehow I know ahead of time *who* it is that comes, and often I know *why.*

I think it must be because of the great love that blooms very powerfully in my heart toward you. As I repeat so often, I love you exceedingly; and so I hear each footstep that comes my way in this silence. And in silence I seem to enter one of the last paragraphs of the Little Mandate: *Go without fear into the depth of men's hearts; I shall be with you.* I know that I will find God there, helping me.

At times, I think I am brought to this silence – this warm but naked silence – in order to become naked myself. To be truly silent, we have to be 'naked' in a manner of speaking. That is to say, we have to shed all the 'garments' that hide and protect our humanity, and allow Christ to bedeck our nakedness with his own garments, which are often those of a pauper.

But I don't wish to bring you too quickly to the later steps in your journey. I simply want to introduce you to the one who is called Silence. As you draw closer to her, let not your feet falter. Walk straight and simply to her doorstep. You are going to a 'person' who loves you exceedingly, and who desires only that you be brought to Christ, for that is love.

Come, share my journey to the home of Silence! Enter her abode and let her serve you. For then so much that is in your hearts, your minds, your souls, will become quiet also.

I know that this is a strange letter to write for Christmas 1976. Or is it? For it is *silently* that the Lord descends into our midst. It is silently that he has stood in our midst for many years, and it is still in silence that he speaks to us. He speaks to us in the thunderous silence of the Eucharist.

Perhaps this is a good time to speak of silence, for it is about the only way of communication these days – the real way.

Lovingly yours in Mary,

Catherine

HOLD ON TO HOPE

Christmas 1976

Dearly Beloved,

This year I have a desire that is almost too great to bear: it is that you spend Christmas and the New Year in the peace of Our Lord. But at the same time, I want you to be armed with cords to chase the moneylenders out of the temple of your heart.

I visualize you making a pilgrimage to Bethlehem, in poverty. You have many of my letters telling you what I think of poverty, so make a pilgrimage – a pilgrimage that is not on foot, not by train, not by bus, but *a pilgrimage of the heart*. Your feet will be doing what the Lord wants you and me to do in Madonna House. Your hands will be working at what he wants you to do in Madonna House ... or in Regina, Edmonton, Yukon, Portland, Arizona, the West Indies, and wherever else our houses are. But your heart will journey forth to Bethlehem.

Don't think for a moment that it is going to be an easy road. Bethlehem is not an easy place to reach these days. You will, perhaps, have to pass through war zones. You will especially have to meet the hatred of man to man. And you will have to go 'two by two' as it were, in the peace of God. You will be unafraid of anything, because the only thing that men can do is to take away your life. But death, as you know, brings a new life! So you walk without fear, with a faith that beggars understanding.

It will have to be that kind of faith this Christmas of 1976. You will indeed have to arm yourself with that faith, for every step of the pilgrimage in this world of today requires faith. You might board an airplane for Montreal, but it will take you to strange regions by being hijacked. You will be at peace, however. And so shall I, because we shall be pilgriming via our hearts to the greatest mystery ever conceived, namely God; to contemplate the Second Person of the Most Holy Trinity becoming a human being, out of love for us!

Truly the Lord has given us hope. *Hold on to it!* Hold on to it no matter what! Hold on to faith. That's the pilgrimage of a lifetime.

Faith is a strange thing. It is something that you enter, something that is given to you by God; but it is something that you can increase *only by praying to God for it.* He will answer that prayer. He always does. So, like the woman who had the loss of blood, stick close to the hem of his garment and tug on it periodically, saying: "Give me a little more faith, please." And power will go out of him and enter your heart.

Christmas is going to be sad this year. We cannot forget Beirut. We cannot forget Rhodesia.* We cannot forget the Third World. We pray that there will not be any more war, but alas, the making of wars is already before our eyes. We have to face it, but we must do so with prayer. A pilgrim is a prayer. Always remember that the pilgrim

---

* In 1976, Syrian troops intervene in Lebanon's civil war, putting an end to the heaviest fighting which had killed 60,000 people. Rhodesia is in the midst of a guerilla war (1970-79). Its access to the Indian Ocean is blocked by the Mozambique government. Henry Kissinger and other world statemen engage in a nine-month effort to achieve a just and durable solution to this and other African conflicts.

does not just pray; he *is* a prayer. That is a real pilgrim. He learns it slowly.

So, my dearly beloved, wherever you are, *be a prayer* and bring yourself to Christ. That will be your pilgrimage to Bethlehem. You will bring yourself; you will bring a prayer to him in your person. There is no room anymore for only childish dialogues; although there will be a time, of course, when you grow in simplicity, and you can play with his little hands and maybe throw little balls at him or have some supper with him, and our Lady will be very hospitable.

This is imagery, of course. But do you realize that one of the greatest tragedies of this world, at least in our Canadian-American world, is that *we have left our imaginations behind,* and we have taken facts as if they were the 'alpha and omega' of our existence? Sure, facts are facts, but who cares only about facts?

It's interesting to know that two and two make four, but I'm not going to spend my life figuring that out, unless I'm a mathematician. If you give me the fact that two and two are four, I'll probably make an imaginative little story out of it; and I don't think that two and two will suffer because I have written a little story about them.

So you see, there is an 'essence' that I want to give you. I want to give you *a desire for the Desired One.* But I want also to give you a certain childlikeness that will accompany you on your way to Bethlehem – not 'childishness,' but 'childlikeness.' It's impossible *not* to be childlike with the Child Jesus. Impossible!

But then, there are other moments ... and you look at this Infant (for he was there in Bethlehem physically as an infant) and you look at yourself, and you understand why you are a member of Madonna House ... with poverty, chastity, and obedience as the 'gifts' that you are bringing to him ... because, you see, it means that *you are a prayer.* Yes, enter the New Year with hope, knowing that you can do nothing of yourself. But you will walk in faith, and it will grow and grow! And you will begin to understand that *he can do all things in you.*

So in total simplicity and childlikeness, in a faith that sings of your desire for him, in a love that celebrates with an untarnished hope, face this Christmas and this New Year without fear! Why should anyone of you be afraid when the Lord is with you?

This might not be a long Christmas Letter, but it comes to you from my heart. I shall journey with you to Bethlehem. Together we shall walk the journey from Bethlehem to Golgotha. Together we shall know (we already do know it) that we live in the resurrected Christ. Together, upholding each other in love and joy and faith, we shall restore that which needs restoring in the Church.

Happy Christmas to you! Even though the whole world should fall apart, it will still be a happy Christmas because, you see, Christ came to make it so! The same is true of the New Year — *it is yours to shape,* in Christ or outside of him. I know that you will do it in Christ, and so it will be a good year. May the grace of Our Lord, and especially the love of Our Lady and Saint Joseph, be with you this glorious season.

Lovingly yours in Mary,

THE COUNTRY OF PRAYER

January 2, 1977

Dearly Beloved,

By the time that you get this letter, you will have already received what amounts to two Christmas letters, one I dictated to my secretaries, the other I spoke into the microphone for all to hear. But it won't do you any harm to get two Christmas 'presents' from me.

This isn't a New Year's letter; it is just a plain, ordinary Staff Letter because I am on my way to the hospital at the Mayo Clinic, and you can contact me there. I am not sure whether or not I will have an operation on my knee. It will all depend on the doctors there, but you will hear about it in due time.

Hospitals and operations are very conducive to thinking about 'the things that matter' and, although I am not there yet (this is being written ahead of time), I look at the Apostolate and my heart rejoices at all of you because you have entered 'the country of prayer' – that strange, beautiful, and yet awesome country of the desert.

Do you know something? Once you enter into that desert, it begins to bloom. Your footsteps are the seeds of the flowers to come, and those who follow you already see these flowers. If you were to look back or retrace your steps, you would see them too. But one never looks back or retraces one's steps in the desert, for Christ is just up ahead, constantly calling and waiting, and all the time he is saying, "Friend, come up higher." There is no time to turn around and behold what was before, for love is like that – *it doesn't look back; it moves toward the beloved; it RUNS toward him!*

This is what is going to happen to all of you. Already it is happening to many. Yes, you have entered the country of prayer and I thank God deeply that this has happened. I want to remind you of one thing, however: those who enter the country of prayer leave all things behind. I often talk to you about kenosis, about 'emptying' oneself, about becoming like Christ ... who, being God, took upon himself our humanity and 'left behind' so much that our minds cannot grasp it at all.

Our minds can understand very well what it is that we human beings must 'leave behind' when we enter the service of God. As we walk the country of prayer (which is, of course, our heart) we become very clear about this renunciation because, unless we make it, our footsteps will be sterile. No seeds will enter the sand; no flowers will bloom; the desert will remain a wasteland.

And what is it that we must leave behind? Obviously, my dearly beloved friends, my dearly beloved children, we have to leave *our wills* behind. You will tell me, of course, that you are perfectly aware of the fact that we have to leave our wills behind and do the will of God. Easily said, but oh, how hard to put into practice! There are so many thousands of ways by which we cling to what is our own: our opinions; our desire to do things our way and not somebody else's way; our reaching out for approval, for acceptance, and so on.

Perhaps it would be much simpler for me to give you the Prayer of Saint Francis, and let you meditate upon it deeply. There are two parts to the prayer. I will dictate it here, although I know that you are already well aware of it. *(But are you? Are we? Am I?):*

> O Divine Master, grant that I may not so much seek
> To be consoled as to console,
> To be understood as to understand,
> To be loved as to love.

Yes, these are the words of one who has entered the life of prayer and the country thereof; for he understands (and so should we) that:

> It is in giving that we receive.
> It is in pardoning that we are pardoned.
> It is in dying that we are born to eternal life.

As I explained, walking in the country of prayer also means walking in the desert. And making the desert bloom is hard on the soles of our feet (and on our hearts). Definitely it hurts. Definitely the Prayer of St. Francis is a *totality of the life of Jesus Christ.* Definitely it is a total surrender of oneself. And it is through this type of life that one *becomes a prayer.*

The phrase I often repeat – that "pain is the kiss of Christ" – is a reality in this land which we have entered. It is a land in which everything that we *own* is surrendered to Christ, little by little. Everything that we *are* is surrendered to Christ until, freed from that 'self' which is so often spoken of in Scripture, we soar on the wings of prayer directly into the heart of Christ. And our soaring is done by humbly walking in his footsteps.

Hospitals are conducive to meditations of this type. I was meditating on my going to the hospital when all of this came into my mind, so I share it with you.

Lovingly yours in Mary,

ON PILGRIMAGE

January 2, 1977

Dearly Beloved,

This is written to you just after New Year's Day, which (believe it or not) I spent in bed, recovering from the flu shot. Though my body is still, staying in the poustinia of my sick bed, my thoughts continue to go 'on pilgrimage.'

This is being written to you on the eve of my departure for the Mayo Clinic. If the doctors there decide to operate on my knee, I will be three weeks in bed, then six weeks on crutches, learning to walk again; and then I will return to the clinic. I am beginning to think that it might be 'a little too much' and that I'd better prepare myself to endure the pain of this rigmarole. We shall see.

I have accepted several lectures, besides the one for the Trappists in Gethsemani, Kentucky, and the one in Dublin, Ireland, so that will carry me until about the end of June. I don't know where I will be in between lectures – maybe in

126

Arizona, maybe in Portland. Wherever I am, I will be in some sort of poustinia of my own while I do this painful pilgrimage.*

I want you to know that whatever I do is for you, because I love you very much. Being very poor, there is not much that I can give you. As the little shepherd boy said to Jesus in the manger: "All I can give you is my heart and my pain." You remember my favorite saying – *Pain is the kiss of Christ* – so consider yourself painlessly kissed by Christ who gives me pain for you.

I am also leaving because I sense that I must. You are growing in wisdom and grace, thanks be to God! But there is a certain sense of ... shall we say, a little 'divisiveness' here and there ... which doesn't augur too well for the future of the Apostolate. It isn't too big as yet, but I think my 'going away' may well resolve this situation better than my staying in Combermere.

Some time away from me (I hope) may erase that adverse mother-figure image that I represent to many of you, and change it into the pleasant mother-figure which I am to others of you. Anyhow, it is time that I made a little break and made a pilgrimage, and a poustinia, for you all.

It is difficult for me to explain to you how much I love you, because I am not a demonstrative person along those lines. I prefer my life to be a witness to my love. So, my dear one, I give you my life.

Lovingly yours in Mary,

Catherine

---

* Catherine was in her 81th year when she dictated this. Because of her health, she was unable to fulfill many of her 1977 lecture obligations. Father Pelton substituted for her in Kentucky. The trip to Ireland was cancelled.

SOLITARIES AND SERVICE

February 23, 1977

Dearly Beloved,

The other day Father Briere asked me: "When you say that no one can just simply imitate the Russian poustinik, what do you mean? How do you think that those living that kind of life here at Madonna House can become poustinikki in the *real* sense of the word?"*

I have often told you that, in the Russian tradition (and in the Eastern tradition in general), there is a style of life which is 'in between' the ordinary life of a Christian lay person and the monastic life of a monk or nun. This in-between point is what we call 'being a poustinik' or 'living in a poustinia.'

We at Madonna House don't profess to be eremitical – that is to say, hermits or solitaries. We are not separated from the ordinary people. But we *do* have some staff members who pray three days in the poustinia and spend four days out of it. Remember, *there must always be some days out,* during which time the poustinik is totally at the disposal of the community. If we take away those three or four days with the community, we would no longer have the poustinik vocation of Madonna House.

Why is this so? It is because both priests and lay people need to exemplify Christ in themselves, in their daily work. Even though Jesus prayed always, he came on earth to serve people in a very definite manner. Now look at what he did. He fed people. He healed them. He spent a certain amount of years with his family. He was a carpenter who made tables, chairs, cradles, other things. I am sure that the carpenter shop was a 'poustinia' for him. He spent his life there, except for three years of a different kind of

* *Poustinia* is a Russian word for 'desert' ... or for any place which fosters solitude, silence, prayer, penance. One who enters that type of life is called a *poustinik* (the plural of which is *poustinikki*).

service; and certainly he must have meditated and prayed in that workshop. But he also worked there.

I often tell you that the Russian people say that you are a contemplative *because you are baptized.* They say that to all Christians. This 'poustinia of the heart' or the 'poustinia of the marketplace' – the marketplace of the family, of a business enterprise, or what-have-you – is open to all of us because we are all baptized Christians.

From the very beginning, from our baptism as a child, we proceed toward union with God. This is the goal of every Christian, as you well understand. It is not a specific goal just of priests or nuns; it is the goal of *every* Christian! The 'poustinia of the heart' is a state of *constantly being in the presence of God* because one desires him with a great desire; because in him alone one can rest. The life of service and love to one's fellowman is simply an echo of this silence and solitude.

We're not saved by prayer, but by love. And love is always at the service of the beloved. In a sense, therefore, I would 'sorrow' very much if any of the priests or lay people of Madonna House thought that his or her individual life was meant to be exclusively a life of prayer. I think that if that were so, God would have sent them to the so-called contemplative orders, and not to us.

If you go through the roster of the saints – whether canonized, beatified, or made venerable – you would find that there are a lot of poustinikki within the Latin tradition. You are not aware of them, however, because these people were out in worldly society, serving others, while in their hearts they remained in a continual state of prayer.

There was Catherine of Siena, who started by embracing a solitary life, but ended up serving others in the daytime and spending the nights alone in prayer. There was Matt Talbot, a solitary, fighting his horrible alcoholism, doing heroic penance, and working in a lumber yard. Benedict Joseph Labre combined being a pilgrim and living in 'the poustinia of the heart' at the same time. He would be hired for a day or two – to help with a harvest, perhaps – then he went on his pilgrimage again. And one could name so many others.

People are lonely, but not solitary. There is a big

difference. They are not attached to God; they are attached to a strange void. And they sense it! In our times, there is a great hunger for God that is so evident. And people are trying desperately to fill this void.

There are many good ways of doing this: there are the Trappists, the Carthusians, the Benedictines, the Camaldolese, to name a few. There are other orders which allow for solitaries also, in a greater or lesser form, but they also exist to serve the community in some way. They work at farming, and often they feed the poor as well as their own community. But, notwithstanding their solitariness, they know that *they have to practice charity and hospitality,* which can often mean performing manual labor as well. They do all of this because Christ said, "I have come to serve!" But their main work is prayer; and they have become leaders in spiritual direction and the practice of the spiritual life.

So then, *love has to incarnate itself in action.* It isn't enough merely to pray for people. Often they need the loving touch of a personal visit, a personal concern – the 'hospitality of the heart' as I call it – so that they can believe in that love.

I know that in the poustinia lies the answer that the world is seeking today. You see, the world doesn't really know God; it only knows *about* God. And because so many only know him by 'hearsay' as it were, they can reject him, be indifferent to him, recrucify him a thousand times in their neighbor. But if people knew him directly, through his own revelation of himself in the poustinia of their hearts, then they would no longer reject him.

The poustinia vocation may, for some people, take on a physical dimension. The answer to the world's hunger, however, lies in discovering this poustinia of the heart. This demands a self-emptying. This kenosis begins with the repeating of the Jesus Prayer* and a silencing of the noise within our hearts. It begins when I 'fold the wings of the intellect' and 'put my head into my heart.' Only then can the poustinia of the heart become a reality.

---

* Adapted from the Prayer of the Publican, Luke 18:14. The longer form: "Lord Jesus Christ, Son of the Living God, have mercy on me, a sinner." Shortest form: "Jesus, mercy!" Other forms of this prayer abound.

When that happens: Now it is no longer *I* doing things; it is *Christ within me.* My words are not my own. They are the echoes of God's voice that comes to me out of his silence. Now I know how to catch fire from his words and become a fire myself, shedding sparks over the face of the earth. Now I can say (with St. Paul) that it is not I who live, but Christ lives in me.

We of Madonna House can best imitate the Russian poustinik in the inner dimensions of his vocation, especially by emptying ourselves of all of our goods – physical and intellectual – and going forth into the solitude and immense silence of God. I feel that, in this silence, the members of Madonna House will be given an understanding of this poustinia vocation, despite the poor and inadequate way I have told you about it.

Maybe some day there will be those who will arise and go into the mountains of Combermere, to spend part of each week in the physical solitude of a cabin in the woods. But most people who join us will be the type of poustinikki who will be absorbed in a deep inner solitude while outwardly living in the midst of men.

Let me put it this way: The Little Mandate of Madonna House calls us to *a combination of prayer-and-service together,* almost running neck-and-neck like a good team of paired horses. In cases of need, the working horse is ahead. The more meditative Arab steed is behind, content to follow the lead of the other. Prayer becomes inner-centered, and work becomes outer-centered. And in the combination of the two is found the Life of Christ, where divinity and humanity are wedded. Prayer-with-action. Action-with-prayer. In a word, the Incarnation!

I don't know if I have wandered too far and made it too difficult for you to understand what I mean. Read this along with the other things I have written about the poustinia, and let me know what you think of it.

Lovingly yours in Mary,

FORGIVENESS

February 28, 1977

Dearly Beloved,

I must be feeling better because ideas pop into my mind all day long. I don't just listen to them; I *pray* about them. The quiet of the night in this Arizona desert* is conducive to prayer and very slowly I begin to understand (or so I think) God's pattern in my life and in our lives.

I feel that the Lord is slowly telling me something – telling us all something – for I am only the 'vehicle for the family' in a manner of speaking. And what he is telling me these days is that the strange pain of Eddie's passing, and the pain that comes from the Apostolate itself, and the pain that has been so specifically mine in the last months or more, were all worthwhile.

It is like moving up on this mountain of mine which I always call 'the vision of the whole.' Every time this happens, I think that I have reached the summit of that mountain; but always the breeze carries the words, "Come higher, friend!" So I go. This time, however, I slowly began to see another dimension, another blessing, of the pain of Christ that we experience (or at least I feel) when he kisses us. And once more I realized that *pain is the kiss of Christ*. Isn't it worth all kinds of pain to be kissed by Christ? I think it is!

So what did these last months teach me? Well, the first step on this mountain that brings us 'the vision of the whole' periodically was an understanding of a new dimension of *forgiveness*. I heard that Father Wild spoke about it, and cried afterwards. I was so delighted that the Lord had given him the gift of tears. I think that Father Wild is a sign for all of us – the fact that God has given one or two of our members the gift of tears. Let us truly thank him, for it is a tremendous gift.

As you know, I mention to you again and again that the

---

* Catherine wrote this letter while convalescing at La Casa de Nuestra Senora, the Madonna House mission in Winslow, Arizona.

Russians are not too concerned about the gift of tongues. They pray, instead, for the gift of tears, which they believe wash away their sins and the sins of others. This is because Christ shed bloody tears in Gethsemane, and probably so did the others. Anyway, a new dimension of forgiveness was asked of me.

As time goes on, all of us are asked to plunge into this forgiveness in various degrees, *especially forgiveness of ourselves.* So many of us are still thrashing around in the net of our emotions which create in us a poor self-image. We forget that we have the 'scissors' of God's grace and the example of His forgiveness to cut that net.

Forgiveness is not something that we practice once or twice; it is not an action that we do a hundred times. No. It should grow into a solid virtue and become a 'habitual state' in which we forgive almost constantly, even while we are being rejected, ignored, spat upon, and so on.

There is something divine about forgiveness; it is truly and closely aligned to charity, to love, to God himself. Factually, it is God alone who can forgive because, as the Psalmist says: "In your sight alone we have sinned." So if we really love God, we must *activate that love* by forgiving ... forgiving ourselves, and others.

I think that this is what happened so beautifully to Father Wild. It has happened to myself and to many others in Madonna House, because we were ready to accept the pain of Christ in whatever form it came to us individually. Perhaps there was no need to have this pain. Perhaps there was no need to accept the pain. But we are human and we had it, and we accepted it; and so we grew in God. Yes, now that we understand (and I hope all of us do!) the reason for the pain of these last months, we can enter more and more deeply into the 'sea of forgiveness' which God places before us.

Walking Hand-in-Hand

By God's grace, I came here to our Arizona house to recuperate. At first I was too tired to take things in, but lately I awoke to what is happening here. The Casa is faced daily with the very concept that I have often presented to you regarding 'identification with the poor.'

Constantly people enter here for a short visit or to linger awhile, bringing to the five young members of the Casa the miseries of their lives. And the identification of the trials of our members blends with that of the people. Because the people see how the staff here live, they try to help them to the best of their ability. There is some kind of coalescence, a coming together which is astonishing to watch. I have been standing in awe of the mercy of God and his forgiveness.

Suddenly I knew that God had brought me here and allowed me to be 'sick at heart' for a while; and then he opened a path from his heart to mine. I am convinced of that because my concerns, my hopes for 'identification with the poor,' took flesh before my very eyes here. As I meditated on it all in depth, I knew that God wanted me to write this letter. I knew to the best of my ability that this is what God wanted – this kind of place where staff and people blended together, helping each other, 'hand-in-hand' shall we say, to grow emotionally and spiritually.

There is something uncanny here. It is as if God took me by the hand and showed me what he wanted. I saw it dimly at first, as if in a fog; and then it was as if a smile of God came over me ... as if God said: "Yes, that's what I want! For all of Madonna House is mine and my mother's." *The smile of God lingers in my heart still.*

My way of expressing things, of course, is in a symbolic manner. It seems to me that I understand better what I am trying to say if I put it into some sort of imagery. Those of you who still like to 'pass things through your mind' will just have to become like little children and accept my symbolic words as the 'toy' that God sends us to delight over and to play with 'in his yard.'

Yes, the Casa is an extraordinary place. It is weak with the weak. It is poor with the poor. Yet somehow it is incredibly strong, because the staff daily enter into the mercy of God and his forgiveness.

Lovingly yours in Mary,

MORE ABOUT TRUST

March 7, 1977

Dearly Beloved,

If you look through the Staff Letters you will find that quite a few are on trust. There is one very interesting letter, which many of the staff will remember, written on February 24, 1962.* It would be good for all of you who are studying the spirit of Madonna House these days to reread it.

As time marches on, and everything grows in depth and height and width, the members of Madonna House grow and mature in many of the virtues, because they are growing daily in love of God and in obedience to his will. Yet, when I consider the virtue of trust today, I find I haven't changed my views very much from the old days. However, I understand better now *what a tremendously difficult virtue it is* for people who have been brought up in pragmatism and have been influenced by Jansenism.† Yes, trust is a beautiful but very delicate virtue.

Trust is a gentle offshoot of faith. It begins when 'reason' as we understand it – the intellect and what-have-you – folds its wings and allows *the wings of faith* to open

---

* See *Dearly Beloved*, Vol. 1, pages 220-223.
† Doctrine named after Bishop *Jansen* of Belgium (who died in 1638). Its austere attitude toward salvation, free will, sin and grace discouraged people from 'trusting' in God's mercy. Portions of the doctrine were condemned as heretical as early as 1653, but it flourished until the early 1700's. Some of its puritanical attitudes continued to influence church-goers in succeeding centuries, even until today.
  Pragmatism is a 20th-century American philosophy, developed by Charles Peirce and William James, which concentrates on what is 'practical' for everyday life. Since ultimate standards are denied and truth is regarded as a relative commodity, individuals can decide for themselves what human values are important, in terms of 'whatever works' for them.
  The famous educator, John Dewey, brought this philosophy into the modern school system, allowing the needs and desires of the student to take precedence over the knowledge or wisdom of the teacher. Disciplinary practices and rote drills were abolished from the classroom. 'Trust' was to be placed in 'learning by experience' and in sharing one's 'opinion about truth' in group discussions. 'Democracy' (in the sense of group decisions) was to be the primary source of ethical values, not the authoritarian views that came from outside the group (from God, church, society, family, or teacher).

up. For trust cannot exist without faith. If I have faith in a person, an institution, a community, a family, I will trust! Wherever there is faith, there is trust.

The first person we must trust is God – the Trinity. Do we really? Most of the time we either question the existence of God or, if we believe that he does exist, we question his ability to help us. We think that our everyday problems are *our own* to solve, and that we needn't have faith or trust in God to solve them. If possible, we would prefer to solve our own problems *all of the time!* It gives us a sense of power, of being our own master. We are willing to have God around and to rely on him *only* when it becomes quite evident that we cannot solve things ourselves.

It is difficult to describe trust. Frankly, trust demands not only 'crucifixion' but 'the thrust of a lance' into our hearts. And that leaves a wide-open wound! Openness always produces a wound. Since the Church came from the side of Christ, the bonds which unite us to Jesus Christ and his Mystical Body are always bonds of faith and trust; or else there would not be any Mystical Body.

Our generation is considered to be an enlightened one, but it has very little trust in the family, in marriage, in religious communities, in one another! One prefers, as the saying goes, 'to keep oneself to oneself.' We are enthusiastic and share the unimportant things, but *we hide the ones that matter.**

To trust someone (and *especially* to 'trust the untrustworthy') doesn't seem at all sensible to us. Yet this is *exactly* what Jesus Christ demands of us when he tells us to pray for our enemies, to love those who hate us, to give our lives for our brothers. He asks us to trust our brethren and himself and the Holy Spirit – the Triune God. Do we? Very few of us have gone into the 'holocaust' of Christ's words by trusting the untrustworthy as he tells us to do. We confide in a few select people, but we refuse to confide in our community, our family, or what-have-you.

Yes, trust is a tender offshoot of faith and is very

---

* Cf. *The Peace Corps Reader,* published by the Peace Corps, Washington, D.C., 1967. It has an article — "The Quiet-Mouth American" by Donald Lloyd — to which Catherine often alluded in her conversations.

136

fragile. Yet, without trust there can be no bonds between husband and wife, between children and parents, between members of a religious community, or between men and women in general – government to government, nation to nation. Because of this lack of trust, we have continual wars; we have no peace. How can anybody have outward peace when there is no inward peace? Inner peace lies in the arms of faith and trust; and, of course, love and hope.

I myself have had to have a sure faith and strong trust in God. I remember so well that, when I had written down what is now the Little Mandate* on bits of paper and checked with many priests what seemed to be the blueprint of a vocation for me, I was truly amazed at it all. And so, taking the first paragraph of that Mandate to heart, I sold all that I possessed, and went into the slums. I did so with a light heart, filled with faith and trust in God and in my spiritual director.

Through the years, with tempests around me, no matter where I went or what I did, *faith and trust in God* were always close to the surface. The result, as you can see, is that we have become quite a group – the 'community' which Archbishop Neil McNeil of Toronto foresaw in the 1930's, when he bade me to persevere in my work. So with fear and humility I could say to you, as St. Paul said to the Philippians: "Be united in following *my rule of life*. Take as your models everybody who is always doing this, and study them as you used to study us" (Phil. 3:17).

There is one thing I really want you to know: my heart is truly open with 'the lance of love' for you. I do love you, perhaps beyond your understanding; for my love approaches you in a way different from that of most people. It has an incarnation that is, perhaps, hard to follow. As I often say, I trust you all (even 'the untrustworthy') and I trust you completely. Many of you, if you chose to speak, could stand witness to my trust of you in so many ways. But you don't have to speak, for the Lord himself will speak in me, today, tomorrow, or the day after; it really doesn't matter.

What does matter is that we grow in understanding, in peace, and in the joy of being together and being *offered to*

* See *Dearly Beloved*, Vol. 2, pages 179-180.

each other by God himself – a family that really trusts one another. This means that we must have faith in each other, and tenderly nurture the gentle virtue of trust which is an offshoot of that faith.

Lovingly yours in Mary,

SACRIFICE

May 2, 1977

Dearly Beloved,

Recently I have had much time to think about many things. One thing struck me so forcefully that I made it part of my lecture at St. Benedict's College in Minnesota. I felt that I had to, for it was in my heart; and, as a ripe fruit on a tree has to fall, so this had to be expressed. It has been in my heart for many months now (in fact, for years ... if the truth be told!).

The United States is being greatly challenged by one man. This man is President Carter. Until very recently, people were asking: "Who is this man?" It was obvious that Plains, Georgia, was not 'on the map' and few had ever heard of the name Jimmy Carter.

But today everybody knows who he is. First and foremost, he is a Christian. Secondly, he tries to govern by Christian principles and is working especially for human rights. He is calling the United States, the North American Continent, and the whole world to sacrifice. *This sacrifice is for our own benefit,* as most sacrifices usually are. He is calling for unselfishness and restraint in relation to the care of our physical environment. All the media – television, newspapers, magazines, etc. – are bombarding us with this need for sacrifice.

I love America. I love Canada. So I prayed a lot to understand what it is that is going to make this call successful or hinder its success. For we are now faced with a question of destroying or rebuilding Planet Earth.

I thought about the many species of wild animals that are dying because we like fur coats. Think of the seals that are being slaughtered by the thousands for the beautification of women and men! Sacrifice is definitely needed here. We are supposed to care for the animals of the earth, not to destroy or despoil them.

It is almost useless to discuss the pollution of our air, earth, and water by chemicals. Recently Ralph Nader* said that it would take fifty to a hundred years to get rid of all the fertilizers we have put into the earth for profit: namely, chemical fertilizers. And so the story of man's disobedience to God continues by man's failure to take proper care of the earth on which God has placed him ... and by not caring for himself properly either. In a word, we have sinned most thoroughly, and we have to atone. We know also that the Lord understands, and he will forgive us if we repent.

So this is really a *call to repentance,* and in Madonna House our repentance must take the form of asceticism, of mortification and penance. This is the time of going back to the beginnings, to reread the story of creation and to examine ourselves on the teachings of the Gospel. Whenever we study the prophets in the Bible, we see two things: *fasting and prayer.* Behind the fasting and prayer, there lies a call to deep abstinence from our passions and from intellectual pride.

Asceticism is the ability to discipline oneself for the sake of God and his law. But all of the ascetic discipline – whether it be prayer, penance, fasting, almsgiving, or whatever – will be as nothing unless it is *the fruit of love,* which comes from faith and hope.

---

* Well-known environmentalist and consumer advocate in the U.S.

Yes, these thoughts have been in my heart for months, and I really 'let them loose' to the audience in Minnesota. I was shaken with the desire to do this, and I feel that same desire to write to you about what has been growing in my heart. I beg you to examine your conscience. Find out if repentance, fasting, abstinence, prayer, and discipline, are the foundation of your life. Unless they become the foundation of the life of the United States and Canada, the 'little sacrifices' that Carter is asking will never materialize. We might continue for a little while to think that we are 'masters of heaven and earth' instead of prostrating ourselves before Him who is Master of All.

Lovingly yours in Mary,

YOURS FOR THE TAKING

Christmas 1977

Dearly Beloved,

In 1915, a monk wrote a Christmas prayer which I would like to pass on to you. Perhaps the word isn't so much 'pass on' as it is 'give' to you, with all of my deepest love. The monk who wrote the prayer is Fra Giovanni, and it begins this way:

There is nothing I can give you which you have not! But there is much that, while I cannot give, you can take.

I pondered over these words and I knew that, truly, there is nothing that I can "give you which you have not" ... except my love. What is love? As I look at it, I know that it is *mine* – mine to have and to give – and it is yours for the taking. Nothing else can I give you; that is true. But here, in the midst of all the Christmas decorations – the shiny and colorful baubles on the tree, the exclamations, the conversations, the feasting – I can give you my love.

Love – I asked myself: "What is it, this love of mine? What shape does it take, what image?" But I have no answer to this question. All I know is that it will fit in your hand. All I know is that it might nestle in your heart. All I know is that it is immense, mysterious, unaccountable ... and it is yours for the taking.

Yes, take my love.
No heaven can come to us
Unless our hearts find rest in it today.
Take heaven.

Yes, Heaven! Like love, heaven is ours for the taking. It might be just some wildflower which you picked up while walking along some secluded path. It might be water which you scooped up at a cool, forest stream to quench your thirst as you passed by. It might be many other things. But then, I hope that your hands will stretch out, as the hands of Mary stretched out, and that you will take in your arms her Child; for after you do, heaven is yours.

No peace lies in the future
Which is not hidden in this present instant.
Take peace.

Peace – Yes, with a heart filled by a strange and beautiful joy, I ask the Lord to give you peace this Christmas. I pray passionately that each one of you becomes 'at peace' – first and foremost with God, then with yourself, and then with everyone with whom you dwell or meet for a day (or for even less time).

I pray the Lord that his peace enters you this Christmas, never to leave you again; and that it may bring with it the Christmas stockings of the English, the wooden shoes of the French, the beggar pack of the Russians. May they be filled with the shining beauty of all of God's gifts, which always go hand in hand with peace. May you be gifted with ... understanding, tenderness, compassion, forgiveness, reconciliation, faith, hope, love.

Yes, take peace.
The gloom of the world is but a shadow;
Behind it, yet within reach, is joy.
Take joy.

Joy – The bells of a donkey (the one that carried Our Lady and her Son to Bethlehem) can be heard in faith, ringing out so joyously. Catch their sound now, and keep it forever. Bells, thousands of bells, still ring across the world to celebrate him who is joy itself! Look at the eyes of a Child, a little Child. Open your hearts and take the joy of his embrace, and your tired heart will become childlike.

Listen to music, for *all good music is the echo of God's voice*. Catch that echo, and you will have joy abundantly.

Take joy.
And so at this Christmas time,
I greet you with the prayer that
– for you, now and forever –
The day breaks
And the shadows flee away.

Yes, were you to open the gift of my love for you, you would find in it a prayer. It goes with the beating of my heart, with the murmurs of my breath. Yes, it keeps moving as incense does. So my prayer, like the incense we often sing about, is offered night and day for you; for I love you, and I hope that my love brings its perfume to you, and that with my love comes peace ... understanding ... tenderness ... compassion ... forgiveness ... reconciliation ... faith ... hope ... love.

I do not pray that the "day breaks and the shadows flee away" in the sense of 'an end' to all trials or tribulations. No. I pray that you may see with brilliant clarity the Will of

God in your life, that you may run passionately toward it, and that *His Will may become yours* forever and ever.

I pray that, as you grow older, your heart may become more and more like that of the Christ Child, and that you will pray with me: "Give me the heart of a child, and the awesome courage to live it out as an adult."

I pray that all, through all your years, you will walk close to Our Lady; for the Child came through her, and it is through her that you can go to him.

Yes, open your heart and take my prayer.

With love,

COMMUNICATION

December 19, 1977

Dearly Beloved,

In the Name of the Father, and of the Son, and of the Holy Spirit! This isn't an easy letter to write. Sometimes I think that I should stop writing letters altogether! Yet my heart tells me that, as long as I live, I must communicate with you in openness and truthfulness. I must do so because I ask you to communicate with one another. I have even written a book about it entitled *Sobornost*.* It beseeches you to enter into deep communication (unity), first of all with the Trinity, so that you and I might communicate with

* Published in 1977 by Ave Maria Press, Notre Dame, Indiana.

one another. It is good, at this holy season, to meditate on the fact that Christ became man in order that we might become united to the Trinity and to each other. I realized long ago and far away that communication is a strange word. For the Christian, it comes from a deep root: *communion*. That is as it should be, because the only time we really can have sobornost is when we are *in communion with one another*. But a human being has great difficulty in establishing communion, first, within himself, and secondly, with others.

This being so, then whence comes that 'key' which will open our hearts to the other, which will remove this strange reluctance that all human beings have in communicating with one another? To us Christians, the answer is quite evident (or should be). The roots of that word *communicate* lie in our *communion with God*. Do we realize what takes place within the depths of our souls when we receive the Body and Blood of Christ? He told us that, unless we partake of this communion, we would have no place in the Kingdom of God.

Why did he say that? Because the Kingdom of God truly belongs to us already – *here and now* – as well as in that future which we talk about, but which we so often don't even believe in (or at least it appears to us as so incredibly remote). And when the Kingdom of God comes to us in its fullness, the first thing that will happen (so Scripture says) is that *every word* that we have thought, spoken, or whispered in the night, or in the most secret chambers of our hearts, will be revealed to everyone else. Why will it be revealed at that time? Why should it be revealed at all? Because the Kingdom of God cannot exist without *this deep sharing between one another*.

The 'Give-and-Take' of Life

When we approach the table of the Lord and receive from Our Lord's own hands (for the hands of a priest are, at that moment, his hands) his Body and Blood, his Soul and Divinity, we have truly *communicated* with him; we have been absorbed in him; we have become one with him. Then, when we move away from that table and return to our place in the congregation, we must become *lovers incarnate,* just as he has become incarnated for love of us, and for our brothers and sisters.

This love must lead us to *communication with others* because we have just been in communication with God. And if we have humbly and daringly become one with God, this means (whether we like it or not) that we have 'become one' with all of our brothers and sisters. If, instead, we choose not to communicate with those around us, if our hearts do not become 'open' to them, then our Holy Communion is not holy at all. It has been in vain, and we have saddened God. Let us not forget that he said, "Whatsoever you do to my brethren, you do to Me." This communication is the beginning of sobornost. Out of it comes a deep and abiding unity – a 'oneness' of mind and soul!

The longer I live in this apostolic family, the more I sense the fact that we don't communicate. Here, I am not discussing 'meetings' in which we openly discuss our ideas and insights about the Apostolate, or even about ourselves. No. I am discussing the ordinary 'give-and-take' between people that should exist every day within the Apostolate. The openness which we are discussing here doesn't mean confession of sins (which is utterly unimportant to the matter, and should be dealt with by a spiritual director, confessor, or priest in the confessional). No. I am not talking about that. I am talking about a person who has the courage to say *what has to be said,* even if what he has to say does not meet with the approval of everybody at once. Slowly, an idea in one mind will penetrate the mind of another. Slowly, ideas begin to gel; slowly, they become one; and then sobornost reigns.

It is time that we faced each other, dearly beloved. So many staff have been telling me recently that they have reached middle age; that there is something about this period of life which hits men and women alike; that it 'slows them down' or does something very special to them. I am sorry, but I have to disagree with that. The moment we go outside of Madonna House and visit our friends, we find many middle-aged couples (of forty, fifty, and over) who are living a normal life and continuing their work and hobbies as before.

Menopause, of both male and female, is well understood today. There is a lot written about it. True, in middle age we may slow down a bit. Our backs may stiffen up and begin to give us trouble; arthritis begins to show its ugly head; our bones are more brittle; our health might be not be all that it should be. But it seems to me that the thing I am most often presented with, by people at Madonna House who are around middle age, is a return to childhood angers and hatreds. Why it should be so, I do not know, but it happens.

Strange, isn't it, that sobornost can be stymied by the fact that an adult man or woman between the ages of forty and fifty will suddenly transfer his or her emotional problems, perhaps with a mother-figure of early childhood, onto some present-day figure of authority (whomever that person might be). This tendency within an individual can be 'acted out' so repetitively as to become a bit tiresome to the community.

Since I love you so deeply in the Lord, *and without any sentimentality,* I try to lead you directly to him ... uncompromisingly so! In doing this, I must deal with this 'transfer of emotions' as peacefully as I can. (Love is like that; it accepts the cross of another and tries to help carry it for them.) It is not easy for me. I feel that I have been battered and pummeled by hostile reactions from staff workers for over thirty years now.

But I come to you today, in this letter, with a great love and (I hope) a deep understanding of what you are going through. I am peaceful about it. The only thing I worry about is that, after I die, someone else will have to shoulder the burdens of responsibility for this Apostolate, and will become the butt of many emotional transfers. Will that person be able to carry them? All I can do is pray; that's all.

God Takes Pity on Our Family

So much for communications with one another across the whole of the Apostolate. There is more that I want to write to you to make you acquainted fully and completely with everything that is in my heart, and in the hearts of others here at the training center. All of this is deep sobornost – this openness, this 'direct talking' to one another. There hasn't been a day that has passed without a demand for solutions and decisions to fairly difficult problems.

Right now, we are in the midst of this holy and beautiful season in which Christ became Man so that we might be united to the Most Holy Trinity and to each other. Yet there seems to be a strange nervousness, perhaps I could say, but I don't really know just what to call it. It seems that there is a strange slipping of morale among the men and women of Madonna House whenever anyone decides to 'leave the community.'

I am not all at surprised when some of our members leave us. As I look back on those who have discontinued their relationship with the Apostolate, I realize the infinite grace of God working in our lives. He wanted to have *free* men and women – ones who, when they said "yes," said it as Our Lady did, resoundingly, simply, and directly. I consider that an infinite grace.

Have we considered a little bit the history of our Apostolate? As I see it, *God took pity on me.* From 1930 until 1952 or so, I was bereft of priests. True, I had some good spiritual directors, but they weren't living with us. They didn't share with us the day-to-day life of our mission houses. They came once a month or so.

The Lord saw my agony and, out of his great goodness, he sent Father Callahan to us. Then he sent Father Cullinane, Father Briere, and Father Nearing to become priests of Madonna House. Then came the most magnificent gift of all: three priests were ordained for us – Father Pelton, Father Zoeller, and Father Starks. Other priests came, and finally the miracle of my husband's priesthood.* Perhaps I haven't the sequence quite right, but you will understand what I mean about God's caring for us. Suppose you go away a little bit and look at it and praise God for what he has done for us. We now have twelve priests, and one in heaven.

Has it occurred to you that, with the exception of these last three (Father Pelton, Father Zoeller, and Father Starks), all of our priests have *changed* vocations, either coming to us from another religious group or from a diocese for which

---

* In 1969, Eddie Doherty was ordained in the Melkite rite, which permits married priests. He died in 1975.

they have been ordained? The proper permissions were obtained, of course. But then consider the next question:

Is it possible that God has brought people to us *to be healed* and then, later on, to go forth to do his work *elsewhere?* You see, I firmly believe that if we were 'one' in the sobornost that I constantly talk about, we as a community could heal more and more people through our love alone, through our oneness, through our simplicity, through the hospitality of our hearts.

Call me a fool. I have been called a fool many times, and I don't mind being called a fool for Christ's sake. There are people who have left Madonna House, and I have wept, and I think God has too. But there are some who have left for other vocations, and those have to be left in peace. Under no circumstances should we lower the morale of everybody by worrying about them. True, we might shed a few tears for those we think should have stayed, and then offer them to our Lady. But to be demoralized because someone left? Even after Final Promises? ... Why? Is it because deep down in our hearts, we feel we might be the next one? Well, it is possible. We will all be tempted, but why not rely on God's grace? Why not throw ourselves into God's arms? Why not use holy water to send the tempter away? And why not accept the seeming defalcations of the one who left, and pray for him or for her?

As I was praying one day, the Lord said to me: *I will replace each one who leaves!* So be of good cheer. Pray for those who have left, and open your arms wide to those who come. But if you are all 'going downhill' over someone who has departed, those who are coming to join us will pause and wonder why. Explain it simply, in truth and humility; and all will be well. Don't be afraid, dearly beloved ones. Where there is perfect love, there is no fear; and that is what sobornost leads to – perfect love. Well, some day I will write another letter, even though I think at times that it would be better to be silent. The Lord doesn't seem to think so, however. Blessed New Year! May it be spent in the hearts of Christ and Mary.

Lovingly yours in Mary,

PREPARING FOR THE FUTURE

April 13, 1978

Dearly Beloved,

I asked the Lord to tell me what to write about next, and the strangest thing happened. In fact, I had to check and recheck it with the Lord and with my own soul. For the answer that I received was simple and direct: *prepare for martyrdom!*

To be a martyr, a person who sheds blood as St. Stephen did, is one thing. But I don't think that is what God meant in this message to me, which is really for all of us in Madonna House. I think that he means for us to enter a new dimension of life. I think that he means a surrender of our will to him. The face of martyrdom is very vivid when we really have to do God's Will instead of our own. It can be easy to follow a routine of work. In fact, it is quite a pleasure, for work is often an escape. But it isn't so easy to follow God's Will expressed by the needs of the Apostolate or by our spiritual director.

Let us be truthful with one another, for sobornost can flourish only in the soil of truth. The face of martyrdom can also be the face of truth, for to be 'in truth' and to speak it to one another – that is sobornost; that is unity. People who were about to die during the period of martyrdom were very truthful with one another. And their truth always bore witness to Christ, and to the fact that they were ready to give their lives for him. So it seems to me that our martyrdom – the one that God seems to speak about so directly and simply – is, first and foremost, planted in the soil of *truth* with one another and thus in the soil of *communication.*

We might be 'in truth' ... but to be in truth 'totally' we must *listen* to one another. We must *hear* what the other says! We must listen carefully and reverently to one another, even though it may seem to us unimportant. At that moment of listening, we must be *empty of everything else,* for we cannot 'hear' if our head or heart is filled with thoughts of self or of other matters.

I think that this is another face of martyrdom: to be like a tree standing by the water.* It combines strength with sensitivity. It is awake and alert to the slightest breeze that moves its branches and leaves, and flexible enough to withstand the storms that might almost bend in two. Something like that.

Yes, preparation for martyrdom has many faces, and I bring you that word *preparation.* It implies a future for which we have to prepare. I begin to understand why I wrote *Poustinia* and *Sobornost* and why the third volume, *Strannik,* will come out in August.† This strange trilogy is like a warning; like a stone which, when dropped into a river, makes eddies reaching farther and farther until they touch the other shore.

To prepare for martyrdom, we must be 'in truth.' We must be awake and alert, listening to one another. We must be 'in communication.' And we must witness to one another as members of Madonna House. There is in all of us a strange martyrdom that we have to face – that is, our lack of communication. Sobornost demands communication and openness. And to be 'open' means to be unafraid to say what is in our heart. (I don't mean confessional matter – God forbid!)

For instance, the other day when I was with a little group, I tried asking everyone how he or she felt, and each one answered, "I feel fine." I looked at them, and then I said again, "Now that you have given me the usual answer, would you like to give me the real answer?" Some laughed; some cried; but some gave me a truthful answer as to how they felt at that moment, and we got together in a oneness that is hard to explain.

There is a martyrdom in entering into that oneness and learning to communicate with one another. We love the people who come to our houses, but we do not have to live

---

* An allusion to Psalm 1, verse 3.
† These Russian words (for desert, union, and pilgrim) became titles for Catherine's books. They were published by Ave Maria Press, Notre Dame, Indiana, in 1974, 1977, and 1978, respectively.

with them. Now, loving people with whom we don't have to live is one thing; and loving people we have to live with is quite another. *And therein lies the crunch!* There is the true martyrdom. We had better begin to accept the challenge of this small pain, because tomorrow (or the day after) our love will be tested in the crucible of tragedies, atomic bombs, inflation, unemployment, economic depressions. We witness to Christ by witnessing to all who come, and to all those to whom we are sent, and to those with whom we must live. And to do this, we must be little and humble.

Martyrdom is seldom a collective kind of affair. True, the Romans allowed some Christian martyrs to die collectively in the arena; and in modern countries (such as in Germany at the time of Hitler) people have been compelled to die together. But this is rare. The great apple tree of love which God has planted, and of which each one of us is a part, must bear small apples. They are easy for children to reach – all children: the very young ones and those in-between. If we are prepared for martyrdom, and someone wants to 'martyr' these little apples – well, apples make a beautiful incense when they are burned. So our martyrdom will become like the Russian prayer: "Let my prayer rise like incense before you."

We have to prepare ourselves, and that means we really have to 'face ourselves' because we will have to be *strong with the strength of God* when these things happen; when the world is fragmented, as fragmented it will be in a little while.

We already know that the twenty-first century belongs to the Third World – the underdeveloped countries that we have maltreated; from whom we have taken all the raw materials that we needed; the 'developing nations' to whom we tried to sell the finished products at fantastic prices. *Yes, the world will belong to them.* You can almost hear the marching feet in the far distance, the shod feet of soldiers from many angry nations. And we will have to face them. We will have to face them, realizing that all we can do is to ask their forgiveness.

But they may not have heard the gentle voice of Christ. That, too, was our fault – we who did not present him to these countries as he truly is. And because they haven't heard the gentle voice of Christ, they may wish to crucify us! That will be one way of atoning for all that we have done to them, or left undone.

But our martyrdom will be 'shot through' with light, because it will be for God! All those who have faced martyrdom in the reality of a blood-martyrdom have been given fantastic graces. It has often meant that they saw the Kingdom of God opening before them, while they were dying. True, we *already* live in the Kingdom of God. But, should we be chosen to die for Christ, we shall see him in his fullness, seated at the right hand of his Father; we shall see the Father, Son, and Holy Spirit, and rejoice at the Beatific Vision.

All of this is possible. So, right here and now, let us begin to prepare for it. And the preparation for martyrdom is peace, gentleness, understanding, love of one another, the sharing of hope, and praying for the constant injection of faith. That is the preparation for martyrdom. It is intensely necessary; but especially there must be a deep conviction and a total commitment to it. (In this case, it is a commitment to the life of Madonna House because I am writing to you who are members.) Yes, it must be a full commitment, meaning a total loving and a total surrender of one's human will to the Divine Will.

I think I will have to pray some more before I share with you the next 'page' of this strange letter I am writing you. But one thing I know: we had better enter the martyrdom of loving one another, and thence loving God; or we shall not be able to face the rest of what is ahead of us.

Lovingly yours in Mary,

MEDITATIONS WHILE TRAVELING

September 12, 1978

Dearly Beloved,

The word that the Lord gave me recently was *hiddenness*. This should have been rather 'obvious' to me because it is in our Little Mandate, which tells us to be hidden and to be a light to our neighbor's feet. But the question arose among us at the Local Directors' meetings, and I would like to clarify it before you read those reports.

Some of the directors posed the question of how we could consider ourselves 'hidden' when I am becoming so well-known. I have just finished around 34,000 miles of planes, trains, and what-have-you, traveling and lecturing and visiting our houses. Many people who have read my books are coming here and want to talk to me. And in the last year or so, I have received the Order of Canada.* So, with all of this happening, a number of members in our group say: "Where does hiddenness come in?"

It is a good question to ask, because *hiddenness is in the heart*. Slowly you or I or somebody else stands slightly revealed. But real hiddenness is a deep resting place in the heart of God for his people. That's what it is and that's what we are discussing at length at our LD meetings. You will read it directly when it is transcribed from the tape. Yes, we are discussing beautiful things. Mostly the beauty of our discussions lies in that hunger which each of us has for the desire to serve God more profoundly, more lovingly.

I am a little befuddled as to what God is doing to me personally. Not long ago, I woke up suddenly talking French to myself; and before I knew it, I had composed several poems and meditations. This rather astonished me because I haven't thought or written in French for a very long time. Father Briere got enthused about them and sent them to Roger LeClerc, a good friend who works for French-Canadian television. He seems enthused too, and

---

* The country's highest award for civilians, to honor Canadian citizens for outstanding achievements in their field of endeavor.

wants to interview me on videotape with his CBC production crew.

How did my 'hidden' self get itself projected into yet another spotlight? I don't know. In the meantime, I'm beginning to dream in German. Perhaps it won't be long before my childhood abilities in the Arabic language come to the fore. Is Madonna House ready to go into new lands?

I enclose some meditations I cassetted during my trip to the U.S.A. They are yours for the having. You are always in my prayers, needless to say:

To make the idea of strannik – pilgrim – known to the West, I think that perhaps we should all read *The Story of the Other Wise Man* by Henry Van Dyke. It is a short book, and a very lovely one.

A strannik is a pilgrim who 'stops everywhere' to do good, not one who is hell-bent to get to some holy shrine and who ignores the intervening steps. By the time a strannik has gone through the experience of poustinia and sobornost, it is a most natural thing to do ... to take one's time during a journey, to be alert to the 'opportunities of grace' that lie along the pathway, to be on the lookout for God and to meet him in another person's eyes.

While I was in Vermont, it rained for a while. There was an elderly lady who couldn't get her raincoat organized. The sleeves wouldn't fall into place, and she couldn't find the hood. So I stopped the procession that was following me, and I helped her. She smiled at me and said: "Thank you!" The woman next to me said: "Do you always stop to do good?" I said: "No. I stop to be of service to my brethren, which I do not consider *being good,* but *being normal."* And I went on. That's what I mean – that sort of thing. For some people, it could be an apostolate in itself ... entering the terrible loneliness of the world, experiencing that loneliness, sharing that loneliness, and becoming wiser for it.

I sense that we have to prepare for martyrdom. What do I mean by that? Frankly, when I am praying alone with God, I think occasionally of bloody martyrdom; and yet, at other times, I think of an ongoing martyrdom endured for

154

others somehow. This demands a great maturity of mind, soul, and heart – a selflessness that surpasses all understanding. It requires a 'real' selflessness, which we do not possess (alas); for we are very self-centered, whether we realize it or not!

Our martyrdom may be given to us by having to endure our self-centeredness, and taking away all means of centering ourselves properly ... such as no psychiatrists, no doctors, no spiritual directors ... nothing to turn to. There may be a desolated landscape in which we have to dig up our own earth (provided it isn't contaminated, and if we still have the strength to dig). I don't know, but these ideas come to me. They spell martyrdom for the West, which is not used to pain and which seldom has experienced the kiss of Christ (for 'pain is the kiss of Christ').

Yes, there might be martyrdom ... I don't know. Yet I know one thing: that Madonna House must be an oasis in the midst of all of this chaos that reigns in the world. As long as it can be an oasis ... as long as it is not eaten up by what is to come: the dragons of tomorrow.

So we have to prepare. But can we do it? It's impossible to convince the Americans to travel in a full car, instead of one by one. They like the splendid isolation of their automobiles. It's the same with Canadians; it is next to impossible for them too. As long as they have gas and oil to do the work of their hands, they will not use their 'hands' to toil for their needs.

I hope and pray that they understand what I say. It seems that they do and they don't. On some days, their backs are stiff. On other days, they are blind. It all depends ... It all depends on their *maturity in the Lord,* and if they can turn their listening heart to his whispering voice. That's all I can say.

I travel on a highway. To look at me, you wouldn't realize that I am in the midst of hell. An 'abomination of desolation' is all around me. Trucks – mammoth trucks that can carry a house or two – swish by like a powerful train at a railroad crossing. A train passes by only once, however, but this abomination of desolation keeps on and on and on. The noise is an abomination, or perhaps *is* the 'abomination' ... and the listening to it is certainly 'desolation.'

Lord, what have they done with their technology? Half of the children in grade school today are partially deaf. Families who live close to the highways cannot stand it; they have to move away because the gasoline fumes and diesel exhausts nearly choke them. Young children are found to have lungs blackened by the cigarette smoking of their parents and grandparents. What have they done to your beautiful earth, O Lord? *What have they done?* They spend millions trying to find out if there is life on other planets and yet people on this earth 'go hungry' – hungry for bread, hungry for water, hungry for air. How dare they do these things?

Who cares about other planets? Do we wish to bring this 'civilization' of ours to other planets, so we can pollute and despoil them? Isn't it enough that we have already seduced and raped the one that you, O Lord, walked on? What can we do? What can *you* do, Lord, except to allow us to sit neck-deep in material possessions, letting our technology pervert all that it touches?

In itself, technology is not evil; for *nothing* that is created by men is evil if it is *in line with your creation.* But the technology that we have spawned becomes evil when it panders to the wealthy and doesn't care for the poor. It helps those-that-have, and it makes those-that-have-not envious. Lord, how can you stand to see those two halves? You died for the poor – for all men. You loved the sinners. You loved the poor. How do you stand this? Or is it the time of reckoning?

There was Babylon and Egypt, and Byzantium and Rome. And where are they now? Is this the fate that you reserve to us? I do understand, God; I do understand. But is there any way by which we can make all those other people understand that they don't have to *worship* oil and gas and money? That they don't have to be neck-deep in greed? That they don't have to trample their brother in order to have more power for themselves? How can we do it, Lord? Teach us, for I know that you are allowing us yet a little time. Though you are angry, do not let this anger fall upon us.

Stop all the greed over gas and oil. Stop the means of that technology, and let us discover better 'means' ... brotherly means ... loving means. Let your enormous hand, O Lord, swipe everything that men cherish today off the chessboards of their minds. Everything except love and hope and faith, which they should cherish. And show them how to build a new civilization, *one based on faith,* for this present one is already rotten and creaking at the seams. Have mercy on us, Lord! Have mercy!

The day is gray. We are traveling over a gray road. I look, and I see farms. Some are in good condition; some in poor condition. Some of the former houses are now just pieces of wood thrown all over, helter-skelter, by somebody looking for something.

I feel sad with a deep sadness that I cannot understand. Yet, in a way I do. Because, you see, I look at all that is so beautiful around me – the bush lands and the fields, the flowers and other things that man has not spoiled, has not defiled. And in my heart I hear a voice: "I give you this earth to love and cherish; all the beasts to name, and the flowers too." And I know that this is what God whispered to man.*

I think of the day that something wonderful and glorious happened. This strange new animal stood upright, and could use his hands, and God breathed into him a strange, incredible, divine breath. Was it a mouth-to-mouth breath as it says in the Song of Songs: "He kissed me with the kiss of his mouth?" Did God the Father kiss man? One does not know, but my heart tells me that it is so ... that the breath of the Lord entered into the soul of man, and man began *to worship* and *to understand.*

Not so long ago, the Indians held this land on which we move. They cherished it. They caught fish and killed bison and deer and other animals to eat, but they always left some intact. There was abundance in this land. And out there in the forest man lived in peace, according to his own ways, and worshiped the One who breathed into his soul eons ago. Yes, these people did not kill for the sake of

* An allusion to Genesis 1:28-29 and 2:19-20.

killing. They did not make a god of sex. They didn't do any of these things.

But somewhere along the road from eternity to eternity, that 'man' who stood upright and felt the breath of God in his soul became 'white' and learned many skills, and decided that he was 'god.' From that day on, he polluted and destroyed, annihilating what God had given him to be steward of.

I travel through many lands, in many ways; and I see the footprints of destruction. I see highways that cut through fields that once were fertile. I see cities arising out of places where they should not be. I foresee that some of these cities will lie in ruins, all because 'man' thought that he was 'god.' I foresee many things. Most of all, I see how human beings have chosen to destroy themselves.

Behold this 'god of the universe' called 'man'! Overly fat ... overly thin ... unhealthy specimens, on the whole. People don't have good food because they have polluted the earth with all kinds of alien additives, things that do not belong in it; and the earth was angry and vomited the stuff back into the crops. So people are unhealthy.

Cities are all vulnerable. How long would it take an atomic bomb to destroy New York, Chicago, Toronto, Berlin, Paris? A few seconds, perhaps? And yet there are men who defend atomic warfare. My heart weeps. It has wept for a long time. Lord of hosts, my prayers have turned into tears; and they are all I can offer you. You have use for tears. They can wash some things away from the hearts of men, and from my own heart.

The Russians always ask for the gift of tears, because Our Precious Mother (and yours) wept at the foot of the cross. And so did you, over Lazarus (who was but myself). So then, Lord, tears I have to give you ... tears on a gray day, on a gray highway, amid pollution wrought by man. Lord have mercy on us, for I understand you! And there is so little time.

I am not restless, Lord. No, I have 'come home' ... and yet, I wonder if there is any place besides your 'heart' that I can really call 'home.' Somehow, I feel very deeply that this is the place where your heart abides. This is the place where you come at night. This is the place where we dance together. This is the place where we cry together. This is the place where we laugh together.

Is it presumptuous for an ordinary person like myself – a person of no account, who is nothing at all – to talk like that about you, Lord? And yet quite long ago (I can't remember when), you came and said to me: "You know, Catherine, you are my friend." Your words entered into all of me. They covered me and infiltrated every part of my being. I was your friend – the friend of God!

I can't remember when you said: "Let us sit down. Make yourself a crown of daisies. I want to tell you something." Obediently, I started to pick some flowers and weave a crown. You said to me: "I want you to be my spokesman." In fear and trembling I said: "Oh! ... Oh no! No, Lord! Not that!" You didn't say a thing. You just looked. You said that all the prophets spoke like that. But I interrupted you again. I said: "My Lord, I am not a prophet. I am a woman!"

Well, you smiled and said that there had been prophetic women. You smiled at me and said: "I have used women to bring my word to you. The first was Mary. I entered her womb. *The Word became Flesh.* That's what I did to a woman. Think about that. So why shouldn't I choose you to be my spokesman. You do not understand." And with that you vanished, Lord. I looked around, but you were not there. I sat there alone, with a half-finished crown of daisies on my lap. I dried that crown and cherished it for a long time. But then somehow it vanished too.

Another time ... I do not remember when or how; I think it was on a very hot day in a Harlem tenement; or perhaps it was a Harlem night, stifling. I saw you moving gently among the Negroes. (You always take the coloring of the men among whom you move. I did not know that until I saw you there.) You took me by the hand and brought me to the river. There were a few steps. We sat on them, and you said: "Catherine, have you thought about what I said to you quite a while ago?"

I replied: "Lord, I haven't thought about it, but I *have* thought a lot about your Mother, and her *fiat* will always be in my heart. I want to imitate her, and I will answer you in

the same way: `Let it be done according to your will.'"
Then you kissed me with the kiss of your mouth, and you
vanished. From that day on, I noticed that the hearts of men
were opening to me. I could see what was in them, but I
was too frightened to say anything.

The time passed, and we came to Combermere. Now I
saw so many things 'ahead of time' that I was frightened
even more. To see what is happening today, tomorrow, the
day after is not given to human beings. It lasted a while.
Remember when I pestered Father Callahan to say a Mass
for Stalin? Later on, we heard that he died. No one except
myself expected his death. Then again I knew that I had
become a prophet. I cried. You remember how much I
cried; you remember how much I was afraid. But you were
there with me, and so was Father Cal. So I spoke
reluctantly, in fear and trembling.

But now I have no fear. The trembling is all gone. I
know I am your voice. I stand ready to speak whenever you
want me to speak, to whom you want me to speak: to
crowds, to people, one by one ... I do not care. I see the
hearts of men. I understand. It's not for me; it's for you.
Maybe, with your guidance and your grace, it will save
your Bride, the Church.

Yes, Lord; speak! Your servant heareth.

Lovingly yours in Mary,

Catherine

EXPERIENCING SOBORNOST

September 20, 1978

Dearly Beloved,

A wonderful thing has happened in Combermere. For over two weeks, there were fifteen local directors, six priests, and the three Directors-General – all gathered together, truly and constantly, in the luminous light of sobornost.

We had absolutely no difficulties in solving problems or making decisions. And we did so with one voice. I could hardly believe my ears, and I was a bit stunned by this fantastic miracle. Each one of the directors will tell you more about it when he or she returns to the houses. But I must admit that words almost fail me. I want to summarize the meetings a bit for you, however.

I had a funny feeling that the Lord was saying to me: "Get out of the way, and let *me* do the job." I had a feeling that I was in his way; and perhaps I was, I don't know.

It seems to me that we achieved what I call *sobornost* – that special kind of unity. And it seemed to me that we have to cherish this unity very deeply and foster it through letters, visits, or whatever is needed, so that we can *continue* to be of one mind. I said to myself: "How is this possible?" And the answer came to me that it is *not* possible, except through God. We – all of us here present – have gone to the poustinia, and I say that symbolically. We were not in a physical poustinia but in a symbolic one. We had all 'gone through' something. After that, God could bring us to sobornost.

What happens in a poustinia, whether a physical one or a symbolic one? First, you withdraw your mind from all worldly concerns. Usually you sleep, because you are very tired, and because there is no longer any outward stimuli to keep you awake. After a time, you wake up and begin to read the Gospel; and you are nourished by it. (That is why you do not go to church when you are in the poustinia. God himself nourishes us through the Scriptures.) Then, sooner or later, you are attacked by the devil. You are *tested in faith.*

The 'food' is always there, and so is the 'sleep' ... but the 'test' is there, too! And after the test, you learn *dispossession.* You learn dispossession of your will, first and foremost. You learn to think of what God wants of you, and not what you want. And then you kneel down and say: "Lord, speak! Thy servant heareth." Yes, there comes a 'moment' like that!

Once these three or four situations arise, you can call yourself a poustinik, and you can face what is going to happen in your life as a poustinik. You can unite your heart with the heart of God. And you can begin to walk in the footsteps of Christ.

Now into this situation enters a strange thing (this is all conceptual, you understand). It is already obvious to you that the poustinia is a 'listening place' ... but now the listening begins to intensify itself. There is a desire to open your ears widely, and now you begin to hear. What you hear is a whole presentation of what is called 'theology' as *God begins to speak to your soul.* You 'see and hear' (but you don't see and hear as we usually speak of it) if you know what I mean.

You see God coming in the twilight to talk to Adam and Eve. You see the breach between God and man. You see that God the Father sent his Son to heal that breach. Then you see and hear all that happened to the Son – the whips, the crucifixion, and all the rest of it. In the poustinia, you enter into the tomb. It is a very dark period ... exceedingly dark. I don't know what you call it, but it is very dark. There is nothing there, and suddenly there is a resurrection. Now you know that you are reconciled to the Father, the Son, and the Holy Spirit. Now you know that you are reconciled to men, and this is sobornost.

Now all you have to do is to be very quiet, not rushing about or anything, but *just listening.* You act as though your feet were on the ground and you couldn't pick them up. Now your heart really becomes one great silent cry: "Speak, Lord! Thy servant heareth." Eventually, a time will come (this is figuratively speaking) when the Lord will say: "Open the door from inside and go forth ... *preach the Gospel with your life.*" (That is what Madonna House is all about – a journey from poustinia to sobornost to strannik.)

And now you will shall *go without fear into the hearts of men.* God will be there to show them to you. You will *pray always* because you have learned to pray from the beginning. You will *love without counting the cost* because you will have gone through the terrible experience of witnessing to what God did to his Son. You shall go forth to *do the little things exceedingly well for the love of God.*

Poor – Obedient – Chaste

It seems to me that we who were gathered at these LD meetings have caught this moment and have been of one mind. Now it is up to all of us in Madonna House to deepen the situation. Let each member of our family take the Little Mandate, and meditate on what it means to be poor obedient, and chaste. Each one of us has to meditate on these things.

What was the poverty of Christ? I could write pages on this, but one word from Christ (and all of my words on paper) will go down the drain, if we aren't listening with an attentive heart. Now that we have experienced this sobornost, our attention should be more alert, so that we will be able to understand things better. I grant you that it may be a dim understanding, but we will understand more about what poverty is (and obedience, and chastity). We will understand dimly because – unless we are fantastic saints like Teresa of Avila, Francis of Assisi, John of the Cross, or Catherine of Siena – we will not understand completely.

What was the poverty of Christ? *Keep thinking, keep reading, keep praying* ... and you will know. God and Our Lady will teach you both spiritual and material poverty. Consider the spiritual poverty of Our Lady, as she held her dead Son in her arms; and you will understand what it means for you, because you will have to do the same.

But there is more to it than I am touching on here. And there is the question of obedience. Why should I do anything you ask me to do? Because I like you? Because I fear you? Because you are my local director? The only reason that compels me to obey you is that *Christ was obedient unto death.* You know, here is the 'essence' of our life. We of Madonna House have been gathered together by God, not by ourselves! He has gathered us into a family so that, like his Son, we may be obedient unto death.

We are going to be tempted; we are going to be scourged. Everything is going to be against us; for the one thing the devil doesn't want us to do is *to die on the cross of Our Lord.* We need to understand what obedience is, not in a narrow sense (like monks and nuns used to do, though they had an idea of the larger meanings) but in a broad sense. In a very broad sense.

At night, before you go to sleep, keep in your mind this thought: "He was obedient unto death." Think of Jesus Christ dying ... dying on the cross. Think of him nailed there, slowly being asphyxiated, dying for you and me. Keep thinking about it more and more. Something will 'break into' your consciousness, and you will cry out: "Yes, I want to be obedient like you!" You will want to be obedient, not in a picayune way, but in a big way. That means to give up your will. It's as simple as that.

Chastity is another virtue we have to think about. It is not at all what some consider it to be. Men and women were created to come together in the sexual act. It is a holy and beautiful act, a God-given experience. But then, along comes this Man who says he is the Son of God. And he states that some people will choose to become 'eunuchs' for the love of him.

That's it! We are chaste, *for the love of him.* That doesn't mean that we reject our sexuality. That isn't so. We simply say: "Yes, Lord, you have created me as a sexual being. I accept that gift. But now you have to give me the courage to overcome my natural desires, for the sake of your Son." God and our Lady will give us the courage.

This doesn't mean that we hide our sexual tendencies from ourselves. Openly and simply, we say: "Yes, it is there." But so what?? So we battle the thing, and that's all there is to it.

I don't know all of the theological answers to this, but I think Christ wanted to show us the way – how we can be chaste for the love of God, *for the love of Someone bigger than ourselves.* Christ became man in everything but sin. So, therefore, he must have been attracted by women. It is a natural, unsinful tendency. (There is a beautiful novel that deals with his attraction to Mary Magdalene.) He could have gotten married. And why shouldn't he? It would have been a beautiful thing. And it would have been a witness to others; for most everyone around him was married. But he chose not to marry. He renounced marriage for our sakes.

Eddie and I did the same thing for the sake of the Apostolate. One day, after we had taken the vow of celibacy, Eddie said to me: "I sometimes feel as though we are already in the parousia."* It wasn't that we didn't desire each other. It was just that we felt as though we were already in heaven "where there is no marriage or giving in marriage." There was a simplicity and a clarity, a certain transparency between Eddie and me, which we could never have achieved if we had continued to indulge in the perfectly permissible marital relation. I think this is a grace that the poustinia gives us.

To return to the topic of poustinia: You realize, I hope, that we must *always live* in 'the poustinia of the heart' even though we may not have access to a physical poustinia. *We must not lose the unity we have achieved!* That unity is still a bit shaky. We should continue to love one another and accept one another, and to grow in that love and acceptance. Each of us may have our own ideas, but let us be simple and direct when discussing them. We must not seek to defend or justify ourselves. And we must not judge others. (I do both of these things, and I apologize. Especially, I beg your pardon if I judge you; and I forgive you if you judge me.)

It has been such a joy to have everyone from our houses present. I could write reams about our meetings – in fact, a book – but I will refrain from it because there are certain things which simply cannot be described. Instead, I

---

* *Parousia* is a Greek word meaning 'presence' or 'arrival.' Christians use it to mean the second 'arrival' of Christ, when he comes in glory to create a 'heaven on earth.'

will leave it to those who were present at those meetings to bring you God's message of sobornost and unity for our family. It happened for the first time in our lives!

Lovingly in Mary,

A VISION OF THE CHURCH

October 23, 1978

Dearly Beloved,

There was a day and there came a night. It is strange how often my days are filled with mysterious footsteps which come and go. At least, it seems so to me; for now I hear them, and now I don't. It was that kind of a day – a day of footsteps that I heard, then didn't hear for quite a while, and then suddenly heard again.

Upon these footsteps came the night. It was a peaceful night. The footsteps vanished. I fell asleep, and a strange thing happened. It was as though someone had reached my heart, and a hand had opened its doors.

I have often wondered what the doors of hearts are like. Are their handles gold or silver, shining as only copper can shine? Or do they look like neglected copper? Are they doors that are easily opened, doors that are oiled with the oil of love? Or are they rusty because they don't want to open to anyone? *Yes, there was a day and there was a night!*

It could be put down as October 8th of a certain year – 1978 – but to me it was timeless. You do not time the opening of the door to your heart; it is part of the eternity in which you live!

Someone opened the door of my heart, and I found myself in a poustinia which I had not seen before. Probably it belonged to one of our houses, but I paid scant attention to it. I just sat down on the hard bed, after I had bowed low before the icon and the cross. I let myself go into the quiet noise of my heart. For since its door was open, someone must have walked into it, and into the poustinia with me. But I couldn't distinguish very much *except that it had been day and now it was night.*

There were strange echoes, too; so I sat there on that hard bed and slowly entered some strange land to which I so often go. I call it 'the land of faith.' Before me in that land of faith was the Church. At first, I saw it as St. Peter's in Rome; then, as the great basilica of Notre Dame in Paris. Suddenly I was transported to the Churches in Russia – St. Basil, St. Isaac (where my father prayed), and Suzdal. A kaleidoscope of churches went around and around in my heart. I looked at them. I walked by them as I moved more and more deeply into this land of faith.

Suddenly all of the churches vanished, and I saw *the wounded Church*. I saw churches which were all broken up, shelled by airplanes and bombs. Then I was in Brunete, Spain, where I had been sent by *Sign* magazine* as a foreign correspondent. The church I was in had been shelled; it was wounded. In the middle of the altar stood a chalice filled with feces, into which a consecrated host had been placed by the communists.

All of this passed before me again like a movie. The churches in their glory, the physical churches, and the

---

* A Catholic monthly, in the U.S.A. Catherine was in Europe sometime in 1936-37 and wrote a series of articles on the state of the Church there. The Spanish civil war broke out in July 1936 and ended in March 1939. Germany and Italy intervened, using the war as a 'training ground' for their own armed forces, in preparation for World War II (which began in September 1939). Foreigners from many nations volunteered to 'help out' the various factions involved.

The destruction was horrendous. One estimate has over 300,000 killed in battle; 200,000 dead of disease or hunger; 100,000 executed or murdered; 500,000 houses destroyed or damaged; 2000 churches largely ruined. Many priests and nuns were cruelly killed in a rampage against the Church. (Anti-Church feeling had been high for years. In the riots of 1931, over 100 churches had been gutted in flames.)

churches that had been broken up, and where God had been blasphemed. All passed before me in this land of faith.

The Singular Church

Then, as if a hand passed over it all, there were no glorious churches, no broken churches! There was just *THE CHURCH* – in the singular, not in the plural. I looked at it and I said to myself: "What is this? It doesn't seem to be a church made out of bricks or mortar. It seems not to be a broken church. Yet it exists."

Slowly it seemed as if I were walking towards this church. From afar it seemed like an architectural picture of a church, any kind of church anywhere. But when I came closer, it was no church at all. It was just people. And I asked somebody: "Who are you?" And they said: "We are the people of God." It was an immense assembly. From it came sounds like the murmur of leaves in the autumn before they fall. "We are the people of God ... We are the people of God ... We are the people of God." It was almost a chant.

But before I could turn around, it had all vanished: the glorious churches, the wounded churches, the people who said they were the people of God. I sat on my bed in the poustinia, and I wondered what was going on. Where was I? *Where was that day? What was this night that was upon me?*

Suddenly I saw another picture. I saw it dimly as though I were looking at a building through a light fog. Again there was a lot of 'something' or 'someone' moving back and forth, and coming toward me. So I walked up to this 'thing' that looked like a church. (It seemed like the outlines of a church; the outlines changed all of the time.)

When I came close to it, there were people of every different race – the whole world was represented – and they were speaking all languages. I asked someone: "Who are you?" And they said: "We are the Mystical Body of Christ." I was not upset, but I was awed, for this thing was all a bit overwhelming. It was a strange thing. I could understand their answers, but somehow they came to me in an unusual way. I was not accustomed to seeing the whole world, the Christian world, in the shape of a church saying:

"We are the people of God" or "We are the Mystical Body."
I was indeed awed by it all, and I fell on my knees and
started praying to God without words, because the
awesomeness of the moment seemed to grow and grow and
fill the very air that I breathed.

Suddenly I saw a cross, and a Roman soldier piercing
a man with his lance. And out of the man's side flowed
water and blood. But something in the land of faith made
me look again; and then, out of it came a church.

I shaped the word 'Church' (it came out of the depths
of my being) and I said: *"That is the Church I was
seeking."* I looked at it again. The Crucified One
disappeared, and the strange form which seemed to have
come out of him began to take shape. It was beautiful, so
beautiful that I cannot describe it! It was also very strange.
I was on my knees looking at it, with my eyes wide open.
My heart was beating so fast that I thought I was going to
die.

The Doors are Open

I looked and looked. The more I gazed at it, the more
beautiful it became. I hardly dared to come closer to look at
it. But when I did, I saw that it had beautiful doors, so
finely wrought that I realized *nobody in this world* could
make doors like that ... if it were a door. For all I knew, it
might not be a door at all! Perhaps it was something else ...
like a heart.

I don't know, but I called it a 'door' because I couldn't
think of anything else. Whatever it was, it seemed to be
opened. As I came much closer to it, I watched it become
the shape of a woman. But it was strange. It allowed
everyone to come in – the people of God, the Mystical
Body. Everybody was welcomed, and 'it' became pregnant
with them. The people seemed to go in empty-handed, and
then come out with babies in their arms. Suddenly I wanted
to ask who she ... 'it' ... was.

Then out of the mist came a beautiful woman, adorned
like a bride with such beautiful garments! Side by side,
Christ was walking with her and holding her very tenderly
with his arm over her shoulder. For some reason, I was not
so greatly awed by it all, this time. I walked up to the

woman and I said: "Who are you?" And she said: "I am the Bride of Christ."

I said: "Well, how could you become pregnant yesterday?" She said: "I'm always pregnant, but always virgin. My symbol is Our Lady. She's always pregnant with the children of God." I said: "The children of God?" And she said: "God the Father begets them all of the time in his mind; and he hands them to me. And I'm always pregnant and always virgin, for I am the Bride of Christ; and my symbol is Our Lady." And then it all disappeared.

Lovingly yours in Mary,

WHAT ARE WE DOING WITH THE SEAL?

November 2, 1978

Dearly Beloved,

It is a strange thing – very strange! I have been reading the lives of founders and foundresses of various orders, and I see a pattern repeating itself.

Take Madame d'Youville, the foundress of the Grey Nuns. She used to do what Mother Teresa of Calcutta does today. She used to go around Montreal, caring for the sick and dying. Often she would fill her house with them; and then she would go out in the daytime, begging food for them, because she had no money. She was poor 'to the bone' you might say! Now you get the picture of a woman who is in love with God and follows in the footsteps of

Christ. She goes around begging for the people whom her compassion envelops like a mantle, and she doesn't care how many there are as long as there is a little corner where she can put them. She nurses them, bathes their wounds, and applies such medicines as are available.

Eventually she has followers, just as Mother Teresa does now. Her followers, who became Grey Nuns, labored mightily beside her. They washed, they cleaned, they scrubbed, they cleansed terrible wounds, and they did a marvelous job of it all.

Finally people began to understand what she was doing, and she got a little horse and buggy to travel around in, so that she might serve the poor better. Young people began to flock to her, and the pope permitted them to become an order which was approved of. Eventually they became teachers also.

Today we have Mother Teresa doing the same thing as Madame D'Youville did. Her work is chiefly with the dying, but she takes everybody, and her work is spreading. People send her money, but she is totally poor. She refuses to take taxis; she travels by subway in Harlem and on foot in India. You might say that *the Lord has put a seal upon her heart.* He always puts seals on the hearts of people like that – those foundresses. It is a burning seal that cannot be eradicated. It spreads through the heart of a human being, and compassion spreads with it. So that is happening to Mother Teresa; and hundreds follow her.

The Call to Radical Poverty

Out in the desert of the Sahara not too long ago (for he died in 1914), there was Charles de Foucauld. He loved wine, women, and song; but God called him, and his spiritual director agreed to it. He tried to become a Trappist, but he was refused for some reason. (Read *The Sands of Tamanrasset.** It will give you an idea of his life and sacrifice). Then he decided to be a humble servant, something like Benedict Joseph Labre. So he hired himself out to the nuns in Nazareth and became a gardener,

* By Marion Hill Preminger, Hawthorn Books, New York, 1961. (Actually, Foucauld *did* become a Trappist, but found that the life was not poor enough for him. He received permission to leave the monastery to work in North Africa as a contemplative monk among the peoples there.)

working for just his food and shelter.

For a while this satisfied his longings, but in his heart he had this desire to go into the desert, not necessarily just for a poustinia (though he had the Russian concept of poustinia, sobornost, and strannik). He wanted to bring Christ to the Tuaregs, a fierce tribe in the desert. So in a mud hut he prayed, and offered Mass, and led a life of great mortification.

His house was open to anybody who came, however. And he wrote several constitutions (which were found after his death). But, strangely enough, he had no followers. He was martyred by the Tuaregs, and he is now up for canonization.

A few years after his death, however, the most fantastic thing happened. His constitutions became widely known, and finally took root in human hearts. Today, in this year of 1978, when other orders are getting so few vocations, the Little Sisters and Brothers of Charles de Foucauld have a great following. (Both the priests and laymen are called Brothers.) They have a strange vocation. They never take jobs where they would be 'in charge of' anything.

The Sisters work as maids in Washington, D.C.; they clean and scrub the Catholic University. The Brothers work in factories and foundries in Detroit, or on the ships that ply the Great Lakes. That is the sort of work they often do. Poverty is their motto, and prayer is their strength.

You can say that they are 'newly organized' because it's not so long ago that they became fully established. But what I am interested in is this: that the distinguishing quality of all of these people was poverty – *total, complete poverty.* I could go on to mention others such as St. Francis of Assisi, St. Dominic, or St. Alphonsus Ligouri. All the big orders were distinguished by their poverty; and everybody who belonged to them in the early days placed their apostolate ahead of themselves.

Among us, something is happening lately; and I ask the question: "What comes *first* in the mind of Madonna House members?" We are such a new group, such a little group of lay people; and yet we make promises to God. Upon our hearts, the Lord places his seal: "You have placed a seal upon my heart" (Song of Songs 8:6). What are we doing with that seal? The seal, of course, is *his call to our tiny, humble apostolate.* But the size of our community doesn't make any difference. Be it as small as a grain of wheat, which dies to bring forth life; be it as large as the Jesuits and the Franciscans; it makes no difference. We are marked with his seal.

We are, I am afraid, beginning to follow in the footsteps of some of the old orders which are losing their spirit in these modern times. We cannot do that! Let us *disband* before we do that, for the very outstanding quality of Madonna House is *poverty.* Because people are good to us, we can abuse their goodness. If each of you would go into the depth of your heart and contemplate the seal that God has placed upon it, would you say to yourself that *you* are more important than the Apostolate? At times it seems as if we do that. (I am not judging anybody. I can only move on facts.)

Time and Money, and the Promise of Poverty

I am speaking here of both time and money as a form of 'wealth' that we can spend on ourselves instead of on the Apostolate. I notice that many people in the world today are traveling to see their spiritual director. Well, I don't care about you doing that, as long as you use money you have been given personally. Certainly you are *not* entitled to use Madonna House money, which should be used for apostolic purposes only, or else should be given to the poor. Using such money for your personal needs must never be done. There is always the mail, by which you can write to your spiritual director. If there is an emergency, there is always the telephone. (I cannot visualize anything that you couldn't ask by phone or by mail.)

But there is also the question of poverty of time, even if you use your own money for this purpose. Taking a train, or plane, or what-have-you, and traveling hundreds of miles to see your spiritual director pulls you away from your assigned job. There is bound to be some dislocation of the Apostolate because of this. No matter how unimportant you might be, your absence still disrupts the work of the Apostolate.

Because people give money generously to Madonna House, I think that we should seriously consider what is happening to it. I would like very much to have a financial accounting from each fieldhouse, as of today, sent to Combermere by December 15th, so that I can see how much each mission has available to it. If there have too much money on hand, it should go to the poor in one way or another. If you have to travel to lectures, yes, it is okay to use 'house' money; or if there's an emergency and your parents or family are ill; but certainly not on private business.

As for the use of time: Lately I notice that there are quite a few staff workers who have used extra time to go and visit their people. I don't want to discuss who or what. (Those to whom it applies will know!) There is something very profound here that could be the destruction of Madonna House quite soon after I am dead, or even perhaps before, because *I am fighting something.*

We had such a beautiful meeting of deep unity and understanding at our local directors' meetings. That must continue to grow in us. We must all be of one mind, one heart, one soul, one person. *Unity!* Out of the poustinia of our hearts, we have to keep that sobornost and become a strannik – one who preaches the Gospel, not only with his or her mouth, but with 'deeds' ... and the main deed is 'the Apostolate.'

God has created an Apostolate called Madonna House. God created this family and called each of us, individually, to come and join it. God has put his seal on all of our hearts. Those who are in the midst of their temporary promises have their seal for a year or two (as the case may be) but those who make 'final promises' have that seal put upon their hearts forever. As was so beautifully said by one of our staff: "I give my life forever."

But it doesn't mean that, just because people are good to us, we are allowed to lead the life of a suburbanite, to travel around and visit our friends whenever we desire to do so. I think that we should go deeply into this unity, and the unity that we should go deeply into is Christ's obedience. *He was obedient unto death. THAT made the unity of the Church!*

So I am a little worried; and because I share with you

all of my worries, I share this. We have to ask ourselves every day: "Which is it – the Apostolate or I?" For if we say '*I*,' we shall perish.

To share more of my meditation on this: Any one of us can say, "Let us figure out the good of the individual person *AND* the good of the Apostolate." Well, my answer to that is very simple. When I observed a bullet hole in the window of our Cleveland house, I remarked to one of the staff there: "You could have been at the other end of that bullet, and might have been killed." She answered: "Yes, I probably could have. But then I would have been a martyr; and *out of the blood of martyrs comes the seed of faith.*"

Which is it – the good of the Apostolate or your own? St. Stephen was killed with stones, praying for the people who killed him. He considered that the good of the Gospel was a little bit more important than his body. Okay ... what are *you* going to do?

The Call to Martyrdom

There was a woman who had an infant son. She was arrested during the Roman times – Perpetua, I think, her name was. After being tossed by a wild cow, she encouraged her brother and a catechumen to stand fast in their love for one another and said to them, "Do not let *our* sufferings be a stumbling block to *you*." The martyrs felt it was better to die for the apostolate of Christ than it was to deny it. And the good of the person became the good of the Apostolate.

Take St. Ignatius of Antioch: when people said they would pray that he wouldn't be thrown to the lions, he said: "No, don't do that. Don't do anything to help me escape this death, because I am going to be torn by the lions and my body will be like 'wheat' out of which you can make the Bread of Christ."

Which is better – the good of the person *or* the good of the Apostolate? If anybody had started thinking that way too much, there wouldn't *be* any Church. "Lord, I throw myself at thy feet, and sing and sing that I can bring you such a small thing."

This does not mean that, in the ordinary everyday life, we should not take care of our sick, our elderly, and so forth. That's the everyday life of Christ. That's what he wants us to do! But when we have to make a choice between the Apostolate or one of us personally, the Apostolate must always take precedence.

Perhaps I can put this in a nutshell. My great desire ... because I love you with a love that you do not yet understand perhaps (I hope I am not blaspheming when I say that I love you with the Love of Christ) ... my great desire is this: *I want you all to be martyrs* if it comes to the 'crunch.' I want you all to be heroes, not for your sakes, but for the Church's sake; because our tiny little Apostolate, if it is to continue to function as we did at the LD meetings of 1978 – *one mind, one heart, one body, one soul!* – must be ready to die for Christ as well as to live for him. If we do so, then *the Church becomes new and revived.* I want you to give your blood for the Church if necessary.

But, of course, those are the great and heroic things that I desire. Everyday life is quite different. When a person gives up a vacation, when a person gives up going to a spiritual director, going to the wedding of a friend or to a christening, or something like this, this is a very heroic and powerful deed. It perhaps might not take the same shades of martyrdom as being shot by the communists or something, but it certainly is martyrdom.

Lovingly yours in Mary,

TIDINGS OF GREAT JOY

Christmas 1978

Dearly Beloved,

I feel like saying to you, "I bring you tidings of great joy." And it is not only a feeling in my heart; *it is reality!*

As I prepared for Advent a bit ahead of time, cars and

planes had me either speeding along God's earth at a breakneck speed, or flying above it in the skies. I met a lot of people* who were all hungry for that very sentence: *I bring you tidings of great joy.*

I know that you, too, are hungry for that beautiful sentence which the Church lays in our outstretched hands, if we make a cup of them to receive it. Perhaps we will hold them in prayer. However it may be, we will open our hands and the 'tidings of great joy' will rest on them like a newborn bird. Or perhaps more like a newborn light.

There are some who will not believe this, who will try to wash their hands so that the 'tidings of great joy' may not cling to them, because – desiring their own will! – they want to wash away every vestige of God's will.

It is for them that we of Madonna House have been gathered together as a family of the Trinity and of Our Lady. It is for those who do *not* want to receive the 'tidings of great joy' – for those who want to *reject* everything about it – that we have been gathered together by God! *SO LET US REJOICE!*

Listen with your heart. It takes listening, a special kind of listening, to hear the tenderness of God; and that is what you are going to hear this Christmas. If you let yourself enter into the immense sea of his tenderness, you will understand even better why we are a family of God – why we have been gathered together by him.

His tenderness will beget in us a tenderness for our brothers and sisters; and the circle of love which he has come to bring this day, this strange mysterious day of his birth, will slowly embrace the whole earth as he desires it to do.

We might not see that we are embraced so tenderly. On the contrary, before us will be catastrophes, tragedies, a blaspheming of the light of Christ, and what-have-you. But listen, listen with your heart ... listen with your mind ... listen with all of your being, and you will hear the tenderness of God! Strange as this might seem, tenderness is usually not heard but felt. However, you will experience it in both ways.

---

* Catherine spoke in Providence, Rhode Island, to a rally of 14,000 people. Then she went to New York City for a television interview conducted by The Christophers.

But in order to do so, my dearly beloved, as he has placed 'tidings of great joy' into our hands, so now we must place into his cupped hands (small as infant hands are, my dearly beloved) our own dispossession, our own poverty. It is deliberately chosen, gladly accepted, joyfully tied up with Christmas ribbon and fancy paper, for we are going to give it – that dispossession, that poverty, that total surrender of ourselves – into the hands of the Great King. We are going to give it into the hands of the Son who is born to redeem us, so that he, in his turn, can carry it to the Father ... the Father who loves us so much!

Yes, I wanted to write you a Christmas Letter, and this isn't at all what was in my heart. It started differently, but as I went on I knew that I had to add to the 'tidings of great joy,' with which I began this letter, the *tidings of great pain*. But somehow or other, if you listen well, my dearly beloved, you will understand that the pain which you undergo in the total surrender, in that poverty which I talk about, in that thinking always of someone else and not yourself ... in that pain lies also the 'tidings of great joy.'

May your Christmas be filled with it. Alleluia! Alleluia!

Lovingly yours in Mary,

178

A YEAR OF CONSOLATION

December 30, 1978

Dearly Beloved,

Greetings, my dears! Happy, Holy and Blessed New Year
to you! All along, my Mass has been for you for courage,
strength, and openness of heart. I want you to have your
hearts totally open to God, so that the year 1979 (which, I
think, is not going to be a happy year) will come to you on
quiet feet, as Christ would have come to you if you had
been his Gethsemane. Perhaps we can all be the stone over
which he wept. But I hope we are not going to be 'like
stone'! We are going to be stones that are *alive,* for the tears
of God would make any stone alive, especially the stones
of our hearts – those hearts who love him so much. Let us
allow him to penetrate them with his tears and his joy, and
let us console him.

I want this year of 1979 to be a year of consolation of
Our Lord by the Madonna House members. Let us forget
our difficulties. Let us forget the pronoun *I.* Let us
remember that God is first, my neighbor is second, and I
am third. I want this year to be 'the Year of the Lord.' Let
us remember him. Let us think of the word *he.* He will need
consolation *from us,* dearly beloved. That is why the
bishops are asking for listening houses.*

We must listen to the tears of mankind ... because, you
see, the tears of mankind flow onto the dark and stony
hearts of *other* men. There are so many who won't listen.
So many worship themselves. So many think and talk only
about themselves. We must be an exception to this, for a
Christian is *one who loves and who ALSO listens.* It is
excruciating to listen to people constantly, but it is very
necessary at this time!

* At this time, Catherine began to establish fieldhouses in which the staff would
mainly 'pray and be available' to listen to people who wanted to 'talk things
out.' She often said that it was possible to *listen* another person's 'soul' into
existence.

Let us listen to everyone without distinction, and pray while we listen. We serve by listening, by consoling, by wiping the tears of children ... and of women ... and of men. My dearly beloved, this is consoling Christ in Gethsemane. Let us think of ourselves as being Gethsemane. It says in Scripture that God has a place for us. He calls it his 'garden enclosed'. (I think it is in the *Song of Songs.*) Well, let us be both. Let us be the garden enclosed where he can rest; but let us realize that the year of 1979 will be a Gethsemane to the world.

Do I make myself clear, or don't I? I want so much to share with you, my dearly beloved. I really love you so much, and I want to share with you all that I can. I want to share with you that we have to also be a Gethsemane to the Lord, and we must console him constantly. We must enroll Our Lady to help us to console him. Perhaps she knows best how to sing him lullabies. Maybe lullabies are a consolation, I don't know. However that may be, let us sing her lullabies to the world, so that the restless ones, the sick ones, the ones who are all tied up with emotions, can go to sleep in our Gethsemane which is open for them. So that we can lead them to the stone and introduce them to Jesus Christ.

Dearly beloved, prepare yourselves. Let us pray and fast. Let us love one another with a powerful love. It is necessary. Yes, that is what I wanted to share with you as a New Year's gift, if gift it be. (Incidentally, pray for me. I need prayers very much.)

Lovingly yours in Mary,

THE ETERNAL FEAST

Easter 1979

Dearly Beloved,

For all of us, but especially for the Russian soul, Easter is *the apex feast*. You know that, of course. You have been told that so many times, and now you are accustomed to koolitch and paska, not to mention colored Easter eggs, the symbolism of which you have absorbed.* All of this, beautiful as it is, is of little significance compared to one fact: *CHRIST IS RISEN!*

Dearly beloved in Christ, how can I ever express to you the immensity of this feast. Factually, it is not just immense; it is *eternal!* It takes you up and drops you into eternity. *Love has come to dwell with us.* We must love one another, for he has said: "Love one another as I have loved you." We ordinary human beings are lifted up into some fantastic, incredible, mysterious, and mystical way.

CHRIST IS RISEN! And on the day of Christ's resurrection, *we* resurrect – at least we should. We should participate in that resurrection by growing in our love of one another. We should become as children. Indeed, our prayer should be: "Give me the heart of a child." For only those who believe in the resurrection believe in the Trinity; believe in the Father, Son, and Holy Spirit.

Just stop to think. ... (Words fail me, and my ability to think is literally nil; it doesn't exist.) ... Somehow or other I am a little child, led by God to become a child in his Kingdom, now and hereafter, because he said: "The Kingdom of God is *now!*"

In my own soul, love is like an ocean which – for a space, a minute of time – has become like a narrow passage

---

* *Koolitch* is a special Easter bread, very rich, containing saffron and candied fruit. *Paska* is cottage cheese enriched with sugar, eggs, and raisins, symbolic of the Paschal Lamb. Eggs signify new life; their rounded shape suggests eternity (no beginning and no end).

to pass *through* me and then becomes an ocean *within* me. *I SCATTER LOVE BECAUSE IT IS SCATTERED IN ME SO TREMENDOUSLY.* I say to myself, "God loves me!" He loves me when I am good, and when I am not so good, because he loves sinners. He forgives them too. His mercy is *infinite* and so is his love, his goodness, his forgiveness. And I behold that which is incredible for man to behold – I behold my Dearly Beloved in the light of this infinite mercy. I look at my hand and see it is a very small hand that nestles quite easily in the immense hand of God, and I shiver with delight. *CHRIST IS RISEN! VERILY HE IS RISEN!* Yes, that is how I am a child before God, and a grown-up person before man. Now the mystery penetrates me deeply, and my love is stirred to its depths. It is a very simple thing. It is so simple that it is hard to understand. "Let us love one another," he said, "as I have loved you."

Well, it is rather clear, so why not turn our faces to one another, no matter what animosity we felt yesterday; and let that animosity of whatever kind fall at our feet like old worn-out garments. We are newly clothed in the shining clothes of one who is baptized, whose garments can be seen from far away, shining ... even through the night. Then we will be a light to our neighbor's feet.

What can I say to you on this feast of all feasts? *HE IS RISEN! ALLELUIA! ALLELUIA! KRISTOS VOSKRESE!**

Lovingly in Mary,

___

* Russian for "Christ is risen." The response to this customary Easter greeting is *Voistinu Voskrese!* ... "Truly he is risen" ... followed by a triple embrace.

182

MY PEACEFUL DREAM

July 21, 1979

Dearly Beloved,

I had a wonderful sleep this past night. That is really extraordinary, for I had not slept for some time because of the 'vigils' and what-have-you.* So I was delighted with this sleep. But I also had a strange dream. This was it:

I was in Russia, and I was in my early twenties. I was going over a path that was somewhat familiar to me. I kept telling myself that it must lead to a little lake, and it finally did. It was a beautiful day, and the water seemed nice, so I disrobed and went swimming. No one was around. It was very quiet, and the birds were singing, so I swam and swam. Then I came out and lay down on some lovely green grass and went to sleep. In my sleep I seemed to have another dream. This time I was dressed in a beautiful cape. It was shining and shimmering, as though it reflected both heaven and earth at the same time.

I was admiring myself in that cape, and when I looked up there was Jesus Christ! He was sitting on a stump with his hands folded, looking at me. I was so delighted to see him because I had so many problems I wanted to solve. So I started talking breathlessly, words tumbling over words.

He listened to me with a little smile; and then he said, "Peace!" I slowly ceased talking, and he looked at me and said: "Peace, Catherine. You have to understand a few things." I said nothing, as I was so excited about being able to talk to him that at first I didn't even kneel down! Then I knelt at his feet, and he said: "Peace. Contain in your heart peace. Your answers will come in due time. Right now you have to open your heart to *my peace.*"

I said, "Your peace is very difficult, because it is always on the cross." He said, "That is true, but I have

* Cf. *Dearly Beloved,* Vol. 3, pages 45-46.

taken you off the cross to give you this peace." I dissolved; I was laughing and crying. I wanted to kiss his hands, but he said: "Don't touch me. I will touch you whenever it is necessary."

So I sat there waiting, and he said: "Look, I am giving you this peace. I want you to take it in and act upon it." So I took it in. He said: "Look, there are so many things that you don't understand, and you are going to continue *not* understanding because I have given you joy recently." I said, "That was a few weeks ago, and I have had such a rough time since."

He said: "I have given you joy, and I am giving you peace, and in between you had pain. That is the way that it is going to be – always together. *Because you follow my life, you will always have pain.* You already know that. And you already have love, hope, tenderness – all virtues from me. But you will be tested in faith again and again and again ... because, while you live, there is only one thing that my Father can test you in, and that is faith.

Many People Depend on You

"So prepare yourself. You must understand that you do not understand. There are many things that you wish to ask me about; but it is of no use, as I am not going to tell you. That is because you have to walk in faith, and that is why you do not understand. *You must grow in faith until the end of your life.* You already have love, hope, and tenderness.

"Look, many people depend upon you because it is this way – neither my Father, nor I, nor the Holy Spirit, nor my Mother can move the will of human beings. We have given them free will; and we will not take it back, because it *is* a free gift. But you can help to change the free will of others. I will give you the grace through your humanity. Faith will be the most important thing to you. You must enter faith. Faith is for everybody, not just for you."

He had to shake me to accept the peace, for at that moment I was not particularly peaceful. He said: "Be quiet. I am giving you the peace, my peace, and it is for everybody." Then he blessed me. He seemed to go away, but then he returned and said:, "Look, that faith and that peace is for everybody, not just for you alone. *It is for every member of Madonna House.* This you must do; you must show it to all."

I was most peaceful during that dream and completely relaxed. I felt warmth and a renewal of joy; and now I feel full of peace and joy.

Peace!

Catherine

COME ON HIGHER

August 8, 1979

Dearly Beloved,

You must be very tired of reading my Staff Letters. It can be quite tiring to read the letters of a woman in love with God. She is like a relentless river, tumbling now in white waters; now running quietly and peacefully (a fisherman's paradise!); now again, running over boulders higher than any white rivers can hold; but always tending toward its goal, almost like a mad woman (or should I say mad river?) holding out her watery hands toward one goal, the Desired One. Bounding or still, white rivers or bleak, always moving toward the sea! Yes, it must be tiring to read the Staff Letters of a woman in love with God!

It is as if nothing, *but nothing,* can stand in her way. She is like a shepherd calling her sheep who might be dispersed or far away. She calls them. She calls them to come and follow her ... no, not so much to follow as to 'go ahead of her' like the Israelite shepherds who walked behind their flock as well as ahead of them. Calling, calling, calling ... in bitterly cold nights; in the summertime when the buds are in flower, or almost there; when the leaves fall one by one, blushingly red upon an almost frozen earth. Calling, calling ... against the wind that tears the voice apart, stopping it (or trying to stop it) from reaching the ears of those to whom it is addressed!

Yes, it must be tiresome to read the Staff letters of a woman in love with God. Tiresome because *relentlessly* she calls everyone upon the mountain – the mountain of the Lord – for in her ears, the words *"FRIEND, COME ON HIGHER!"* constantly reverberate. She knows only too well that very few want to come on higher because they are well situated right now among green grass, fragrant flowers, and trees singing their eternal lullaby. Why should anyone leave this lovely spot to go up higher? From where they are, they contemplate that higher place. It is cold; the wind blows the snow all around the boulders, the trees. There is no green grass, and there are no flowers. Alone, Christ stands on a boulder and says, *"FRIEND, COME ON HIGHER."*

Years have come, and years have gone. And the refrain of the woman in love with God is always the same – so monotonous. "Come on higher," she says, "to brave the rain, brave the tempest. Come on higher ... Christ is waiting. *Come on higher!"*

So, dearly beloved, I know that a letter like this isn't going to take up much room. Maybe you'll read it; maybe you won't. But all I can do is sign it ...

A Woman in Love with God,

THE HEART OF POVERTY

August 11, 1979

Dearly Beloved,

I wish I knew why poverty *possesses* me; but it is true that I am so possessed! Stewardship is well practiced, not only by me, but by all of us in Madonna House. Everything is accounted for. We are grateful for each item, each gift that people send. When things are sold in our gift shop, the money goes to the poor ... to the 'boat people' and so forth.*

It seems that I am truly poor. There is nothing that I possess in my own right – except maybe a few pieces of clothing which I got from the clothing room, just as the other members of Madonna House do. There is the one-room cabin in which I live, which has a bed, a table, a few chairs ... as well as the desk and filing cabinets necessary for running the Apostolate. But all this really belongs to Madonna House, not to me personally. Although I am poor, I can say that 'I live on an island' quite comfortably and pleasantly because of the island itself – its moods, its winds, its sunshine, its trees, its snows. I should be satisfied; for I can say in truth that, officially, *I am poor.* (What I am really trying to say to you, however, is so much bigger than anything that I can put into words.)

Poverty – does not the sound of that word enchant you? Are you listening to Lady Poverty? Can you hear her siren song saying, "Come, follow me"? You arise and

---

* In 1978-79, the Vietnam government began a wholesale resettlement of its population from cities to forest areas, banned all private business and confiscated all wealth. Hundreds of thousands of refugees fled Vietnam, many in small antiquated boats (usually leaky), thereby becoming known as 'boat people.' International agencies attempted to help these refugees.

Evidence mounted that the Vietnam government was extorting millions of dollars from refugees before letting them leave. Pirates on the high seas attacked and stole what little the refugees had managed to bring with them. 'Boat people' became a term to refer to *the poorest of the poor* ... those who had nothing, not even a country in which to live ... such as the 500,000 Cambodian refugees who fled to Thailand after Vietnam took over that country in 1979.

follow her, and she leads you to strange and unknown depths. Here, she stops before a cave and bids you enter. So you do; and, in that cave, you begin to learn *detachment.*

You were poor ... (I know that I was, but was I detached?) ... *It is one thing to be poor. It is another to be detached.* The Russian spiritual writers say that real poverty begins when 'the need to have' becomes 'the need *not* to have.' That is true detachment.

Now the cave becomes deeper. Lady Poverty grows more beautiful, and she holds before me the invitation to go into her depths. Suddenly I understand that poverty is *total* detachment – from everyone and everything. In my own cupped hands, I offer to God all that I possess: husband, son, brothers, sisters, family, earthly goods – whatever! And, having offered it all, I remain indeed 'naked' ... or perhaps one could say covered with rags. Yet, at that very moment when I have lifted up my cupped hands to God and allowed the wind of the Holy Spirit to carry my gifts to his feet, he takes what I am giving him, and at the same time *he attaches me to himself.*

Then I begin to see Lady Poverty as she really is! I look at her, and she is bedecked in splendor because, for me, *God is everything* – my beginning and my end – and since he owns the world, so do I!

Nevertheless, Lady Poverty, resplendent in her robes, still beckons me to follow. She walks in shimmering garments up a mountain. I have left 'detachment' behind. I am 'attached' to God, and all seems to be well. I possess nothing. I have given everything up, *and yet I know that I am not poor enough.* Sometimes an irritation creeps into some of my days. Sometimes anger enters them (and one is never poor, if anger or irritation are still in one's heart). So I sit in my poustinia and contemplate my lack of poverty, and pray God to take from me any kind of anger or irritation.

Higher, Still Higher

Again, Lady Poverty beckons me. And I hope, in Christ, that my irritations and angers are diminishing minute by minute, as I try to follow her footsteps. Then – quite suddenly – she doesn't seem to be around, faithful companion that she was. I am left to myself, and the winds grow stronger.

When that happens to you, my dearly beloved, you will find that the winds are not quite like a hurricane, but they are strong. The rain that they presage is an 'acid rain' that is going to fall onto your soul, and the result will be an endless temptation. You will find yourself alone on the mountain ... with the wind, the thunder, and the lightning as your only companions. The rain is lashing you as though it wants to punish you. You turn around and look, and Lady Poverty is nowhere to be seen. You are drenched. Such garments as you had are falling off under the impact of the rain. You become naked and cold. If it isn't the rain, then it's the wind that lashes you.

Suddenly (as you sit there, naked and defenseless, against a tree trunk of some sort) you smile! Now you know that you have reached 'the heart of poverty' – you have opened yourself to be tempted. The name of God is on your lips, and the *Pax-Caritas* cross is on your breast, and the tempter leaves you. Now you really know that you are poor, that you have nothing except God; and it is *by his grace* that you have overcome the temptation.

When that happened to me, I understood then why I was *possessed* by poverty. It was because I wanted to be possessed by God!

Lovingly yours in Mary,

FAITH – A GIFT OF GOD

September 3, 1979

Dearly Beloved,

I thought that I would share with you a meditation that I had recently. Maybe you will enjoy reading it. I hope so, my dearly beloved.

At the moment that Jesus entered the water to be baptized, all the waters of the world became holy. Did you know that? Yes! All the waters of the world became holy. Just one step from the hot sun of Palestine into the cool water, with St. John the Baptist watching ... John the Baptist who said that he would come – he whose sandal he was not worthy to unloose.

Faith is a mantle so big that *all the world is covered with it*. It is a gift of God! Perhaps a gift of Mary, too. Did she weave that mantle as she wove the seamless garment of her Son – the one that the Romans wouldn't cut but threw dice for? I wouldn't know. All that I know is that *faith is a gift of God* found in the baptismal waters. It is immaterial if the water is from a river, a lake, or a sea. Once it touches the forehead, enveloped with the holy words, the gift is ours – yours and mine.

We have faith. Now we must make it grow. Perhaps 'grow' isn't the word, for faith doesn't grow – faith *expands*. Yes, it expands, and it gets firm and strong – strong as love; for, in the ultimate, faith is love. Faith looks upward into the eyes of God, and from them draws its strength; and when it does, it is immovable. Death can threaten it, dance around it – in fact, capture it – but faith laughs. Faith laughs at death because it knows that death has no dominion over it. Faith knows that if death for a second seems to conquer it, it is just an illusion. It is just for a second. For all that death does is to open a real door for us – a door of love. Yes, it stretches its body half-forward and twists in some sort of way a clasp that holds the door; and then it retreats. It retreats because it cannot confront life again, for beyond that door is life. Life eternal! Life of joy! Life of song! Life of beauty! *Because it is LIFE WITH GOD.*

So faith grows in you and me (or it should). The Church helps us along the road by giving us the beautiful sacrament of confirmation. It is a funny word, that word *confirmation*. What does it confirm? Do you know? I do! It confirms the gift of God. It confirms our faith. It makes our faith strong and immovable. Yes, it is a confirmation of depths unplumbed and mysteries unknown and yet familiar to us all.

The anointing with oils: holy feet walking into the water. They will very soon walk *on* the waters, and God will immerse himself in the waters and make all waters of the earth holy. Then he will come back in the soothing oil that *confirms* his immersion, in our baptism, and make us whole. This becomes understandable even to children – or perhaps mostly to children.

Faith! Faith confirms. Faith now calls its retinue. Behold there is hope! There is love! There come all the seven gifts of the Holy Spirit, and even more! It is so hard for us to understand.

And yet, while we are on earth, faith stands taller than all of the rest. We shall be judged on love; but we shall also be judged on faith because, you see, it is a very simple thing – that mystery. Yes, very simple. Those who have faith in God love him beyond all measure, and those that love God beyond all measure have faith in him. Two separate and distinct faces of sacraments; and yet, are they two? Or are they all one? Is faith always 'pregnant' with love and hope? Whichever it is, it is a mystery beyond our ken. Yet it is a reality which we must – now, in this hour of need – make strong, as strong as love can be. Strong as hope can be ... and stronger! For we can make it as strong as faith can be.

Lovingly Yours in Mary,

Catherine

A BEAUTIFUL MEETING

October 1, 1979

Dearly Beloved Family,

Again I have been very silent. Of course you know that we had the LD meetings, and there was no time to do much more, as everything was concentrated on the local directors. My heart was completely at their disposal as it should have been.

Already you know that we had a 'miraculous' meeting. *Sobornost* reigned supreme. I suggest that you read my book by that name, perhaps at spiritual reading, for it will make our LD meetings more vivid to you. Your local directors may have spoken of it to you. Reading it will help you to grasp the essence of that spirit, which means being *one with God and one with each other.* Anyhow, I leave this to your decision. It was a beautiful meeting that we had – peaceful, relaxed, and holy.

It was also a meeting in which I was able to present my thoughts to the family without interruption or difficulties. We talked mostly about the things that matter. And the thing that matters most is *sanctity.* I don't mean the type of sanctity that is the question of being declared a saint via Rome and so forth. No, I mean that hidden type of sanctity that stems from a heart in love with God. We talked a lot about being in love with God. It involves so many things.

Above all, it means totally emptying oneself. Reading about this in a book may make it *seem* easy, but it takes a lifetime – or half a lifetime, or maybe a quarter of a lifetime – to even *begin* to empty oneself from self. Of this we talked; and somehow as we talked we knew that we were obeying Christ's words, "Friend, come on up higher."

So we kept talking, and a fantastic vista opened before our dazzled eyes. It seems as if we all suddenly understood what it really meant to belong to Madonna House. We understood that, by the grace of God, we had plowed and harrowed the field of faith. What was given to us at baptism began to grow as it should, and it became a big tree with lovely leaves. And in the shadow of those trees, people began to rest and feel that Christ was near – which of course he was! Yes, our faith grew and grew and grew. It was beautiful to behold, but this is what we must do, dearly beloved. *We must have faith,* faith that is unshakable under any circumstances, including martyrdom. For this we must pray.

We understood this perfectly during our LD meetings; for, on this earth, faith is master of hope and love. When we die, faith vanishes and hope disappears; and we shall be judged on love alone. It is not quite so on earth. Here, faith guides our steps. It points to hope and love, and it shows us when and how to use them.

As far as I am concerned, the LD meetings truly taught me to begin sweeping from my heart every little speck that shouldn't be there, so that God might feel 'at home' in my heart. I rise to his full stature and speak; and yet I don't speak; he speaks with a loud voice to all those he desires to reach.

Yes, it's been a beautiful meeting. There is still so much that I want to share with you; but for today there is one thought that is, I think, sufficient: *To be in love with God.* Yes, to be in love with God! To say that one's soul is being emptied for him to feel 'at home' in it. Yes, that is sufficient for one letter.

Lovingly yours in Mary,

PRAYER AND ZEAL

October 5, 1979

Dearly Beloved,

I haven't written you because I am recovering from the flu. I had a little temperature, much tiredness, a few aches here and there (but then my bones always ache, so that is nothing new). But now I am slowly recovering. And do you know something? Being in bed gives you a lot of time to think and pray. The thinking continues as usual; but, in a way, the praying overcomes it.

What do I mean by this? Well, when a priest once asked me how I prayed, I said, "I *am* a prayer, Father." I suppose this answer probably sounds terribly arrogant and vain, and contrary to the idea of what people generally think that prayer is. Yet, I would repeat that same answer anytime to a priest or lay person who asked such a question. "I am a prayer."

How did I arrive at this answer? It is rather simple; it begins by being in love with God. I have been in love with God since the age of six. This sounds funny, but God was my playmate! And when I had other playmates, I always included him. So when I began to grow up (say, at ten or twelve or fifteen years of age), it became perfectly normal for me to talk to God about all kinds of things, no matter how seemingly unimportant. We had a poustinia at our house, of course. It was a small cabin with a cross and bed and a Bible. Many times in my youth, I went there to pray; and that also helped to bring me closer to God.

As I grew into womanhood, I began to be faced with other ways of praying. There had been the way of prayer through which my first spiritual director had guided me (I have always had a spiritual director). It was called 'vocal' prayer; that was the usual way to talk to God at first. Then you were passed on to somebody who (your spiritual director thought) knew more about prayer; it could be a

Carmelite, a Dominican, or maybe a Franciscan. They were to teach you 'mental' prayer.

Obedient to my spiritual director, I went through all of this. I entered a new land, the land of meditation. Somehow the vocal prayer fell off like old rags. Avidly, I read the Gospels; and slowly (very slowly!) I began the practice of meditating on each word. The Gospels became my favorite prayers. It seemed as though the Lord himself explained things. It ceased to be meditation in which my intellect sought to find some answers. No, it was God, pointing to this passage or that and making it clear. (To be absolutely frank, I was lost in God in those days!)

Prayer is very much like a love affair. You first get to meet the person; and you talk, because you want to know all about him or her, and the other wants to know all about you. Then the love affair progresses. You begin to think about what that person has said to you, and the memory of it is sweet both in your mind and on your lips. And then there comes a day when you get married to that person. When people marry one another, contemplative prayer becomes part of their married love. They belong to each other, totally, intimately. After the sexual act, conversation does not take place because love is too 'big' for conversation. Love – when God is your lover – does not need conversation either.

Because He Loves Me

Now you will ask me, "Where did you go from there, Catherine?" And I will give you a very strange answer, one that is difficult to understand – especially for people who are theologians and Scripture scholars. They will probably reject my answer, but I will give it to you very straight: *I BECAME A PRAYER.* There is no explanation of this state. It could be called 'the prayer of the presence of God' but it would be false, because it isn't that. It is simply *being a prayer.* You could say that it closely resembles the Jesus Prayer, but it is not that either. If you ask me point-blank (which is what you are trying to do) I would simply say, "I am so in love with God that he has made me a prayer." If this answer is not satisfactory, I have no other.

Now, in all humility and simplicity, I say that I had

become a prayer, not because I was so great, but *simply because he loves me.* He loves me so much that he died for me! And when I had absorbed all of that, what else could I be but a prayer? So the answer that I gave this priest was, in my mind, a very humble one and a very direct one because that is the way I feel.

What really matters to me is that I pray with all of you. When I pray, it suddenly seems that the door of my cabin opens and you are all there, everyone of you. It seems as though those who have left and those who have stayed are there, and my room becomes very large, and you are all there, and we pray together. I watch all of this and I say: "How nice of God! We truly have sobornost!" You know God; he knows you. We pray together, we communicate together, and I am filled with joy, a great and immense joy.

But there is pain too. In my case, the cause of this pain is very simple: not everybody is in my room. Some stay away. I don't know why, nor dare I even ask why. Those things are the secrets of God, and I don't ask anything. I just pray a little harder. I miss some of you sometimes; I miss others of you quite often; and there is a pain in my heart that I cannot describe. It is just there.

As my years go by, and my encounter with God comes closer, I talk to him more. There are so many things that I want to say to him about you. I know it is foolish because he and Our Lady will take care of Madonna House – the Triune God and Our Lady will take care of it. But I am a human being, and I ask myself: "What is happening to us lately? We had such a beautiful local directors' meeting, and I was so happy over it, as I am sure all were who participated in it."

Perhaps I am simply foolish, but something bothers me. I wish I could explain it, could reveal it to you as one shows a moving picture; then everyone would understand. Perhaps it is a question of our ... call it indolence, call it tiredness, call it 'old age' even. But then I often read the lives of saints who lived to a ripe 'old age' and are not afflicted with this problem. St. Teresa of Avila, for instance. St. John Bosco, with tired feet that were swollen, walked up and down the streets of Turin (and he probably had a heart condition too). If sometime you have nothing to do, read what people have done in their old age.

There is some kind of a ... I don't know. I can't call it laxity; that would be unkind and untrue. But there is something that isn't ... You see, I stop; and I don't know what to say. Maybe you feel it more than I do; and yet there is a tremendous compassion in me for everyone who has this strange attitude. You see, my words are stumbling; they don't really go anywhere. I am sure they don't penetrate very deeply into your hearts and souls. And when I look at what we have to face in this world, I fear.

My father always said to lift two arms to God – the arm of fasting and the arm of prayer. Quite a lot of us fast, and a lot of us pray. So what is the matter? Everything is fine; and yet there is something that *isn't* fine. Is it an attack of the devil? Does he, once in a while, throw himself against Madonna House and try to change its way? I don't know. I don't think so, and I hope not.

I am not sure whether this letter will upset or console you. In it is so much compassion, so much love for you, so much desire for your perfection; because I never forget that I have always tried to lead you to Golgotha, no matter what it costs me. I try. I really try, because I love you so very very much.

I think that I have said enough for the time being. Maybe later I will say something again. But you are in my room, my well-beloved. You are! We are all praying together – most of us anyhow – and my love, compassion, understanding, and my strange knowledge are deep in your hearts. Sleep well.

Lovingly yours in Mary,

READINESS AND SIMPLICITY

October 27, 1979

Dearly Beloved,

It seems that I have just written you a Staff Letter. In fact, I am sure that I have. Yet somehow, my heart craves dialogue with you. I miss you very much. At this time, you are probably reading the excerpts of our LD meetings in September, and are beginning to realize how beautiful, peaceful, and filled with sobornost they were.

I want to tell you that I love you so very much because, quite simply, *I have laid my life down for all of you.* It is quite simple to lay one's life down for those one loves. Don't you think so? You are so very close to my heart. As you come closer and closer to me (or perhaps I am coming closer and closer to you), I must share some things that are in my heart. These are things which ... I wouldn't say they bother me, but they make me feel as if I were in a boat, a small boat on a large sea, and the boat is rocking. Nothing is going to happen to it, but it rocks. And when a boat rocks like that, you don't feel very happy. You usually get seasick.

Well, this is what is happening to me. I often spend my nights in vigils. (You are getting used to the fact that I do this regularly.) I spend a lot of nights thinking about what I have *left undone that I should have done* to help you. By 'helping' you, I mean bringing you closer to Christ. You see, dearly beloved, again and again there is one thought that dominates my whole life. It is not easy for me to take a hammer and some nails, and to nail you on that cross, even though I know – with my whole heart, my whole mind, and my whole being – that God takes you immediately off it. It *still* is not easy. The sound of nails passing through human flesh is very difficult to bear. But I know that this is what I have to do.

What I am telling you is symbolic, of course; yet it is

also a reality of daily life. And we meet that reality constantly! I look at you, all of you everywhere, and I must admit that I see holiness – as yet with a small 'h' (smile). I see sanctity – as yet with a small 's' (smile). But I do! I know that you are on your way. *I know that you are walking in the footsteps of Christ.* All of this I know. What is it that bothers me, then? What is it that wakes me in the night and sends me (since, with my bad knee, I cannot kneel) to 'stand before the Lord'? What is it that leaves me uneasy?

As I said, I was very happy – and I still am – over the local directors' meetings. Our sobornost is really a big cornerstone to Madonna House, one that makes it stand firm. But since those meetings, as I have told you already, I have been uneasy. What is this uneasiness? I try to get into its depths because, with God, *everything is depths and heights.* I have continued to pray; but thoughts strike me like little arrows and then depart. Later, they return again.

As I said before, sharing is not easy ... not because I am unwilling to share, but because you are (perhaps) not always willing to receive my confidences and my sharing. We are still not facing what tomorrow will bring; and *tomorrow will bring pain.* Are we ready? Are we ready to endure that pain, to offer it up to God because it is His Will to give it to us? Are we ready to reduce our 'lifestyle' (as they say) to great simplicity ... to a *very great* simplicity?

There is a book in our library that deals with the spirit of simplicity. It is a good book to read. If you don't have it at your house you can write to a Cistercian Order. It is characteristic of their simplicity. It is worth reading. It is called *The Spirit of Simplicity.**

Do I desire simplicity? Yes, my beloved sons and daughters, I do. I desire simplicity with a *passionate* desire, as I desire poverty. Poverty and simplicity are linked in my mind. Yes, I desire a great simplicity. Our houses are too 'magnificent'! There are carpets from wall to wall, cheap as they may be. There is, perhaps, too much furniture. I don't know about the most recently founded houses. But do we have a simplicity that hits the eye of the beholder? Not in

* Published in 1948 by the Abbey of Our Lady of Gethsemani, Trappist, Kentucky.

order to hit that eye, but in order to invite the person to enter into that simplicity and that poverty. Because it is time now that we should divest ourselves from much. *It is time!*

Lovingly yours in Mary,

MY LAST WILL AND TESTAMENT

November 26, 1979

Dearly Beloved,

Here is the beginning of my Last Will and Testament. It will continue, by and by, as the Spirit moves me. In the meantime, I thought that those of you in the field should 'share in' what I gave to the Combermere staff at one of our Friday night meetings. Here it is.

There are several things that I want to discuss with you. I tried to write a Last Will and Testament, but I find it very difficult. In the first place, I have nothing to will. I have a few dollars from my old age pension, but I am giving it away, so don't worry about it. All the clothes that I have and other things belong to you. So I have only certain ideas that come to my mind, and they are powerful ideas and won't leave me alone.

The first idea is that you should never sell any of the property that we have because, in due time, it will be needed for others. That is how it comes to me.

The second thing that comes to my mind is your future attitude, your future ways of approaching various things. (These various things are really written in my book, *The People of the Towel and the Water.*) For instance, I would consider that St. Raphael's, our handicraft building, should be very precious to you. Three generations later, when Father Cal is dead and many others are too, you will have to make decisions about these things. It took me thirty years (or thereabouts) to build an adequate place for handicrafts. It is a dream that came and went in my life, and has now come true ... as so many dreams do, when they are put into the hands of God.

Always I dreamed about handicrafts! The reasons for this are: first, I love handicrafts; secondly, I know their therapeutic value; thirdly, I know what it does to people when they learn things that they had never tried to do. I would never, never, never (I put this in my testament!) ... I would never touch this place. I hope that you will never feel that this building would make a wonderful place to have meetings (except, perhaps, once in a great while to teach liturgy or something). This place is 'holy' because it collects and it sorts.

You have to understand what I mean by collecting. I am a person who will always seem to you very contradictory. That's because you have a very literal mind – a European-type literal mind – *and I haven't!* My idea is that this place exists for *many* reasons, of which I have named only two or three.

One reason it exists is to 'sort things out.' Let's say that a liturgical vestment, or a broken statue, comes in and needs repair. This has therapeutic value, of course; but that pales before the fact that somebody is going to restore *something that belongs to God.* This is 'custodianship'! There is beauty untold, and often not understood, in the fact that these belong to God.

Father Briere was telling us about a man he met in Russia who was putting together thousands of little pieces of a church that had been destroyed by the bombardment. It would probably take him about ten years, and very likely a successor would have to finish it; but he worked patiently at it. That is the way that I feel that you should think about this handicraft building. *It is a place through which the grace of God passes like a river.* I come here, and I sit downstairs sometimes, and I allow this river of grace to pass through me. The charisma of God, the grace of God ... a broken statue restored, a vestment repaired.

This Place is Holy

What is the purpose, the goal, of all of the things that we are trying to 'sort out and restore' in this building? You might say that the goal is salesmanship; but my friends, I wish I could tell you what 'salesmanship' means in this house. Salesmanship is *money for the poor!* That is what I call it, and Father Cal stands witness to the fact that "by poverty I am possessed!"

Whenever you see me looking at this item or that, I am thinking of how it was 'crafted' by one of you. I know that a sheep originally had this wool, and that it was cut, and washed, and carded, and spun; and knitted, or crocheted, or woven on a loom. Out of this wool, you have made objects that are good, and warm, and beautiful! So when I meet somebody in our gift shop, I present these woolen things *almost as an offering* because I know that so much work went into them: from the time the sheep was first born at St. Benedict's farm, until the finished goods are displayed on our shop counter.

I do not hesitate to say about this handicraft building: *Walk softly ... the place is holy.* There is something to cherish here – to hold, but not to have. Never to have for yourself, unless you have a real need.

Salesmanship in our gift shop is not just selling something for profit. It is salesmanship *for the poor!* You hold something in your hand – a chair or whatever – and *you bless God* for the fact that it is there. You know that one of our members (or a visiting guest) has repaired that item. Into the thing went a lot of brawn and tiredness and a lot of other things. The Lord picks that up: the tiredness, the sweat in the summer, the cold in the winter, the infinite patience over little details ... the wheels, the chair, the wool.

The Lord bends down and picks it all up and lays it at the feet of his Father; and he is justified. As a human being (which he was), he feels justified. He has not died in vain.

He sees young men and women, and middle-aged ones, persons who don't think they amount to much. He sees them working at Madonna House. And as long as they remain humble in spirit and continue doing humble service, the Lord lifts it all to his Father and says, "I am justified."

To change this handicraft place, to make something out of it that it isn't ... well, I can't say that I am going to throw 'bricks' at you!* But I can say, in faith, that the Lord is going to 'turn his face away' from you, as he has done when this sort of thing has happened with other groups. *Be careful!* Don't touch certain things; because they are not ours, they are God's! When you look at all of those expensive art books, when you look at all of the handicraft stuff that we have in this building – where did it come from? Out of my heart? No, it came from God. Be careful; be very careful to keep it as it is. And not only keep it, but *pass it on* to future members of Madonna House.

Pass It On!

The spirit of Madonna House is that of 'passing on.' What I mean is this: pass on what you have learned in your heart. Pass on what the Holy Spirit has given to you. Pass on what Our Lady taught you. Pass on what the blessing of the Father has given you. Pass on what Jesus Christ taught you. It is not only the little three-by-five card;† it is much more! In that three-by-five card lies all the wealth that is in this place ... in the handicraft building, the gift shop, the pioneer museum, the religious museum.

What is the religious museum? What is the pioneer museum? You know much of what is in the pioneer museum was collected by me when I was nursing in this area. You can tell the story of how I nursed the sick in isolated cabins, and how they repaid my services by giving me these things. But you can go much more deeply. *Follow*

* St. Therese of Lisieux is known for sending 'rose petals from heaven' to those on earth whom she favors. Someone once asked Catherine if she would do the same after her own death. Catherine's unsentimental reply was that she would more likely 'throw brickbats from heaven' if her followers strayed too widely from her spirit, or began to compromise the teachings of the Gospels. This was her no-nonsense way of saying, "Friend, come higher!"

† This apparently refers to a card Catherine had made, on which was printed the words *Pass It On!* Later in this letter, she refers to a different three-by-five card, on which her *Little Mandate* is written.

me, and then walk alone. Watch! Watch! Keep your eyes open!

But in order to keep your eyes open, you have to have an open heart. To give you a little example: I was passing here just a few days ago, and I counted six apples which had been eaten just a little bit and then thrown away. That, to me, is a waste! So I collected those apples, washed them, and made myself a compote because I couldn't see this waste. This type of thing happens all over the place. Why? Selfishness? Thoughtlessness? I don't know.

It seems to me that this kind of custodianship, which extends to such fantastic depths, is really a mystery – a mystery that people seldom understand. You remember the parable of the rich man who takes his retinue and goes away for a while. He leaves his land in the stewardship of other people, but has trouble with them later on. Lots of things happen. He even has to send his son down; but they kill the son. And so he 'did war' on those people.

This is something that is in my heart. I don't want to war with God. And I don't want you to find yourself at war with him either. You can delude yourself and say: "Oh well, such and such a thing was okay back then, when Catherine was around in 1979 or 1980. But now in the twenty-first century, it's different." No, my dears, nothing is different with God. A mystery is a mystery. Love is love. Nothing has changed. The crucifix is still over the world, and God is God!

So be careful not to touch these places – St. Raphael handicraft center, and the gift shop. The gift shop might change; we might not have any antiques. But we will always have sheep and wool, and other things that we can fix or 'make over.' And your eyes should be wide open, watching everything. You must be watchful, as I am over the apples.

Watch and Pray

Begin to be watchful. It is so very important. It is important because watchfulness is not a question of apples alone. Watchfulness is *waiting on God.* You pass by and see an apple on the ground. Pick it up; it can be made into something. If you don't need it, you can bake it and take it to some poor woman. *WATCH ... WATCH ... Because this is God's way of gathering up what you have watched and presenting it to his Father.* If you have not watched, his hands will be empty. Tragic, isn't it, to have God's hands empty?

For instance, what is the reason for a nurse in Madonna House? To look after the sick. That seems easily understandable, but it isn't always. For some reason again, the approach to the sick is strange. What does a nurse do? A nurse has to rely especially on God's mysteries. She has to pray very much. She has to ask God to give her the grace to distinguish what is emotional sickness, what is physical sickness, what is both, and to act accordingly.

Believe me, my friends, if she does that, if she really prays, it will happen to her. It will happen that God will always point to this woman and that man, and he will tell her what is the matter with the person, provided she is wide open to constant prayer. That is healing. The healer must be like Christ (or very nearly like Christ) – which one can do by praying, by entering the fantastic mystery of Christ's healing. It is a beautiful thing. (It isn't just the nursing staff that I'm talking about. I could take each of our departments, one by one, and once more present to you something like I wrote in *The People of the Towel and the Water.)*

You have to pass on the vision of Madonna House; and *the vision of Madonna House is not limited* by that little three-by-five card. It is as big and as wide as the world; and it should be understood that nothing narrow or picayune should enter into it. I leave you one of the most beautiful gifts that God has given to me. I didn't give it to you – GOD gave it to you. God showed you how to live the nitty-gritty life of the Gospel, and I would like you to continue to do that.

Don't go in for long studies or anything like that. No! You might come with a good education and all the rest of it, but cherish especially ... cherish like a great gift of God ... the fact that *he has taught you to be ordinary.* The ordinariness of our days in Madonna House, the simplicity of them, the hospitality of them – THAT is the essence of Madonna House.

Don't break that. Don't try to break it because, I repeat, the face of God will disappear from you, and in no time. It won't take long to break it if you are unfaithful to that ordinariness, to that simplicity, to that living the Gospel in the reality of its life.

So many are trying to teach the Gospel this way and that way and the other way. It doesn't work. Pre-evangelization will work only one-by-one, so that we meet each other and we love each other. And because we love and trust one another, the person who doesn't know Christ will trust enough to allow us to tell him or her about the Divine Lover.

This is part of my Testament for you.

Lovingly yours in Mary,

Catherine

BECOMING A PRAYER

Christmas 1979

Dearly Beloved,

As usual, during Advent and on the great feast of Christmas, I think of and pray for all of you. There are so many things that I want to tell you, to share with you. But it seems, somehow, I never get either the time or the opportunities to do these things. Maybe when I get to Arizona in January, I will be able to answer more of your letters because I am taking with me Helen, my secretary. Mostly she will be transcribing the books that I am going to write (I hope). I ask you to please write me your personal letters, which will be directed there, and you and I can share what is in my heart.

Yes, this is an Advent letter and also a Christmas letter. This should usually be a joyful letter; but I can't feel joyful when I see the United States going down, down, down ... and Canada following it. Instead of joy, I offer to the Lord the pain of it all. For let's face it, this Advent and this Christmas – though wrapped in the tinsel of joy – are not very joyous in depth, except for those who have understood that pain is joy and joy is pain.

Above all, I want to almost implore (though I know that this is a rather stupid thing to do, because you are already a prayerful people), but I implore you to be *more prayerful than ever*.

Someone once asked me what prayer is, and I explained that it began with vocal prayer, and with faith that God is listening. By and by the beginner became proficient in that and entered into the prayer of meditation, and later into contemplation, as he or she came closer to God. Then, one day he or she *became a prayer!* Those of us who 'become' prayers do not have to say very much. We just allow our hearts and souls to be like a movie screen over which pass the people about whom we want to pray. The Lord knows all the people on earth, and those we want to pray for; and he will pick them out and attend to them. So will Our Lady.

'To be a prayer' means to allow yourself to be what a prayer should be – a prayer of joy, a prayer of pain, a prayer of faith, hope, and especially of love. It is not easy to be a prayer. It is painful because you have to become the screen, the reflection, the virtual 'incarnation' of a given person. Yes, it is not easy to become a prayer, but we have to try. We have to try to see if we can abolish ... (no, that's not the word, we can't abolish anything) ... but we can implore God to abolish everything, including a third world war.

Think Before The Lord

Yes, Advent and the forthcoming Christmas Season must be seasons of prayer. They must also be seasons of pain because there is no one in Canada and the United States who is not going to feel that searing pain which will go through us again and again as our country gets humiliated, pushed around, and so forth.*

This is also the time in which we have to think before the Lord. To 'think before the Lord' changes the process of thinking. We have to begin to understand what kind of a lifestyle is before us, and we have to 'buckle down' to that lifestyle.

The season of Advent and Christmas will teach us how to become poor as the Infant was in the creche because, fundamentally, we will have to choose between a Child in a manger and an atom bomb. It is not an easy choice. It will rend our hearts, but we will be whole again ... if we pray, and if we refuse to let our faith be troubled, no matter what, because Christ is in our midst – he who rose again is with us. No matter how bad things seem, we know in faith that all is well because he is with us.

I don't know if you have thought of it but, between two Masses, *anything* can be borne. Yes, it can! As long as we can receive the Body and Blood of him who was borne of the Virgin, we will function. And he will see to it that, if we are not allowed to have a Mass every day, we will at least have a Mass on some days. And if he leads us into the catacombs, all we have to do is to follow his footprints.

This doesn't sound like a Christmas letter; but frankly, dear friends, it *is* a Christmas letter. "Follow Me," he said. He entered her womb. Nine months later he was born, and she remained a virgin. He grew obedient to her (and to his foster father, St. Joseph). And then one day he left her and started to preach. The wind still brings his words to us, if we but listen; and we have the Gospels to read in case we are deaf to the winds.

He preached as no man has preached before or after him. He gave us a blueprint of happiness in the Beatitudes and many other ways. Most of us rejected them, although we 'think' that we believe them or practice them. There

* On November 4, 1979, Iranian terrorists seized the U.S. embassy in Teheran, and held over fifty Americans hostage. The Iranian government refused to negotiate the release of the hostages, and a U.S. attempt to free them by military force failed in April 1980. With the help of Algerian diplomats, the U.S. hostages were finally freed on January 20, 1981.

was hypocrisy in us, and this hypocrisy is being found out. They found him, they tortured him, crucified him, and he rose on the third day; and that's why faith, hope, and love all dwell among us – because he died for us and lives among us.

And so, dearly beloved, I wish you a Christmas in depth. A Christmas in which you will really evaluate your service to God and increase it. I wish you a Christmas that will be a prayer. And may the Lord have mercy on us all!

Lovingly yours in Mary,

Catherine

A LIFETIME OF CHRISTMASES

January 4, 1980

Dearly Beloved,

I spoke to the staff on Tuesday, December 18th, instead of my usual Friday night talk, because of Christmas and my going away after it. I asked everybody to write to me because I will be able to answer letters now, I hope. The rest is as I spoke it that night; I leave it to you to read.

First, I want to bless you, for I have the right to bless you because I founded Madonna House. Also, I want to wish you a Happy Christmas ... not so much happy as holy ... so that you enter into the *real* Christmas spirit, which is poverty, *great poverty!* There was just a cave, you know – with a Child, a woman, a man, some animals, some straw.

That was all there was for the first Christmas. To journey to that cave and to sit down and look at that Child – *that is a lifetime*. So I wish you a lifetime of Christmases.

You will have to walk behind him across many miles, for he walked so much. Up and down mountains, over hills and dales, he walked and walked, preaching the Good News to the poor. Therefore, my wish for the New Year is that you realize how poor you are, how poor we all are! Then you will hear his voice, because it was to the poor that he preached.

John the Baptist sent two of his disciples to question Jesus about who he was. And one of the answers of Jesus was that 'the poor' were having the Gospel preached to them. Always when he spoke, he spoke of the poor. *The poor were his beloved!* Isn't it wonderful to be poor, so as to be his beloved?

So I wish you a *poor* New Year. A year of great poverty and great simplicity. I leave it to you to decide *how* and *when*. I am a little tired of telling people what to do; and I don't think it is necessary any more because you yourself understand what it is you have to do. *Be poor, be simple. Kneel or sit on straw and watch the Child.* Then arise, as he arose! Follow him across dales and mountains, until you come to a very small promontory (a sort of little mountain) called Golgotha.

And then, because you love him, you will be crucified with him. And when you are crucified with him, you will be the happiest person in the world; for he will take you off the cross and into his arms, and thank you that you followed him. *It is a beautiful thing to be thanked by God.*

Yes, that is what I wish for you for the coming year: simplicity, poverty, prayer ... and the understanding that joy and pain always go together when you follow Christ, and that you will *take a risk* every time you follow him. This is my hope.

It is so beautiful to be present once again at the birth of Christ. When you stop to think about it, what do you see? A woman wrapped in silence. How wonderful! She really was wrapped in silence. They questioned her (they must have – she lived in a small town). *She never tried to explain.* She grew bigger and bigger, as pregnant women do, and she was silent as a grave. It will help us if we begin to meditate on being silent when we are very much perturbed; when we want to tell somebody (anybody, everybody, whoever is present!) that we didn't do such a thing; that it is not our fault. Let us try very hard this year not to be always negative, but to be positive once in a while. We so easily become negative.

In my heart – constantly, unceasingly, in all my years of the Apostolate – one thought prevails: *poverty*. It is certainly one part of my testament to you. I say, "by poverty I am possessed." And nobody who knows me will deny it. I am in love with God, and by poverty possessed. It is very lovely to be 'possessed' by poverty. (It frees you from all of all the troubles that are inside of your heart, of all the worries that come to you.) I will probably be away about three months, because the doctor says that I am very tired, 'accumulated' tiredness they call it. Maybe I am; but I'll recover. God willing, I shall return to Combermere. But my great desire is to live poorly; and I find that our headquarters in Combermere is very 'rich' (but that is of God and not of me). I sense that in your heart there is an answer to my call for poverty ... there is an answer to my call to love the Lord ... because you are here, because you are part and parcel of this humble but tremendous Apostolate. I know that you are attracted to poverty, to simplicity, to love of God. And may this attraction grow and grow!

I have a feeling that Combermere, with or without me, will be a center to which many will come. Many priests will be healed in this place, and perhaps a number of nuns. But the laity especially will *hunger* for this place, for they are hungry for poverty, simplicity, and the love of God, whether or not they know it. So we have to make a 'nest' for them to rest; for many, especially the youth, are wandering across the world, searching.

The Hour of Atonement
We have to face a few things, however. We live in a century of anger. White people are now reaping the results of their sins. As white people, they are not going to be a center of attraction to anybody. Man is angry against man

because for centuries we have exploited the Third World. It is the hour of atonement, for God is angry too. We have to do penance and make atonement. It is the hour when Christ comes to atone for us before his Father. It is time for us to atone before each other for all the misery we have inflicted on the Third World everywhere.

It is very difficult to explain to you how much you mean to me, how deeply I bless you with my whole heart and soul, and how sad I am at times that we do not love one another as he wants us to love. *We must love one another;* and it has to cease to be this superficial loving. We love so superficially. We do not go deeply into loving one another. That is what we have to do. That is what I offer you as a Will and Testament: *to love one another as he has loved you,* and as he expects you to love one another.

I wish that I could open my heart to all of you. I take you all in my heart, whoever you are, wherever you are, here or out in the field houses. You are exceedingly dear to me – in a sense dearer than my own family (of which there are now only a few left). *You are my family!* God has begotten in me this family. I have 'called' you here to love him. (In all humility, I could say that I have been the 'telephone' of the Lord!) It is *his* family, really, and his Mother's. She nursed you, and she continues to do so.

You are beautiful people, greatly loved by God. I take you all in my heart, and I will bring you all to Arizona. There in that poor, simple, little house, I shall lift you up to God constantly because I love you very much. I ask you to pray for the world because the world is like an immense and heavy cross that has been with me for these last few weeks.

But there is great joy in these sufferings that God sends me. There are moments when I think that I can carry the whole world on my shoulders; however, that is just 'little me' with big ideas! But I want to call you to come and *share with me that suffering and that joy* ... because it is not 'my' vocation, it is 'our' vocation. And it is that vocation which will bring people to us. It is that vocation which will bring Christ into the hearts of people who seek him so vainly.

This is the answer. In the ordinariness of everyday life,

we live the 'extraordinary' ... for what he has given us is extraordinary: to be like everyone else, but to be in love with him.
God bless you all.

Lovingly yours in Mary,

REMEMBER WHO YOU ARE

January 4, 1980

Dearly Beloved,

I got together with one of my secretaries a day or so before I left for Arizona, and she suggested that what I said should be shared with the field houses. I trust her judgment, so I am writing this letter to you. I have already shared with the staff what was in my heart, poor and simple as the words may be. So here it is now, in print:

I want to tell you that you should begin to understand how exceptional and wonderful you are. I am not joking. This is not a fairy tale; it is the truth! It was written to me by the pope's representative in Canada, the Pro-Nuncio. He said: "You are one of the most extraordinary groups that I have encountered, and I have been all over the world. You preach the true doctrine of Christ. As far as I have noticed – and I have read all of your books, and I have talked with you – I find no heresy. I find nothing except a straight, direct teaching of Christ that does not deviate to the left or the right."

He said that he would pray very much for us that we would never be seduced, but would always 'make straight' the paths of the Lord. That was a great compliment for you people (and also for myself) because, all through the fifty years of our Apostolate, we have never moved to the right or the left. We have stood firmly and have followed Christ; but the cost was very high. We stood straight and followed Christ.

I think you should know that in our weakness, in our smallness, in our hiddenness – (for we are very weak, and we are very small and unimportant) – lies the strange combination that Christ calls for. This is the kind of people he desires to surround himself with. Oh, we might have a little bit of education here and there; but that doesn't amount to too much with Christ. *What matters is the heart.*

What kind of dispositions do we need in our heart to follow him? So far, many of you have followed him under great difficulties, as far as you personally were concerned (and there were great difficulties as far as I was concerned also); but *you followed him!* This is called 'perseverance.' Perseverance ends only when you are buried; then you really have achieved it. But now it keeps on growing and growing until it becomes a great tree under which you can rest yourself; and you can allow many other people to do so also. It is your simplicity, your ordinariness, your faithfulness to 'the duty of the moment,' your lack of desire to shine before the world, which makes Christ 'at home' in Madonna House. And because Christ is at home here, priests and nuns and laity feel at home also.

This is the secret of the spirit of Madonna House. It is the spirit of Christ passed on through Our Lady. He gave his love to us through the heart of a Woman. We all need a shoulder to cry on. We need to be held and kissed, and Her shoulder is there to embrace us and hold us. Never forget that you are Madonna House. Those words mean *The House of Our Lady.* That is what we are.

Christ was very fond of sinners, of prostitutes, of unpleasant people, of pleasant but unknown people – all kinds of strange people. If ever you want to read about them, read Dostoyevsky and Tolstoy, and you will know what that means. We are just that kind of people. We may have done all kinds of strange things, but God feels 'at home' with us just because we are sinners, and because he came to save sinners. That is why God feels at home here; I want you to understand that.

The Memory Lingers On

People say, "What is Madonna House?" That can be answered very simply; it can be said in a few sentences: It is an open door; it is a cup of coffee or tea; it is an invitation to work for 'the common good.' (Those of us who work are always working for somebody else.) If you wash your linen, you are washing that linen for your neighbor. If you cook, you are cooking for yourself, true; but you also cook for everybody else who comes to partake of the hospitality of Madonna House.

Madonna House is a house of hospitality. It is a place where people are received, not because of their education, or how wonderful they are as painters (or whatever else they might do). They are received simply as people; and what I hope is very evident is that *they are loved.* They don't have to stay here longer than twenty-four hours to know that. They come and they go, and the memory of Madonna House lingers on. Something happens; what happens nobody knows, but something happens.

I want you to know who you are. *You are very wonderful people!* It is true; and it would be a lie to say that it wasn't true. For some unaccountable reason, God chose me to found Madonna House. You followed him. (You didn't follow me!) You followed Christ and Our Lady. And you followed something that your heart hungered for. Oh, it wasn't easy. No, it was difficult, and it *still* is difficult. And it will be difficult to the day that you die, because that is the way it is. But at the same time, *you are following him!* You hear a voice saying "Arise and go" ... and so you arise and go, and that is your beauty. It is such a great beauty!

And you are also beginning to understand poverty. Slowly, painfully, with great difficulty, you are beginning to understand poverty – not only poverty of the spirit, but poverty of the heart, of the clothing and all that. But poverty-of-spirit is something really difficult to understand. It is a complete and total surrender to God, no matter what he asks, no matter where he asks us to go. You surrender; we all surrender.

He put me through a lot of trials to prepare me to found this Apostolate. And then, suddenly – in the midst of it all – he says to me: "Catherine, I want you to give up this Apostolate ... not to really 'give it up' in the deepest sense ... but I want you to turn your face to writing books, so that I can use them as seeds to be planted in various hearts." This is the moment that I have to lift up to him and say, "O Lord! My husband, child, Apostolate – all are yours!" This simply means that God has asked me to cleanse my soul of all attachments and offer him that which is most precious to me. This is why I once wrote to you on a little card: "I have nothing more to give you, except my life ..."

I am so happy that I have nothing to give; so truly happy! I am so poor. There is so little that I can give you that 'giving my life for you' is a joy. I look at you, and I see beauty – a strange, unearthly beauty. Oh, you are in the mire; your feet are deep down in some kind of dirt or something, but your heart is not in the mire. Slowly, painstakingly, with great difficulty and a lot of turmoil, you fight on! You don't understand [the implications of the struggle], but you do so [continue on with it] because God loves you (and me, for we are all sinners). He makes his home 'contentedly' with us. We shall be the place to which people will come.

I sense that a catastrophe is coming upon the world. It is coming nearer and nearer. We should not worry because maybe this catastrophe will bring people back to God. We don't know. All that we have to do is to have an open door. Let our hearts be open. Let them be completely open. Let us take the key of our heart and throw it into God's lap and say: "Here is my heart; do what you want with it. Let it be, if necessary, a [door]mat for those with tired feet." Because there are going to be tired feet pretty soon.

I want you to see your beauty. I want you to see, not in mirrors but in the eyes of God, how beautiful you are! How my heart sings your beauty! Strangely enough, as I sing this song, the Trinity and Our Lady join me. That is what I think about you. You would never know that, would you? I scold people sometimes, but all the time I just love them. That's my 'problem.'

What I really want you to think about is that you do not realize the effect that you have everywhere by your presence. It is very important, I think, to know that this ordinariness, this dish-washing, this cleaning, this terrible everyday monotony that exists among us, makes people go to God. That's it!

The Chemistry of Love

As I have said before, there comes a time when all prayer ceases, and *YOU become a prayer* – each one of you. When you become a prayer, something happens that I am not capable of explaining. There is a sort of opening-up of one's heart and, by becoming a prayer, you somehow encompass the whole world. *You become one with everyone!* It is a very great miracle, as far as I can see, because it encompasses a person. When you become a prayer, you *become* the other person. You encompass people in the totality of their being. At the same time, your heart opens wide; and all of those whom God has called to come and drink ... they enter into your heart and become part of it.

People have some very strange ideas about prayer. With them it is a sort of folding one's hands and 'concentrating' or something. Nobody says that you shouldn't pray for the dead and the living and all of that; that's part of life. But, as life continues, something else, something quite different, happens to you. Something falls away like raggedy garments, and now you are free; and then you just 'encompass' everyone. This is done by the strange chemistry of love. A person walks through the door. You don't know his name, you don't know who he is, yet something out of your heart jumps into that person's heart. You encompass him, and he is your friend. It is quite simple; that is the way it is.

Remember who you are. *Remember always who you are.* You are the image of Christ. Look in the mirror and you will see the image of Christ. "Whatsoever you do to the least of my brethren, you do to me!" Be careful. Be very careful. This particular person or that particular person is bruised and wounded. Like the Samaritan who picked up the traveler left along the road by robbers, you have to deal gently with the person who comes before you.

That is why I very seldom talk to people right away when they arrive. I find that they often want to blurt out their story immediately. And while that story is not false, per se, it just doesn't go deep enough. I like to sit down two or three weeks later and say: "Tell me what hurts you. I have lots of medicinal herbs and salves. I can put some on." I don't talk very often to people, because I am always waiting ... waiting for them to talk to me. I do this, lest I tread on the place that hurts.

I chose this card to send you for Christmas: "Give me the heart of a child ..." because I have realized from my youth how hard it is to live that out – to really *be* a child. Even today, I have it always in mind that I have to remain childlike. To be childlike requires tremendous courage. Children are very courageous. Children know how to live. The trouble is we adults don't. If we only had a childlike attitude, then life would be a very easy thing. But we haven't.

If we started being more childlike toward one another, we would become very happy people. You were very happy this Christmas; did you ever realize that it was because you were childlike? You were, you know! You were open, ready for music, singing, dancing – for anything. That is what a child is. Let us try to be a child during this New Year, my dearly beloved ... as simple and free as a little child who is loved by God and Our Lady.

Lovingly yours in Mary,

PLUNGE INTO THE WATERS

February 29, 1980

Dearly Beloved,

I am writing this letter, sitting in Winslow, Arizona, surrounded by floods. Even the road from Flagstaff is closed. Closer to Phoenix, there really is a 'disaster area' ... just as President Carter has declared Arizona and California to be. California is worse; but Arizona, down near Phoenix, is in incredible shape. There are three bridges down, and only two left for traffic. (I suggested that people should walk, but they haven't yet reached that stage.) Let us pray for both California and Arizona.

It is interesting that today we read from the prophet Joel (2:12-18). It is so fitting for Lent:

Even now (says the Lord), return to me with your whole heart, with fasting and weeping and mourning. Rend your hearts, not your garments; and return to the Lord, your God. For gracious and merciful is he, slow to anger, rich in kindness.

Oh, beloved of my heart, I wish that I could pass on to you the joy and the pain of Lent; but truly each one of you is carrying that joy and that pain. I beg you to enter Lent. Here is the key. Open the door and follow Christ's passion with Our Lady, from his childhood to his death; and then enter his resurrection and rejoice beyond all rejoicing. But there will be rejoicing even *during* the pain of following him; for his voice will ring in your ears ever more loudly, ever more closely, calling you ... calling you ... calling you to follow him, no matter what he asks. Leave behind you all anger, all dislikes, all that rends garments but not the heart.

We live in the midst of chaos. Governments are powerless to stop the surge of the downtrodden toward those who have enjoyed wealth with impunity. This is the time ... time to 'share the wealth.' Perhaps it is already too late. Perhaps they will come and take it away from those who have it and distribute it to those who have nothing.

Whatever it may be, whenever it may come, we are living in a time of chaos. Before us are the steps of the mountain of the Lord. Let us crawl up them. On each step, let us 'offer up' our sicknesses, our pains, our emotional difficulties. Let this be the moment of surrender to God – of total surrender.

I don't know whether or not this is a good Lenten letter. I really don't know, my dearly beloved. But I hope that you can hear the cry of my heart, that you can hear my desire that *we love one another as he has loved us,* and that we should acknowledge him before men, so that he will acknowledge us before his Father.

I remind you that the prophet Joel said we should "return to the Lord God. For gracious and merciful is he, slow to anger and rich in kindness." And it is so; but we forget about it. This is the time to 'take the plunge' into the holy waters of God's chastening. Yes, that is where we shall be washed of our sins. It is not an imaginary water; it is a true water. It is the water that he spoke to the Samaritan woman about, telling her that if she drank it she would never be thirsty.

So, dearly beloved, let us take that plunge. Let us cleanse ourselves of all that is against sobornost in our midst. Let us love one another; for only then can we stop this war that is coming. Only then can we regain his peace, which he alone can give.

All that I can do is to pray; and I am doing that. I am praying for our little family that we will be 'one' in mind, heart, and body because we are people of faith, people of love, people of hope. God has chosen us to come together to 'pass on' to others this faith, this hope, and this love. Let's get busy, for the time is short!

Lovingly yours in Mary,

FROM THE ARIZONA DESERT

March 12, 1980

Dearly Beloved,

The Lord has placed me in a desert. It is a real desert, geographically speaking; and yet it is also a spiritual desert, symbolically speaking. I walk in the bloody footsteps of the Lord (although when he walked upon earth, they were not yet bloody, for he had not yet been crucified). Somehow, step by step, clearly outlined in the desert, I see the imprint of his feet. Each one is bleeding, and (reluctantly, I must admit) I place my feet in his footsteps.

It is a strange life that I live, here in the Arizona desert. It is, in a manner of speaking, a desert in itself because *I am left alone*. I rest, I sleep, I write letters, I write books, and I write my meditations of 1965. Yes, I do all of these things while I 'walk' in the bloody footsteps of God, facing every day, in the morning or the night (or maybe at noonday), him who tempted Christ 'in the desert' so long ago.

There are no ways of describing this life, because no words fit it. It is a life of prayer – constant, unrelenting prayer. It is also a life of fasting. You can call it a 'diet' or you can call it fasting, I couldn't care less. The main thing is that I lift my two arms. As my father used to say, "When you beseech the Lord, don't forget to lift the arm of fasting alongside that of prayer."

To put it another way: All of these expressions of mine are but shadows, shadows of a heart that cries out to God night and day for one thing and one thing only – that everyone in Madonna House comes every day closer to God. That all the hearts of the Madonna House members, whether they are priests or lay people, may be open to the Lord. That the shadow of 'self' – as understood by the words selfish, self-centeredness, and so forth – may disappear before his luminous presence. Yes, that is my constant prayer.

This is a strange letter to write you; perhaps I shouldn't write it at all. Perhaps the agony in which I live should remain hidden and silent. But again, I think it shouldn't ... because it isn't a concern only for Madonna House, the members of which, priests and laity, I love with a love that defies all ways of expressing it. I have loved you all for a long time – since the beginning of the Apostolate. But this letter has to be written because there is *another* love in my heart that blossoms forth in the desert, like the strange desert flower that it is.

It is the love of America and Canada. It is the love of the world. It seems that I am 'kneeling' before the face of God all the time, though I can't physically kneel any more. God lets me symbolically do the kneeling and prostrating that I am used to. So I 'kneel' and I am 'prostrated' before him, asking him to have pity on us – on all of us, wherever we are.

I sorrow that the predictions I made many years ago, trying ... trying so uselessly it seemed at the time, to get into Madonna House hearts the need for prayer, surrender, total surrender that alone will save mankind. But you didn't hear, nor did mankind, as I went throughout the States and Canada lecturing. Attention was not paid to my words. Perhaps my words did not need to be paid attention to; but I think that they should be ... because this time I really do feel like 'someone crying in the wilderness.' Before us, whether or not we believe it, is *the breakup of a world*. At long last, the poor have rebelled against the rich. What Pius XII said has come true: "If we push the face of the poor into the mire, as we have done, they will rebel and kill us." And that's exactly what they are doing in many places.

I beg you, dear hearts, to pay very much attention to the simple words that I say. *Mankind needs an oasis!* It is walking in the desert ... a desert that is a thousand times worse than the Gobi or the Sahara or Death Valley, or any other kind of desert that you can imagine. People are dying from thirst because no one is giving them Bread and Wine or anything, except a few who really care. Think of all of the millions all over the world who do not receive Our Lord

– not even in their hearts, let alone in their bodies. Think of it! (I think of it always.)

So we must be a center, as I have said before ... an 'oasis' with cool water to drink. Didn't he tell the Samaritan woman that he had enough water for the whole world? He was referring to his Body and Blood again. But he also has the water of faith, the water of joy, the water of love and hope. But it seems that hope is dying; joy is seemingly nonexistent. *Love?* One has to go around with a lantern to find it. And *faith?* Well, I just don't know!

Expect a Miracle!

I don't know about you, but I am glad that Father Cal suggested that Madonna House have Exposition of the Blessed Sacrament on Sundays during Lent; and that people go and pray, especially to the saints, throughout the day. Prayer is the only answer to the whole present 'mess' that is absorbing us like quicksand.

You know that at St. Kate's, my little cabin on the island, there is this little motto over my window sill: *Expect a Miracle!* It prevails against all of the storms which sometimes rock St. Kate's. I do believe in miracles; and in this case, the miracle of prayer, of surrender, of a total, uncompromising surrender to God.

We have a very special role to play in all of this 'mess' that I talk about. We must continue to love one another ever better, ever more closely, so that people who come to visit us see the reality of Christ's commandment to "love one another as I have loved you." Implement it!

I was writing my meditations of 1965, and I came across these paragraphs which, I think, describe the world today:

> It came to me that Christ had been, and is, and *will always be rejected* because, in our modern lives, he desires our happiness. Loving us, he asks us to arise in faith and, with his grace, to depart from our selfish existence of anxiety and guilt, and to enter a new healing by being fully his disciples in love in the kingdom of heaven, which begins here and now ...

The problem is clear. We are *used* to our anxiety. We are *secure* in our selfishness. We do not *want* to mature; to grow up; to accept the awesome, terrible, yet totally liberating freedom which comes when we enter the Law of Love which God gives us ...

So we can know only the alternative: rejecting him because of the seemingly unendurable burden which he places on our shoulders and our souls. This passage, this eternal 'pass-over,' we must make through the Red Sea on faith and love ...

This wandering in the desert to which he calls you and me; this entering into the healing of anxiety by love and faith, by a total surrender to him, is a terrifyingly dark night to the majority of us. Besides, the land beyond all of this, the New Jerusalem, he offers to us at such a seemingly high price.

Yet it is available to us while we are still on this earth. To me, this New Jerusalem, this kingdom of God, begins here and now – if we will to *accept Christ and his teaching totally, absolutely,* knowing that he is the Absolute. Then, indeed, all will else will fall away, and we shall be free.

But we do not believe this – children of the modern, technological age that we are! It is all so speculative, so unproven ...

Perhaps I shouldn't write this letter, and yet this is what is in my heart. Night after night, it seems that God has asked me to write it ... to call, at least you, my beloved ones, to really form a Christian community. (By 'Christian' I mean in depth, in totality, in surrender, in poverty.) Long ago and far away I wrote that, unless we become poor, we too will be trampled underfoot by the marching hordes of the poor. *Only our poverty will save us.*

So there is nothing more I can tell you. Each of your houses must be what poverty teaches you to be. Each one of you must be open to Christ in whoever comes. Yes, it is possible that you might be killed, or die a martyr in some of the houses; but what is that? Martyrs are the seed of faith. I don't expect to be martyred; neither do you. But I implore

you – I, who live in this symbolic and godforsaken desert, who pray and fast, and try to walk in the bloody footsteps of Christ, while being subject to the whispering words of the devil. I begin to pray, pray for countries, especially Canada and America, but I also pray for the entire world. Will you pray and fast with me?
With much love from a very loving heart.

Lovingly yours in Mary,

THE CHRIST OF THE GARBAGE CANS

Easter 1980

Dearly Beloved,

It is time to write an Easter Letter. Would you believe it, I find that kind of hard, humanly speaking. There is no question that my heart sings its alleluias. I praise God unceasingly, together with you, for the resurrection! Yes, he really did resurrect, and he is in our midst forevermore.

He was in our midst before, but in a remote way. It is only when he became a human being, and walked and talked and ate and slept, as human beings do, that *he became one of us*. And to think that he took all the sins of the world upon himself! That's the cross we always talk about, but never accept very well ourselves.

After his resurrection he asked us to love as he did, to love one another as he did, to treat one another as he would have treated us. He said that we were to *pray always and serve always,* because that's what he was in our midst for – to pray and to serve. He was 'meek and humble of heart' and asked that we should be likewise; and then he proclaimed his Beatitudes.

You know that I occasionally write poetry. Maybe some of you read them, and some do not; but here they are – some old, some new, from the storehouse of my heart. I share them with you because I love you. (Love is like that.) Sometimes poetic thoughts speak louder than ordinary words can. For what can ordinary words say in the face of today's immense crisis that surrounds us?

The greed, the desire for money and power, the 'business as usual' attitude of some Western nations is destroying the economies of developing countries. No wonder the Third World is rebelling. One way or another, the people of the world have had enough of unbridled capitalism. It is no longer the way to prosperity or joy. (Watch out what the new budget will cut; mostly it will be services for the poor.) Only lip service is rendered to Christian principles.

You know, Christ is truly in our midst, and he suffers like we suffer because he loves us. He is with the woman who tries to stretch the impossibly small amount of pension that she gets toward living for a month. No wonder she picks things up in a garbage can! But the most horrifying thought is that *this is CHRIST who is picking through the garbage cans* ... and we somehow or other created this situation. (I don't mean we of Madonna House, but we of the Western nations.)

What can mankind choose from today? Capitalism? Marxism? Those are the two broad highways that he can walk (or, at least, I think he can). There is, of course, the small path that leads to God. But no one wants to take it, because pride, arrogance, selfishness, and greed rule the world.

What a tragic Easter Letter I am writing you. But here in the desert, where I walk often at eventide (I walk slowly, and not too far), the air is clear and one can see far and wide. And life becomes as clear as the air, and one can see

even 'over the horizon'... as I do. Hence the poems, which
you might read or might not. They express better that I can
in a letter all that I have to say about Easter.

Lovingly yours in Mary,

POEM #1:
YOU WHO ARE CRUCIFIED

You who are crucified
You know that day and night
I dream and fight
To take You off the cross
Of hard, cold human hearts.

Tell me, You, my Beloved
Who hang So high ... and yet so low
Against a fearsome
Sky aglow ...
And drink the bitter,
Bitter draught
Of mankind's old
Endless pride
While, at its feel, you let
Your precious blood seep ...
Seep ... to be trampled
By its clay feet.

Tell me, Beloved,
How I can change these
Stony hearts ... You see,
If you helped me ...
I could become a fire
Of desire
That would melt stone.

For You have come and
Walked with us and worked
And played – perhaps You sang ...
But then, why should You sing?
Each word You said
Contained all music.
You came ... You lived
In our midst ... You preached ...
You lived ... You died of love ...
And you allowed the Holy Women
To walk with You.

So now, if only you will
Tell me how ...
I, too, can make my soul a veil ...
Nay ... not my soul alone ...
ALL OF MYSELF! ...
And show your love, and
Thus, perhaps, take You off
The crucifix of men's proud ...
And dead ... hearts.

O my Beloved, there must,
There *must* be a way ...
To take You off that
Crucifix of death
Where men continue
Endlessly to crucify
You on their living-dead
And hard hearts.

Make me a chisel.
Make me an endless drop
Of water, cool and clear,
That I may break the
Crucifix of human hearts ...
Or drill them into tiny
Stone that would become
Soft, loving sand
Just by falling, falling ...
An endless drop
On their cold hearts.

228

For You know, Beloved,
That day and night I fight
To take You off
The cross of hard, cold
Human hearts ...
And in so doing,
Make them a loving
Inn to rest in.

POEM #2:
EASTER 1955

*Today, exile
Is real to me.
I feel, indeed,
A stranger
In an alien land.*

*The alleluias sing joyously
And make such golden
Steps
That few, there are,
Who can
Resist
    Going
        Right up.*

*But I am silent,
Sad, and slow
To feel their joy.
For I behold
My Lord still
Hanging on a cross ...
Behind curtains
Of iron.*
   *Or are
   They just
   Prison bars?*

When will the Easter
Of my people come?
And will it be
In our time?

It seems to me
I see a vision
Of the Bride ...
Crucified ...
With Her Bridegroom.

The shadow of
This crucifix
With its
Double load
Falls on the world,
And half of it
Knows it for what
It is – Golgotha –
Mystically extended
Into our days!

The other half of
The world (our own!)
Does not know it.
It goes around ...
Selling, buying,
God-denying,
Or rendering
Lip service
To Him Who hangs
With her ...
     His Bride,
          His Church ...
From a thousand
Crucifixes
Over half of the
Land of the earth.

O perverse generation,
— STOP!!! —
Fall on your knees!
Declare days, weeks,
Of fasts, of prayer,
Of penance, of pain ...
To atone for
Your neglect;
To bring your hearts
A SACRIFICE OF LOVE
For them whose
Easter is ...
not yet.

POEM #3:
AN EASTER MEDITATION

RABBONI ... I see You, Gardener of my soul, in
    splendor clad ...
and yet, my heart is heavy ...
for I behold Your beauty, unsurpassed,
in a thousand hungry faces ...
and I have *empty hands!*

RABBONI ... The alleluias of my joy make jonquil
    carpets
for Your pierced feet ...
and yet, my heart weeps before the thousand wounds
that cover You in the cold and naked,
who stand so silently before ...
my empty hands!

RABBONI ... My eyes are dazzled by Your resurrected
    glory ...
Lumen Christi ... and yet my heart beholds
the black night of Your loneliness
in the forsaken who wait for help from ...
my empty hands!

RABBONI ... The fragrance of Your unguents brings
    ecstasy to me ...
yet the bitter-sour smell of Your poverty
is wafted to me from the endless line
of the pinched, gray faces of the poor.
They cry to me from many places, without words.
My answer to them is just a display of ...
empty hands!

RABBONI ... Exultant is my soul with songs of
    gratitude
and joy at the conquest of death by You, Lord ...
Yet, I see Your Bloodstained face, so still
in Mary's hands, in the poor dead!
How can I be Your Nicodemus, and bury them
with *empty hands?*

RABBONI ... Will You once more enter through the
    closed door
of human hearts ...and show them Your wounds?
Your pierced and loving heart? And make them see
that they still must believe your words ... and You?
For You have said ... that all that is done to
the least of Your brethren is done to You! Then ...
perhaps ... they will open their hearts and purses ...
and fill *my empty hands* ... with silver and gold
that will allow us to feed the hungry ...
clothe the naked ...
house the forsaken ...
bury the dead.

RABBONI ... Please!

———————————

POEM #4:
EASTER VIGIL IN RUSSIA

Twilight is long.
The nights are longer
There in Holy Russia!

But at long last,
The darkness fell
Bringing silent, recollected,
Motley crowds upon its
City streets; its old,
Mysterious, country roads.

The streets were dark.
The lamplighter
Would light them after the
Resurrection of the Lord.

Along the doorways
Of open churches
Poured streams of thousands
Of golden candle lights
Into the outer darkness.
And men hastened to
Be absorbed into
That Holy Light.

The singing started
Within the Golden Light.
Time ceased to exist as
Prayer chant grew louder.
Hope in the Parousia
Soared like a glowing sword.

Suddenly again, all was
Silence and darkness,
Once again, within
The hallowed walls.

Slowly the Holy Mysteries
Of Mysteries began.
And men lit now
Their candles anew
At the Christ candle,
The Lord.

Melodious ... gentle ...
The choir swelled slowly to
Unbearable, unknown heights.
With them went human souls
Ascending to God
On scales of naked love.

Suddenly the priests
Sang out:
"CHRIST IS RISEN!
VERILY HE IS RISEN!"
Men almost died with joy.
All words ceased.
Alone the "ALLELUIA!"
Pierced the dawn
With its unbearable
Delight!

Bread ... Wine ... God ... I ...
One! ... He conquered death ...
NOW HE IS MINE!

The streets are
Alight with lights.
The lamplighters
Have passed this way.

SEEK OUT THE LONELY ONES

April 16, 1980

Dearly Beloved,

It seems that the desert has a very cleansing effect on the human heart, even on one that imagines that it is already clean! This is the effect that the desert has on me. It affords a strange deep look into the very depths of my heart, to see the deep wounds inflicted there. But the wounds are good, for each one of them has been allowed by God. And all things that come from the hand of God *are* good.

Yes, the desert cleans well, cleans deeply, and brings from the width and depth of my heart the thoughts that I dare to think are God's to me. The desert does its work. It does not allow me to blink away the reality, to turn away from it and try to hide somewhere among the cacti and piñon trees. No, there is no place for hiding. I have to 'face' that which God tells me to face, whether I wish to or not, for the simple reason that I am in love with God, and *His Will is my will.*

It seems, these days, that the world is on the brink, not only of a catastrophe, but a disaster. You are intelligent enough to know this. The United States stands alone in the world, in a manner of speaking, for its allies are not following its leadership. They are afraid of only one thing, an economic blockade by the U.S.A. (which, of course, would be a disaster too).*

But in the desert I am not so much concerned (strange as it might seem) with wars and the rumors of war. I am used to them. For a long time, I tried to tell you about them. But that's neither here nor there. What concerns me is the

* In December 1979, the Soviet Union invaded Afghanistan. In January 1980, the U.S.A. stopped its grain shipments to the U.S.S.R., suspended the sale of computers and other high-tech equipment, and organized a partial boycott of the summer Olympic Games being held in Moscow.

wastelands of the big cities. There are towns and villages that are deserts, too, but mostly my concern is with the larger urban areas.

I am tormented. I am tormented with the situation of the old, the helpless, the hopeless, the ones that 'die' from loneliness! My torment is not in hospitals, nor in nursing homes. (There are people who are already doing good work in that area.) It is the others – the forgotten ones, the rejected ones, the 'humiliati' – who need our help. How we are going to do this, I do not know. We have to pray, and we have to search. God will show us the way.

It is a very simple thing I am asking. We are already doing much of this already, but we have the capacity to do more! *Go out ... be free ... do it!* They are on the streets, in rooming houses, in offices, in condominiums. They are the hidden ones, the overlooked ones, the neglected ones.

The 'real' rejects of society already knock on our door, seeking our help. But these others we have to look for! They may be very poor (in the economic sense of the word). They may be very rich. They may be politicians, or civil servants, or wards of the State. It is up to us to seek them out. It is up to us to make friends of them, to help them in a very special manner – the only manner by which they can be helped: *love!*

Is this a silly sort of letter, or isn't it? I really can't distinguish, so I am just sending you what the desert told me. It's all yours – a post-Easter gift.

Love,

236

COME TO BETHLEHEM

Christmas 1980

Dearly Beloved,

I greet you in the Lord! It is the great day of his birth. I invite you to follow me to Bethlehem, for we have need to go where he was born. We have need to enter the cave, so as to learn humility – the humility that should be the foundation of Madonna House, and that I hope is.

We need to go together to Bethlehem to find hiddenness – hiddenness that is truly hidden. Vainglory is not for us. No, not for us. Nor is boasting about anything such as our degrees, if any; our achievements, if any; our talents, if any. Because in our hiddenness, in that cave of Bethlehem, we understand, or should, that all that we are and all that we have comes from God and returns to God. To him be all glory. Alleluia!

We have need to go to Bethlehem to have a *wounded heart* because that is what Christ had as he grew up. He allowed everyone to pass through his wounded heart. It was pierced by a lance when he was dying. But he had a wounded heart when he was born. We couldn't see it, but it was there.

We have to go to Bethlehem to have *listening ears*. It is in Bethlehem that we fold the wings of our intellect and allow the voice of man and the voice of God to blend in our mind and heart, so that they become one. So that we may kneel at the crib of the Infant, realizing that we are the basin; we are the pitcher. True, he is not washing our feet because he is too small, but we are washing each other's feet in that basin; and from that pitcher comes a water that is blessed because we received it at the crib.

Yes, let us arise and go to Bethlehem to learn *danger* also. But above all, before we speak of danger, we have to learn *faith*. The faith that comes to us from baptism and must grow with us. Yes, grow with us in peace and in war.

When I speak of danger, I simply want you to learn that danger is all around you. But if you have the faith, which is like a tree standing by the water and which cannot be moved (as the song says), you will face that danger with a smile because God stands before you.

It is a strange Christmas letter that I am sending you. It is a letter filled with longing – longing for his coming. *Maranatha! (Come, Lord Jesus!)* Are you longing for his coming? You know that you must be longing for his coming because your feet follow his feet ... in the hot desert in which he once traveled; in the cool waters in which he was baptized; and in this long, painful way of the cross; in his flogging and in his crucifixion.

Christmas is an incredible feast. The creature has given birth to God. God who became Man, who knows all about us, has brought us knowledge of heaven and the knowledge of his mercy.

Fear not, little flock, fear not. Come with me to Bethlehem. Let us celebrate a joyous Christmas. Let us be merry and happy, no matter what, because *Christ is born.* He is in our midst, and from now on he will be with us until we die. And when we die, *he will be the first one to greet us.*

Yes, let our Christmas, this year, be one of joy. The greatest joy that we can have is to share our joy with others. Let it be a poor Christmas – like a cave, like a man, like a woman. A woman who gave birth in the midst of animals, and thereby, I am sure, blessed animals too.

Yes, let us be happy. Let us sing all the beautiful songs that we can find because they will all become one – a song that will lift itself up to the Trinity and to Our Lady, and perhaps console Our Lord too! I am sure that, even in his childhood memory, he shed a tear or two for the heralds of our time.

Happy, Holy and Glorious Christmas to you, my dearly beloved ones!

Lovingly yours in Mary,

REVEAL MY DEALINGS

March 2, 1981

Dear Family,

[... This is Father Briere writing ...] What I say to you in this letter is very very important. You could meditate upon it throughout this Lent. It is concerned with a most recent word from God that Catherine received. The word is: "Reveal to others My dealings with you."

It came about in the following way: As Catherine was wondering about what to say, what to do during her European pilgrimage, God himself took over in very powerful ways and strengthened her spiritual being, making her ready to face whatever she has to face, and especially to speak his word with power wherever she goes. It was quite a lesson to me. We need never worry about what to say when God gives us a mission to perform. He himself will fill our hearts and minds, and his words will flow out of our mouths.

The four enclosed meditations – recorded by Catherine on February 19th, 20th, 23rd, and March 1st – constitute one of the ways in which God strengthened her and drew her more deeply into his mystery and thus prepared her.

I hope you will meditate seriously on what she has dictated and be strengthened yourselves in your spirits, and speak only the words of God during these blessed days and forever. Remember these words are also addressed to you namely, "Reveal My dealings with you to others." We used to speak of 'the secrets of the King' in days past [which were to remain secret], but now the word of God, it seems, can only come to people from a *personal witnessing* to his action in our lives. I hope that this is clear to all.

I bless you in Our Lady of Combermere,

Father Briere

CHRIST IS NEAR

February 19, 1981

Dearly Beloved,

This is simply a cry of my soul at 10:30 on the 19th of February. Father Briere was trying to make believe that I was being interviewed by the French TV and, as he was talking, many things moved in my heart. You see, it is so very hard for me to pass on to others what is in my heart. Perhaps I am absolutely stupid; perhaps I am absolutely foolish; perhaps I am filled with the foolishness of Christ (which always appeared idiotic to men). I can't tell. I simply feel that Christ is near, that he is right in this house, and that I am very close to him and that he is speaking to me.

Yet, his voice is strange. (His voice is always strange.) You have to have a passionate heart to hear it. By 'passionate' I mean a heart totally in love with him; a heart that beats in rhythm with his heart. Then, slowly, quietly, you can hear. And what do I hear? Well, it is strange, very strange, but I *hear* tears. Do you visualize that? Does anyone visualize the ability to hear tears? Sometimes people cry big, heavy tears, and they fall onto your hands, and you hear them falling. But lately I hear them clearly as if they were little bells, and yet they are not bells; they are the deep and profound bells of Christ crying.

There are very few records of Christ crying in the Gospels, but there are some. That is what I hear. I hear Christ crying, and I know what he is saying. It seems as if he says: "Why did I hang on this Cross? Is it all in vain?" And I say to myself: "Does Christ have doubts too?" And I remember his time in Gethsemane, when he cried out to his Father to let the chalice pass by. He bled from his forehead, so anguished was he – emotionally anguished just like us; just like you and me. We call it depression or anguish, but I think that he had that too. And they all slept – I mean the apostles. He was all alone in the Garden of Olives. Did you ever see olives grow? They grow gnarled – sort of twisted. And there he was, his face against a stone, and I could hear his tears fall on that stone. Of course he answered himself that his death was not in vain because, obedient to his Father, he came and saved us in this manner and not in any other. His death and resurrection are proof of our immortality. But, in the meantime, there are his tears. *I dream about his tears all of the time.* Do you?

How can I explain the depth of the wounds in my heart? How can I explain that I seem to lose all senses and be lifted up. I don't know where or how. You call me a prophet. No, I'm not a prophet. I just repeat words, like a little monkey or a budgie (or any of the other birds who repeat the words of their master). I repeat what I hear in those great depths where God places me.

Why is he crying? Because he sees a whole civilization 'going to pot.' I used to use the words *an era is cracking.* An 'era' is some time, and right now I hear it 'cracking.' Everything has disappeared. Everything is backwards. Right now robots are coming in. Can you imagine that? Instead of men, there are robots. Medicine is going into depths that are unwholesome. Nothing is left to God anymore. God is shoved aside – God the Father, God the Son, and God the Holy Spirit. And Christ is crying because his Father is totally neglected and forgotten. People don't even know the Creed and the Ten Commandments. The very basics of our religion are erased somehow. And the Father who created us, the Trinity who makes us live *the life of the Spirit,* is shoved aside as if It didn't matter.

True, people begin to pray. People again turn around and look for faith. But it is happening so slowly. Now, I cannot sleep ... or I sleep too much because I cannot endure. I say it simply; I say it in complete and utter simplicity. *I cannot endure the sea of God's tears.*

Lovingly yours in Mary,

BROKEN PIECES

February 20, 1981

Dearly Beloved,

It is 10 o'clock at St. Kate's. Outside it is raining. I have just had a meeting with the women and I was extremely tired when it was over. I feel a bit better now, as some food and tea have refreshed me.

Again I feel lost. I don't know why I dictate all of this. It seems foolish to dictate the impossible, the incredible. But somehow, I need to talk, even through this [cassette tape-recording] machine. It is something that I can forget about – this machine, I mean.

Again I feel the presence of Christ in this room, and this time it is very powerful. It is as if he were right here, sitting where Father Briere usually sits, on that green chair. He is talking to me. This conversation, these strange dialogues with God that come and go in my life, are difficult to put on tape; and I ask myself why I desire to do so. I don't know why, but it seems to me that it is because God wants them on tape. He speaks very softly, and at times, it is hard to hear him. At other times, it is very distinct, and I begin to understand what it is that he is saying.

Strange as this might seem, he is, as it were, 'complaining' to me – a creature of no importance – and yet, I don't imagine that God complains. But there must have been times, when he was here on earth, that he did. There certainly was much to complain about. Maybe it wasn't just a complaint. Maybe it was a 'sharing' that he did with Mary and Martha and his few friends.

It seems as though God shares with me. Why I don't faint, why I can talk, why I sustain a dialogue with him, I don't know. I just don't know. You see, there are so many things that I just do not know. But they don't seem to bother me because it is all so simple to me. Why shouldn't

God talk to his creatures? God the Father talked to Adam and Eve in the garden. Why shouldn't his Son talk to me? I think that it is kind of natural; perhaps supernatural.

Father [Briere] keeps saying that I know God. He means 'from within' as it were; but many just know him 'from without.' It is very hard to understand what he says. I am not cognizant of knowing God from within. I don't think that anybody can know God from within. I know God simply because I love him. It is so very simple. I love him; yes, I do.

To me, my service to him must be total. There can't be any lacunae. I never do desire my own will. Long ago and far away my own will disappeared, and his will took its place. That's dialogue; I'm listening. When I listen, I begin to know what he wants done, and then I do it. It's so very simple. It doesn't require any particular knowledge of any kind. I think that it requires only faith and love; predominately love, and a belief, of course.

So Christ seems to be very close today – very close – only I am not frightened. But the words of his dialogue are heavy; they fall across my back, as a cross would fall. *He is sharing what he sees!* Maybe I am all mistaken. Maybe these are hallucinations, for all I know. However, what he says makes sense.

My Hands are Trembling

It seems that God is thrown away – God the Father and the Holy Spirit, and he knows that God cannot be mocked. He explains that the wrath of God will descend upon us, and it is a 'just' wrath that cannot be stopped. We have thrown away all of God's Commandments. We have broken them into pieces; I can almost see the pieces! Could I gather them up? I don't know, but there they are – the Ten Commandments, the Creed, and even my favorite Gloria, the *Glory be to the Father.*

They are strewn around this room in little bits, and I want to gather them up and make them whole again. But my hands are trembling. I am afraid. I can't pick things up anymore. And it is as if the hand of God touched my two hands and said, "Let them alone. Let them be. For they are the judgment of men today."

And I look back [in time], as if with the eyes of Christ. It seems that I really do so. And I begin to see the Renaissance, secularism, and all that happens now. I suddenly understand how God understood that, when the pagans were worshiping their gods in forms of matter, they were worshiping God the only way they knew how. But now, *now – look!*

I can't cry. I can't do anything but stand before the broken basics of our faith. No thunder comes from God to break it up; we break it up ourselves. Lord, how can I walk with pieces of your Commandments, your Creed, under my feet? They are too sharp. Lord, have mercy! Have mercy! For if those pieces fall on us, it will be worse than any atomic bombs. Lord, have mercy!

Lovingly yours in Mary,

PASSIONATE LOVE

February 23, 1981

Dearly Beloved,

Tonight I find Jesus Christ very close to me. One of the men of Madonna House wrote me a letter that left me wondering. This is what he says:

"I am immensely proud that you have been chosen for a semiprivate audience with the pope. It's an honor to you and to all of us in the family. I am happy for you because of the talks that you will be giving in Paris and London. I see these as a sign of God's approval of your long years of service to his people. It seems to me that what matters here is that the people of Europe will see *who you are*. What you will say, though important, will be relatively secondary. They will see the person whose *life* speaks for her, who preaches the Gospel without compromise by her *being,* and the one who reveals the wisdom of God the Father and the mystery of Jesus by her *presence.* ...."

I must admit that the closeness of God with me (or close to me today) is very powerful. I am going on that trip simply because he tells me that I must; because I must preach the Gospel without compromise; that is, *his* Gospel ... not mine, but his. I don't understand, in its full implications, what this person is trying to say. I just don't. He seems to speak of something important about me; but I am not important. It is very strange. When Christ is so close that I could stretch out my hand and touch his hand, I realize my total nothingness.

As I read this letter, however, I am very honored that this member of Madonna House wrote to me. I feel very happy, in many ways, that he did. But I do not understand it; and when I speak of 'understanding' it, I do not mean intellectually. Sure, I understand his letter intellectually. But spiritually, in the depths, the great depths in which I seem to abide periodically, I don't.

Because with Christ present in this room, I sense my utter insignificance, my utter almost-nonexistence before him. And I feel his hands reaching for me; and he is making me stand up because I feel prostrated before him. In my simplicity and my faith (I have a very simple faith), I believe that God is *in us* and, at times, he is next to us, almost physically present (so it seems to me); and I rest in him.

When he lifts me up, I rest in his hands, sort of 'in the palm' of his hand. I cannot explain all of this. I really can't. It is as though he picks me up and sends me on and says to me: *"Fear not, child. Go where I send you. I will be there."* And so, though I fear this trip, humanly speaking, I don't fear it all, spiritually speaking, because God is sending me on this trip.

How are you to explain the closeness of God? How are you to explain what stymies people so much: what it is to have a *wounded* heart? But you are wounded with the wound of love. It's such a simple thing.

Everything is so complicated. I don't know who I am – God knows. I don't know anything – God knows. But trying to explain that to anyone is impossible. I love God with a passionate love. I love God in his totality. I love God the Absolute One. I love God because he is who he is, and I am who I am. He is God, and I am his creature. But he *sought* my love; he wanted to be loved by me. God the Father created me to love him; and I do. And that is all there is to it. There is nothing about me that should impress anybody, except one thing: that I am passionately in love with God.

Lovingly yours in Mary,

[signature]

PREACH THE GOSPEL WITH YOUR WHOLE BEING

March 1, 1981

Dearly Beloved,

It is 10 p.m. on the eve of my departure. Today, when I entered St. Kate's, Father Briere said, " This place is kind of holy." It was holy because Christ was present; Christ seems to be always present. I don't quite understand it all. In fact, there is so little that I understand that sometimes I think I am too simplistic, almost too childish – not only childlike but childish. Because right now I feel the presence of Christ as powerfully as I felt it a few days ago.

There is no denying that I am afraid, with a sort of strange fear, of the trip – France and England and all the rest of it. Strangely enough, I feel that I am being sent this time – definitely, It is as though Christ were sitting here on this green chair and telling me, *Arise and go!* And, once again, this 'arise and go' comes to me clearly and simply. That is what I have to do. I have to arise, and I have to go. Go where? The answer is very simple: where he sends me; where God sends me. And he is giving me his Mother to guide me.

I don't know what is going to happen on that trip. I am a little frightened, humanly, of the French audiences and so forth. But that is perhaps because my faith is a little too weak. But I don't think so. Though I am humanly a little afraid, I count on him so powerfully, so ... I can't explain that; it's a matter of faith. You see, when you believe, then the great Absolute – the real reality who is God – becomes touchable, visible, in this sense. You don't see him with your earthly eyes, but you can see him with the eyes of your soul, and you can touch him with that same heart. The heart has eyes; the heart can touch.

But today I am a little excited with all of those people saying goodby and everything. That makes no difference, however. It's as though Christ blesses me and says, "Arise, child, and go and preach My Gospel over the borders of the United States and Canada and the usual places where you have been. You even left footsteps in Rome. I knew them." (He talks to me; can you imagine?)

I said to myself, "Why is he sending me?" Well, the answer comes very simply: "Catherine, I am sending you to preach the Gospel because your words are *words of fire.* You don't know that. You don't know. And perhaps you will never know that your words are words of fire to the listeners ... that is what I need. I need people who preach the Gospel with *all* that is in them. You do that, Catarina Mea."

And he seems to smile at me with such gentleness, such tenderness, that I seem to dissolve completely. It is as

if I were not, and yet I am. I am lifted up into his arms. I
don't know what I am saying. I'm simply trying to explain
to you – whoever will listen to this – what God is to me.
What joy, what infinite joy that seems to grow out of his
pain ... and mine.

Lord, bless me on this venture. You're here. You're
near. Bless me. (And he has, can you imagine? In a little
isba* at the end of nowhere, in a little village called
Combermere, God blessed me. Alleluia! Alleluia!)

Lovingly yours in Mary,

Catherine

---

*Editor's Note: In the early part of 1981, Catherine visited
Cardinal Lustiger in Paris and Pope John-Paul II in
Rome. In June of that year, she was on her way to
Moncton, New Brunswick, to visit the mission house there.
But on June 22nd, while in Ottawa, she was suddenly
struck down by her 'great sickness' and was forced to
remain in that city for three weeks. She returned to
Combermere without ever visiting Moncton.*

*On August 18th, 1981, Catherine was found in St.
Kate's, her cabin on the island, lying unconscious on the
floor. She had apparently been in that condition for some
time. She was not expected to live through nightfall, so
preparations for her funeral were put into effect.*

*Catherine did not die, however. She rallied, but her
health deteriorated considerably from 1981 onwards.
During 1982 and 1983 she was able at times to come to
the noon meal at the main building of Madonna House,
and to conduct spiritual reading after the meal. In June
1984, however, she began to go into a final decline and
spent her remaining years in bed at her island cabin.*

* Russian for a little log cabin in the woods.

THE REJECTION OF CHRIST

August 25, 1981

Dearly Beloved,

I am sending you the transcript of the staff meeting [held on Monday, July 13th] after I returned from Ottawa. Because the Pro-Nuncio, Archbishop Angelo Palmas, told me to share it with you, I do so with great love.

Catherine: ... One day it was as if Christ were speaking to me, and he said: "Catherine, I want you to share my pain." I said, "How can I?" He said, "I will help you to bear My pain." And so he did; but it didn't lessen the pain. The whole thing was spiritual. It had nothing to do with other things or anybody else. It was my heart that cried out to God and said, "Lord, how can we help you?" And always the answer came, *"Bear My pain."* So that was it.

What happened to me was like a lightning flash. It was an understanding or realization that *Christ was not loved.* Clearly, totally, obviously, I saw that the Lord was not loved. I saw that he was rejected. True, he had been rejected ever since he left his mother's home, right up to his crucifixion. Oh, he was accepted by some people, and in some places; but most of them were not very strong in their acceptance.

Like a picture, I saw all of this in one moment. It hit me as nothing has ever hit me before. I couldn't go anywhere. I could only lie there in bed like a person that has lost her mind and body. I was just completely numb. For several days – I don't know how many – I didn't know anything except one thing: that Christ, across the whole Christian world, *was not loved.* It annihilated me. I moved, I got up, I ate a little. But all the time, I knew from the very depths of my heart that Christ wasn't loved.

I haven't much to say to you about it because it is not possible to put it into words. The only word for it is agony.

Father Briere: Well, what she says is true. She underwent a real agony. It started exactly at 2 o'clock on Monday, June 22nd. And it lasted nearly two weeks. She came out of it only on Sunday morning. It was quite a painful thing to see what she underwent. It took some time for her to realize what was going on – that it was an agony for the world. And, as she said, the agony was to see that Christ is rejected by Christians. Others who are not Christians, of course, reject the Lord because of the wars, the violence, the rebellion, the injustice, that exists in the world.

The Nuncio was a consolation to her after this terrible thing. And, after we visited him, for the next twenty-four hours she was like in a cocoon. She relaxed in the 'cocoon' of his love, of his understanding, of his blessing. The visit with the Nuncio was of the same caliber as the meeting with the pope and with Archbishop Lustiger in Paris. It was that same kind of friendship, intimacy, and total understanding. There was no need for many words, for self-explanation, or for defending one's convictions. There was none of that. It was a total openness and oneness of heart and mind.

One of the things that the Nuncio mentioned most strongly was this: He said that Christ, after his resurrection, always acted in great silence and in great hiddenness. He said that before his resurrection, the Lord spoke openly and performed miracles, etc. But after his resurrection, he did not appear to Pilate to confront him and say: "Look! See what you've done!" He didn't confront the Sanhedrin or the High Priest. He appeared quietly, at dawn, to a couple of women.

The Nuncio said: "Christ works in silence. God works in silence. I'm always afraid, I always feel distressed and disturbed, when I see a priest who becomes personally popular, or when I see a bishop who attracts people to himself. The things of God are characterized by silence, by hiddenness, by prayer, by simplicity, and poverty."

He said very specifically to bring this message back to the Madonna House priests as well as to the Madonna House laity, but he was talking about priests in a special way. Cardinal Rossi in Rome had said, "As priests are men of faith and dedication, then the Church will be renewed." It was in that context that he said these words: "Tell the priests of Madonna House that the crisis of the Church is basically *a crisis of the priesthood,* and it will be renewed by priests who are simple, hidden, prayerful, and who live a life of poverty."

Several times, when we were leaving, the Nuncio said: "Tell every person in Madonna House – in the Madonna House family in Combermere and elsewhere – that I bless them, that I pray for them, that I love them. Be sure to tell them that."

The thought that came to me during those days of Catherine's real agony was this: we are 'in the breach' ... we are 'in the trenches.' We are not to expect peace. We are not to expect to be without pain. We are not to expect to be without a battle. The devil is attacking us with all his might, and we are in a battle; so let's not expect that it's going to be easy. These are not depressive thoughts. It's just 'reality' – the reality in which we are, the reality that Madonna House is in the Church.

Catherine: You must realize what Madonna House is. Incredible as it might seem, the Nuncio said, "You are the door that holds Lucifer away." Cardinal Rossi said that he had read our books; and he said, "This woman is holding up the Church, keeping the doors open."

Now all of this seems like a lot of exaggeration. But in another way it isn't ... because, for fifty years, I tried to hold everybody and everything properly in their place. (I didn't succeed very much with the priests and the nuns and so forth. Hippies, yes, perhaps.) But it didn't matter. I was there, praying and trying to help the Lord.

But it's the first time that I heard his voice. That's what the Nuncio wanted me to talk to you about. It's very hard to talk about it, because so much seems to be imagination. But when a person so high up as the Nuncio tells you that it's so, you begin to believe a little, you understand? It's very hard for me to believe. But I *make* my will believe; I *make* my heart believe; and Father Cal and Father Briere are helping me through these terrible days.

So I came here today because I want so much to be with you. You see, I love you. You will never quite understand my love until I die. But I love you with the love of Christ — because he is in my heart, because I am in his heart — so I love you as Christ loves you. Perhaps not as well, because I am human; but, nevertheless, you are very very dear to me. You have no idea how dear; but that, in due course, will reveal itself to you. In the meantime, we have to get busy. We have to do little things *exceedingly well* for the love of God. We have to open our hearts to people.

We have to open our hearts because, you know, my friends, our hearts are still closed. Yet, bit by bit, they must become open. For, you see, Christ comes into them, into our hearts. *With each person, he comes in.* Remember; don't forget! We are to share his pain. That's why we will share his joy ... because to those who share his pain he will give infinite joy.

I want you to understand simply that the Nuncio said: "Talk to your staff. They are the door that holds Lucifer back. They must share in that pain." These words are not easily shared because they are very profound.

Some of you wonder if you should stay in Madonna House or go someplace else. Think and pray, if you have those thoughts ... because God is not loved, and you must remain to love him. And not only that. *You are a door.* Remember that. You are a door that keeps Lucifer away.

The Nuncio said to me, "What do you think is the reason that so many priests are in misery?" I said: "Your Excellency, it is very simple. They are guilty of the same act as Lucifer was. Lucifer said, 'I shall not serve, nor obey!' And the priests say, 'I shall not serve, and I won't obey.'" So the Nuncio said, "Pray for them." I said, "Yes, we shall ... always ... constantly."

As far as I can see, a Director General or a Foundress has to carry the burden for quite a while, until she can share it with the rest of her family. So today I share it with you. Today I say: "God is not loved. Arise and love him, no matter what the price." And here you have the eternal question: Are you ready to really obey? Are you ready to go wherever you are sent? Do you consider that the

Apostolate is for you, instead of you for the Apostolate? (I'm just asking questions. I leave it to you. It's in your heart. I have to first suffer these things; then you come in and share them.)

This is the hardest thing I ever had to do. I couldn't have done it if it weren't for the Nuncio. He said, "Do it!" ... so I am doing it. It is not easy to tell things like this to a group of people who may or may not believe. But that's not important. The only thing that is important is that I obey the hierarchy, the authority. It is not easy, but what God asks of us is beautiful.

Above all, I desire in my heart that we should be 'one.' I desire it with a passionate desire. That is so important. I realize that we have no tomorrow; and yet, we have. Whatever happens, you know (neutron bombs and all the rest), if we are one, we are a power, we are a great power. And I realize that power, and I implore the Lord to use it so that you will be one. And the way to be one is to bury the word *I*. Take a big shovel, make a big hole, stick the word *I* in there, and put a cross on top. Because the word *I* is the greatest enemy of *he, she,* and *we.* Remember that; it's very important. So try not to use it the word *I,* especially: "Oh, *I* need this ... Oh, *I* need that." No!

I got a letter from Raleigh. She says to me, "... don't come to North Carolina because it's very hot." When I think that I was in Harlem at 120-degree weather for eleven summers; and we survived! Now *that* was very hot. It doesn't matter. God gives grace for heat and cold. Let's use it!

A SHORT CHRISTMAS MESSAGE

Christmas 1981

Dearly Beloved,

How wonderful is this Christmas! Really beautiful! I send you my greetings. I may or may not be home in Combermere for Christmas, but you are all in my heart, and I love you very very much. You are a very nice group of people.

Let me tell you, you obstreperous and non-obstreperous ones, that I love you very much. Here I am sick and have landed in the hospital, but it is very nice and they treat me well.

This Christmas is a very special one because I put the Child in your arms, and I ask you to care for him as if he were your very own baby. Turn to Our Lady, and she will teach you how to care for him.

I love you very very much.

Lovingly yours in Mary,

A PICTURE OF CHRISTMAS

Christmas 1982

Dearly Beloved,

Happy Christmas to each and all of you! You are all gathered in my heart, and I offer you up to the Lord, especially, on this Christmas day. It is such a deep and profound day, this Christmas day.

You know, I always think of going to the Infant and of really being present at his birth. I don't know why that picture of Christmas is always before me. I even wrote a poem about it. Here it is:

Christmas! They talk of Christmas ...
I see fire descending from above ...
And all men's desires fulfilled by Love!

They rejoice in tinseled toys ...
I see stars dance and fall ...
In an ecstasy of love
At the Fire passing them
From above!

They prepare food, costly and rare ...
I hold a Child, singing to him
My lullabies of love.

How can it be that he — so small
Fills my hunger with Bread and Wine
Divine ...
While they are hungry ...
Eating food, costly and rare,
Which their servants
Prepare?

I share that poem with you because it is the closest I could come to sharing that thought with you. So, Happy Christmas, my dear ones! Happy Christmas of 1982! Let us thank God for a New Year too. Alleluia! Alleluia!

Lovingly yours in Mary,

Catherine

CATHERINE'S LAST EASTER MESSAGE

Easter 1983

Dearly Beloved Ones,

This year I haven't written my usual Easter Letter, but you have probably heard that I became ill quite suddenly, and I have been in bed for quite a while. Thanks be to God, the doctor arrived, and he cheered me up. He is a wonderful man, that doctor of ours.*

Anyhow, I am all right now, and I am getting up and about ... slowly. In three weeks, I will be going for a complete checkup, and the doctor will tell me whether or not I can visit all of you. I want very much to visit you, and he thinks it is a good idea. But he just wants to be absolutely sure that I will be all right.

You know, this was a wonderful Easter. Although I spent it in bed, the Lord was so close to me that I really wanted to share him with all of you. I realized that what we have to do, (all of us, whoever we are) as members of

---

* Dr. Joseph McKenna of Toronto, who was Catherine's doctor for some time and a good friend of Madonna House.

Madonna House, is to open our hearts. Truly open our hearts to him and to our brothers and sisters. This is really the vocation of Madonna House – *a heart-opening vocation*. Each one of us has the key to our own heart, and because of it, to the heart of Christ. Let us truly understand what we are saying this Easter: *Christ is Risen! Verily he has Risen!*

Truly, what does that mean to you? What does it mean to me? It means that we must preach the Gospel. Preach the Gospel honestly, constantly ... constantly. I spend nights and days praying just for one thing: that people begin to *live* the Gospel. We say that Christians are those who have a Christian point of view: a love of one another, and mutual support and understanding; and that this will be the salvation of the world. But *will* it be?

Look around you, and you will see that Christ is forgotten. Do you understand that? Do you understand that Christ *is* forgotten? Isn't it tragic? Isn't it a terrible thing? We must make him known to each and every person with whom we come into contact. So let us pray, all of us together, mentally and spiritually holding each other's hands, that we may bring Christ to the world. Do you understand what I mean, my darlings? Do you really understand? My whole life is in that one sentence: *Preach the Gospel!* God love you and Mary keep you.

Lovingly yours in Mary,

P.S. I want to thank each one of you for all your cards, good wishes, and wonderful gifts. God bless you!

CATHERINE'S LAST CHRISTMAS LETTER

Christmas 1983

Darlings:

My love is as close to you as your own heart, for you are constantly in my prayers. Sometimes I cannot write too much because I am still sick. Nevertheless, I am feeling much better, so this kind of a letter will cheer you up because it cheers me up.

To each one of you my love comes (or goes). I don't know which it is in English – comes or goes – but one thing is for sure: I am close to you, and that's the main thing.

I am not writing very much this year because I am trying to be as well as I can, and I am not yet in very good shape. Anyhow, with all of my love: Happy and Joyful Christmas to all of you!

Lovingly yours in Mary,

Catherine

On December 14th, 1985, around 5:30 a.m., in her 90th year of earthly life, Ekaterina Kolyschkine deHueck Doherty passed into a new and better life.

On December 18th, Catherine's body was buried in the local parish cemetery, a half-mile away from her beloved island cabin.

ACCEPT THE CROSS OF RESPONSIBILITY

May 24, 1958

Carissimi,

Greetings in the Lord! May I begin this letter by congratulating each of you on the wonderful work you have done in the last year. Both Father Callahan and I were deeply impressed and edified by the results of our visitation. Notwithstanding some setbacks here, a few difficulties there, and a number of unclarified points everywhere, the overall picture is wonderful. We thank God for it. He alone, through his grace and your cooperating with it, can achieve these results.

We realize that all of you, individually, have had a 'hard row to hoe' indeed. Some of you an especially hard one, either in the area of the apostolic work itself or in the area of personal relations with those around you ... and at times in both. Yet you came out of it with 'flying colors' because you understood the fundamental truth on which our Apostolate is built – that these difficulties are part of the interior cross that you were given when you received your metal one.*

You understood, sometimes at a very high price, that the goal of our Apostolate, personal and general, is crucifixion; and that you, *as the leader of others,* have to be in the vanguard of that slowly-moving 'via crucis' of ours, which inevitably leads to a Golgotha of suffering, and in years to come, to a final and complete crucifixion.

The ways of God are strange. He doesn't follow the regular Stations of the Cross, the ones created by the pious and loving imagination of St. Francis of Assisi. Instead, Jesus places you – at his own choice and in his own time – now in one spot of his passion, now in another. Slowly, lovingly, he puts you through his own novitiate so that you

---

* When individuals become members of Madonna House, they make promises of poverty, chastity, and obedience, and they receive a metal cross on which the words *Pax-Caritas* (peace and love) are inscribed.

might be 'fit' to be presented to his Father. For he loves you passionately, and has specially called you to be an oasis of *peace* in this immense and desolate desert of modern life, a pioneer of *love* to our chaotic twentieth-century world.

Even though you only see this pattern dimly at times, you have 'held onto the cross' during the midday darkness of your Good Fridays. Father Cal and I are happy about our visitation, though we share and understand the pain that went into the past year. We hear the Lord saying, "Well done, good and faithful servants!" And we echo his words.

In the spiritual life, *to stand still is to go backwards.* So I want you to face the coming year with renewed courage, with a determination so strong that nothing can shake it! Keep on at the same pace, and even increase it, no matter how black the darkness at noon nor how hard the stone of Gethsemane on which you might, at times, have to lay your tired head. Keep going!

There is still much clarification for you to do, to see how you are to be a pioneer of *love,* an oasis of *peace,* to your particular surroundings. Remember that the Directors in Combermere stand ready at any time to undertake the role of Veronica and Simon of Cyrene to you, and to those you have charge of. We are here to help you in any portion of the apostolic work which might baffle, stymie, or worry you.

One of the practical findings of our last visitation is that there is not enough contact between the Directors General (the DGs) and the Local Directors (the LDs). We in Combermere cannot properly direct the Apostolate if we don't know the situation in the field. A constant, flowing exchange of information is the 'life blood' of our family. Without that vital flow, we are like a head cut off from its body. And you understand clearly that, if such is the case, both the head and the body are dead. They cannot live without one another.

Once this is thoroughly understood, then a wide range of information between the DG Office and the LDs in the field will be passed back and forth. This communal knowledge is needed for the proper 'co-direction' of our activities, and it will redound to the good of the entire Apostolate. This deeper rapport between us will soften much of the pain that LDs must struggle with. The burden that is left can more easily, by the grace of God, be borne. The staff in your fieldhouse will also discover that they can implement the particular mandate of your foundation much more effectively. Their work will become more orderly; they will live in an atmosphere of peace and clarity, instead of the fog and mist of uncertainty.

Because of this close contact between fieldhouse and training center, the DG Office will better understand the day-to-day problems of a particular house as well as the overall situation of the entire Apostolate. Better training programs will come forth, a deeper implementation of our spirit will follow, the formation of new staff members will take place at a more rapid rate.

The training of Local Directors must go on, too! That is why I have decided to begin writing you this series of letters. I may be repeating ideas already said during my visitation to your house, but I want these thoughts 'on record' everywhere, in every fieldhouse, so that you can refer to them in between visitations. In the line of communication between us, I want to see two essential points of communication implemented by you: (1) a weekly newsletter from your house and (2) a report of your weekly staff meetings.

Your Newsletters

The newsletter is not a jovial little letter that recounts only the funny incidents and frivolous tidbits that happen. It is serious document, the purpose of which is to give the other houses, and especially those at the training center, an honest picture of a life led by Madonna House members in one of its foundations. There's no reason for it not to be lighthearted, relating anecdotes and incidents and even jokes at times. That, too, has its place. But it should also present to us the problems and difficulties in implementing the mandate you have, the monotony of routine activities, the trials and frustrations of apostolic work.

Every person around you carries a hidden cross. Perhaps entire populations are being pulled and tugged this way and that, suffering a strange crucifixion from opposing forces and urgent needs. How do they shoulder their cross? What are their problems of wonderment, of adjustment, of pain? Tell us about the beauty and courage that you find in other people's souls. How do they find the 'never say die' attitude that is necessary to 'live out' their life? What difficulties must various levels of government cope with? What good and wonderful things does your city or town take pride in?

Let staff workers in a fieldhouse each take a turn at writing a newsletter. Even if they don't know how to 'write' (in the professional sense of the word), they have their own individual thoughts and feelings, insights and dilemmas. What personal wonderments and adjustments can they share with us?

These things are important to us all. We want to share your burdens, to share your rejoicing, to unite our prayers with yours. And we especially need it for the training of the young. Realize that you are writing for your family. You are writing an important document that may shape the future of our Apostolate. View it in a more serious vein that you have before ... and remember that, at least for now, it should be done weekly.

Your Staff Meetings

The first point to remember here is that each house must have a weekly staff meeting. Having just finished visiting you, having comprehended and taken into full consideration the difficulties of time/work/space that make an LD want to postpone such meetings, nevertheless – notwithstanding every difficulty possible and imaginable – a staff meeting should take place weekly ... catastrophic difficulties impairing it only.

These meetings are tremendously important as 'morale builders,' especially for houses that have only a small number of staff. It gives them a feeling of sharing more profoundly in the work, knowing the mind of their LD, being able to discuss their own opinions and to launch discussions on techniques, problems, etc. All this clarifies and soothes. It also makes for good teamwork, and for the ever-growing ability to assume more responsibility.

Sending to Combermere a report of each meeting gives the DGs a working picture of the strengths and foibles of your foundation. It becomes for each of us (and any future holder of the office of Director-General) a vital aid to which he or she can consistently refer to see what progress/regress has taken place in the work or the morale of any given house.

Here in Combermere, our membership has increased to such an extent that – what with many new staff to be trained, and a group of volunteers not as yet integrated into our work and our spirit – we will begin to have weekly meetings of the Heads of Department (i.e., the senior staff) to give them an ever-greater share in the running of the house. The department heads, in turn, will hold workshops with their staff, to discuss matters in detail. Several times a year we will have general meetings for all the staff, in which we can discuss all-embracing problems, techniques, etc.

All of this is being done, you understand, not only to give each individual *a more intimate share* in the workings of the Apostolate, but to prepare them to participate well in the staff meetings that you are having in your fieldhouse. If any LDs want a copy of the 'minutes' of our workshops, meetings, get-togethers, etc., to use as helpful examples for their own meetings, please let me know.

The young staff still in training at Combermere find it difficult to visualize themselves being sent to a fieldhouse. Since this last visitation, however, they seem more alert and aware of the possibility. What about yourselves? One of you will have to 'fill my shoes' someday. We all walk under the shadow of death, and soon one of you will take over the reins of government. You will have reached the summit of Golgotha and be crucified on the cross of responsibility. You will be grateful for the sponge of cool clear water that is given you in your thirst. Then you will know the thirst for reports-on-file – for good, intelligent appraisals to help you in this burden of governance.

Lovingly yours in Mary,

OPEN THE LINES OF COMMUNICATION

May 24, 1958

Carissimi,

I hope my letter to you about weekly newsletters and weekly staff meetings has made clear the vital necessity for establishing a strong 'cable' of communications between the DG Office and the LDs. It is our first line of communication, but it is not our only line. A second 'cable' that connects us together is that of personal letters. We in the DG Office want to help you learn *the art of responsibility.* Our main role in this regard includes being a listening post, a broad shoulder, a confidant, an advisor, a teacher, a helper, a director, an outline maker, a report generator, a mandate implementer – with you, and for you.

Feel free to write us personal letters about anything. Write about yourself, your problems, your health, your questions about life; ask for help in any phase of your apostolate which is troubling you. Encourage your staff to write us personal letters also. Urge them to write as children do to their mothers (and in my case, being the foundress of Madonna House, I occupy a special place as the 'mother' of missions).

Letter-writing is important to us in the DG Office. We need to hear from even 'the littlest ones' of Madonna House their personalized version of the Apostolate, their point of view about life in the missions. They are focused on details. Little things are still important to them. Consciously or unconsciously, they give vivid pictures of daily life, and touch upon minor problems which could later become major ones (if not solved in the early stages of their development). They provide us with very interesting reactions and insights as to the mandate of a given house and its day-to-day implementation. It is most valuable data to the Office of the DG.

Make clear to your staff that their excuse of "the poor

DGs are too busy and read and answer letters" is pure 'baloney'! That is what the DGs exist for – to be vehicles of communication. That is what love is all about – caring for the other, being of service to the other. And nobody in our family is ever 'too busy' to love. If they are, they shouldn't be members of this Apostolate!

That goes for the DGs, above all. They should be the most dedicated and the most organized (with regard to time, I mean) because, as you know, *it is the busiest person who has always time to do more.* Most definitely, the DGs should exemplify in their lives that "the impossible takes only five minutes longer" and should be an example to the LDs and the staff in this matter.

So, my elder children, please encourage your staff to communicate with their DGs. Clarify for them that they can always write about their personal relationships with you or with each other. If they mark their letters *personal and confidential,* the contents will be handled the way a priest treats 'the seal of the confessional.' Instructions are left to burn any letters of this type without reading, under pain of mortal sin, should I die unexpectedly and could not do so myself.

As an LD, you can help to develop a deep rapport between your staff and the DGs. Encourage these communications, both confidential and non-confidential, because tomorrow (or the day after) you will yourself reap the fruit of such seeding.

Responsibility before God

Having clarified the need for a constant and close contact between DGs and LDs, between LDs and their staff, and between staff in the field and the DG Office in Combermere, I want to draw your attention to the necessity of having 'open lines of communication' with God. The implementation of the mandate given to each individual fieldhouse is not always clear. The LDs of each foundation should prayerfully reclarify the fundamental mandate of their house, lest misguided charity or simple misunderstanding lead it astray. Pathways that at first appear to be 'somewhat within the mandate' can very soon lead you far afield. Check and recheck with the DG Office before undertaking any unusual deviation (seemingly logical though it may be) because we must remain crystal-clear about the source of this mandate.

It comes from the hands of a Bishop, *from whom all apostolicity stems*. It is definitely the mandate of Christ, given through the Father and the Holy Spirit. It is our beginning, and our goal. It is the road which each foundation must travel, strictly keeping to that road and taking no side paths of any kind, looking constantly for signposts (especially at crossroads). Pray for your Bishop, in whom the grace of the Holy Spirit resides in a special way.

One of the LDs said at a recent meeting with her staff: "Our prayer life is the most important part of our day. It is not something we 'fit into the schedule.' It *is* our schedule!" This classic sentence sums up all I would say about 'the prayer life' in each foundation. To add anything more would detract from these beautiful words, spoken by one of the most harassed LDs in the field, in a house whose work schedule is the hardest of all our foundations.

Besides having a common prayer life, I would recommend that you meditate on ways to cultivate a 'family spirit' within your fieldhouse. I leave it to your ingenuity (charity is ingenious and has a thousand ways of making the impossible possible) the various methods for implementing this. It may be a matter of common recreation, or picnics, or 'getting away' from the house for a time, or whatever. Staff meetings, a common prayer life, a common family life ... it all helps to unite us, to give strength and purpose to our being. It disposes of many problems that otherwise would arise if any one of these means are neglected.

Affectionately in Mary,

Catherine

TRAIN YOUR STAFF

May 24, 1958

Carissimi,

We all must keep before our eyes the fact that the fieldhouses are never going to receive a 'finished product.' Each foundation is the continuation of the training center at Combermere. We must realize that the training of a staff worker is finished only when that person is buried; for none of us ever ceases our training in 'the novitiate of the Lord.'

Therefore, each of you LDs must condition your mind, your time, and your fieldhouse to be a *continual* training center. You have a tremendous responsibility for all the people coming to your house, whether they are junior or senior staff. You must evaluate, train, check and report the progress of these people to Combermere, because we cannot here simulate conditions in the fieldhouses. Yet upon their ability to adjust to the various problems encountered in the missions will depend their final acceptance into the Apostolate of Madonna House. A vocation, and a 'life' in a manner of speaking, depend upon this extended training.

Because of this need for continued training, there is often a request for 'more staff' in a given house. Before you request this, examine your conscience and your techniques. Make a survey of work habits and plans. Pause prayerfully before the Blessed Sacrament and imagine yourself to be a DG instead of an LD. First, view the whole Apostolate in the light of your needs; and then focus on those particular needs and evaluate them accordingly. You might even ask the DG to make a special trip to your house and help you in this survey of personnel and work. Oftentimes, our familiarity with a situation blinds us to 'other ways' of doing the same work more effectively.

This brings me to the next point of clarification:

simplicity. Sometimes work suffers because an LD is very tired or ill, and (out of mistaken loyalty to the LD) the staff in that house feel they should not report this to the DGs. Such situations should be reported in utter simplicity and trust, so that something can be done about them. Unless you trust the DGs at Combermere, there can be no efficient direction and help from them. Mistaken loyalty plays havoc with the spirit of the staff, and its effect on the spirit of the Apostolate can be disastrous.

While we are discussing this, let me mention that the same openness applies to 'personality clashes' in a fieldhouse. A simple, truthful statement of this situation would eliminate many heartaches for everyone involved. The staff must be indoctrinated in presenting their personality problems to other staff (or the LD) in simplicity and truth. People *can* be changed and problems *can* be solved, if one is simple and trusting and open.

I must close this letter for now, but I'll mention more at a later time. Let me know your reaction to it.

Lovingly in Mary,

ALWAYS AIM AT SANCTITY

January 14, 1958

Carissimi,

In our discussions here at Combermere, we came to some clarification about training. We considered the 'foundation stones' we must give to the newcomers, the requirements we feel are important for any staff worker going to a fieldhouse. We will try to implement this training here as far as we are able to. They were discussed under three headings: physical requirements, mental requirements, spiritual requirements. (You will receive a list of various kinds of instruction covered in the training here. Please add any special skills that you feel are needed in your particular house.)

I would also like to ask you for any suggestions that you might have regarding our training in mental health! Because of the fact that nearly all modern youth are more or less 'neurotic,' a serious attempt is being made at Combermere to solve the principal emotional problems before young staff go to the fieldhouses. We have given courses on psychiatry and religion, and much individual counseling is done. But frequently, when people go to the missions and face the manifold problems of everyday life there (after having the security of the training center), old emotional problems reappear. This is where the LDs must try to continue the training begun at Combermere, realizing that they are always and forever teachers. (If serious problems persist, the person may need to return to Combermere for more help.) As stated above, there must be openness and trust about it all.

With regard to the *spiritual* requirements for staff of the Apostolate, there are two basic errors that LDs might be guilty of. The LDs might say that the spiritual life of the staff is not their concern, that it is something for the priest to handle. Or they might go to the other extreme and meddle in the affairs of a soul. The right position is, of course, in the middle. The priests and the DGs at Combermere are fully cognizant (and believe you me, most thoroughly concentrated) on the spiritual training of our membership – that is to say, on the spirit of poverty, chastity, and obedience – and on the in-depth growth of each person in their care. But nobody becomes a saint in a day; and *we are aiming at sanctity.*

I know this is utterly clear to you. But remembering your own struggles that each of you continue to have, you must understand that two years, three years, even ten years at the training center would not give your fieldhouse a completely finished product, i.e., a saint. Therefore, it behooves each of you LDs to understand that *your own sanctity* depends on finishing that job which has been begun at the training center. Each individual who comes under your care is a unique personality and so has to be treated with deep reverence, immense understanding, infinite charity. At no time must you interfere with the workings of the Holy Spirit in a soul ... or, of course, with spiritual direction.

Let us clarify this point, as I wish to give you the benefit of our ever-growing findings. I know that neither you nor I would dream of asking for a revelation of 'conscience' nor wish to interfere in any way with the souls in our keeping. But as I have realized (and probably you have too), *every act of a human being carries a moral connotation.* So every Director, from myself on down, has a right and a duty to attend to the 'spiritual fruit' of a particular person, as it exists in the external forum.

To illustrate: A room might be swept by a given staff worker in an hour, when it usually takes only a half hour (and the person *knows* it!). So the act of sweeping, in this case, has many possible connotations. The staff worker might be doing this to spite the LD, to show revolt to the 'obedience' that has been given, etc. (I needn't go any further with examples; I know you are familiar with them.) You would, of course, reprimand that staff worker for the bad example and the bad sweeping. And then you would take up the spiritual matters inherent in that particular act. As I said before, an LD can fall into two basic errors here. You can consider the spiritual life of your staff as solely the concern of the clergy; or you can go to the opposite extreme and meddle in the affairs of a soul. Your position, of course, should be in the middle.

So these are my ideas on training. I would deeply appreciate having your ideas on this; it would lighten my organizing load tremendously.

Lovingly in Mary,

LOOK TO COMBERMERE FOR HELP

June 14, 1958

Carissimi,

This last visitation, plus my discussion and trip to Rome and contacts with various secular institutes, have shown me that there must be a great unity between all levels of Madonna House. Here in Combermere, I have inaugurated a rather bold and imaginative way of doing this. Now it is up to me to translate the same technique into letters as I have been doing face-to-face, to continue the job of training and clarifying our life here.

I want to extend every possible help to each individual, from the LD to the youngest member in the field. *You are the key person in the fieldhouse.* I rely on you to implement this idea, and to help me 'share' as much as possible in your life in the missions ... its joys, sorrows, difficulties, bewilderments, problems, etc. Only then can I direct well, and my successors too. We need this exchange of information. We are gathering a tremendous lot of experience, each in a separate field, but with a common denominator. *And this must be shared.* This is a time of inner growth and consolidation for the Apostolate. The sands of time are running out for me, and it behooves me to pour out everything that the Lord has entrusted me, to give it to my oldest children ... as well as, in part, (as much as they can absorb) to my youngest ones.

I will write (God willing), starting now, a history of both Friendship House and Madonna House, a series of directives to Local Directors, and letters to the other 'children of my spirit.' It is time for us to face the fact that we must really grow in spiritual stature, that we are not 'playing at marbles,' that the issues at hand are 'souls purchased by God' through the Incarnation and the

Redemptive death on the cross. This is a vital and serious business, one which spans heaven and earth, encompassing life and eternity.

You can begin looking to Combermere for help of all sorts. But you will need the proper tools to benefit from the training we are going to share with you. Can you beg or borrow the use of a tape recorder, movie projector, slide projector, filmstrip viewer, and phonograph? This is vital equipment, the more so because of the latest encyclical from the pope, *Miranda Prorsus,* which is on films, radio, and television.

To be *alert,* to be *awake,* to have *boldness and imagination:* these are the graces that God gives to our LDs who have to pioneer in the 'marketplaces' of life. Don't waste those graces. Pray and think! (There is much that I want to say to you yet, but a little at a time is better than long letters; and this one is pretty long already.)

Lovingly in Mary,

CHERISH THE FLAME

August 25, 1958

Carissimi,

I thought it was high time I wrote to you, our LDs, who are my co-directors in the Apostolate. Maybe this is a good time, too, to give you my idea of what an LD is and what place that person occupies (as I see it) in the Madonna House Apostolate. We have been having many discussions to clarify the roles of the various people who take responsibility in the Apostolate. If you have any questions and contributions to make, please think and pray about them and let us know what they are.

I see the LDs primarily as *people of prayer,* even though their daily life will be a very active one, for ours is an active/contemplative apostolate. Yes, I see them as 'contemplatives' ... and by this I mean that they will have an inner awareness of God's presence. As one LD in a very busy fieldhouse told her staff: "We do not say that we 'set aside' time for prayer. Prayer *is* our work."

I see LDs also as *prudent people* ... prudent with the Prudence of God and his Wisdom. They are stable, loyal, totally dedicated to their vocation; and (through it) to the Lord and his Blessed Mother. They are thoughtful people, concerned least of all with themselves, concerned most of all with others – those on their staff, and those whom they serve in their apostolate. Their prudence is especially directed toward safeguarding and developing the spirit of Madonna House within its members.

There is also a prudence and wisdom which the LDs have in regard to the world that lies outside their doorstep. I expect them to know when to speak, and when to be silent. I expect them to be good listeners and (at times) slow talkers. At other times, however, when it is 'in season,' I expect them to be good speakers – speakers *on fire with the Holy Spirit.* I expect them to be guided by a *flaming* charity ... for no one can ever sin in charity! Nor can anyone ever have enough charity, nor give enough charity. *Love is limitless!!* (I urgently ask you to take 1st Corinthians 13 as your constant meditation. I seriously recommend that you read the book *To Govern is to Love.** Women especially should ponder Proverbs 31:10-31.)

LDs are very important people. They are staff workers who, before their appointment, were imbued with the spirit of our Apostolate, and I expect them to grow constantly in that spirit. I look upon them as custodians of that spirit, *carriers of the flame* ... that flame which will renew the face of the earth! That is the main job (to my

* Written by F. X. Ronsin, SJ; published in 1953 by the Society of Saint Paul, New York.

mind) that they have as LDs; all the rest is added to that.

The LDs must also be *people of vision*. Even though they may not have that vision to a great extent when they start their important assignment, they will (with the grace of God) get it after a while, and will grow in it. They may start small, but they should be constantly open to an enlargement of their spiritual horizons. At least I hope and pray this will happen. It would be tragic for the whole Apostolate if the LDs did not grow in vision, for the Apostolate is only as strong as its weakest link.

The LDs must pray unceasingly for a growth in faith. For the 'impossible' is always possible to God. Miracles of grace happen every moment. Our Lord told us that, if we had faith, we could move mountains! This is abundantly illustrated in your foundress. Whatever sins and imperfections I have (and their number is legion) I have constantly received *the gift of faith* from God. (And I have never ceased to pray for it, too!) Your foundations, your very presence there along with others of your house, stand witness to what may be termed the grace of God to me – *a flaming faith!*

From now on, you can expect to get a lot of letters from me, clarifying what is the role of an LD. Prepare yourselves, therefore, to open your minds and hearts to (perhaps) a very unusual set of ideas. I've always taught you that the difference between lay-apostolic groups and the more traditional religious congregations is that the laity have the ability to 'change with the times.' That *flexibility* ... like the highly tempered steel of a rapier, which has been refined many times to remove its dross ... like the malleability of wax, which changes its form when warmed by God's love ... is what is needed if we are to keep pace with the eternally enlarging 'vision of the whole.'

We are entering a new phase of our Apostolate, a phase of great internal and external growth. You who are the commanders of the 'Commandoes of God in the Marketplace' must begin to bear the brunt of these changes. I know you will do so with your customary generosity, charity, and understanding. At no time can you ever allow your vision to become static. Nothing is ever static in the Madonna House Apostolate. Nothing can be!

It must always be dynamic, ready to discard the old and take on the new, but always for the sake of love – love of God and of one's neighbor.

Lovingly in Mary,

Catherine

IMPART THE SPIRITUAL ASPECT

January 15, 1960

Carissimi,

A week or perhaps a little more than that ago, you received a Staff Letter dealing with *thoughtfulness** and the true implementation of 'little things done well out of love for God' in practical day-to-day living. I should have expanded it a little further and dealt with the spirit of poverty, too; thoughtfulness and poverty have a deep relationship. (Some day I'll write another letter on poverty.) You may have wondered why such a forceful and agonizing letter was written. I must confess that, when I wrote it, I was in darkness and agony (which doesn't happen often, even to me who realize the pain of Christ somewhat 'deeply' if you know what I mean). Let me tell you what spearheaded that letter.

The first thing was the two meetings I had with all the women staff who live here – junior, intermediate, and seniors. Then came some LD letters from various houses.

---

* Catherine is apparently referring to the Staff Letter dated January 14, 1960. See *Dearly Beloved,* Volume 1, pages 154-159.

Lastly, there were many letters from staff in the field, which seemed to show a complete 'oblivion' (shall we say) of that relationship which connects the spiritual life with the practical life. Let us take these three items separately and analyze them.

An Unawareness of Life

I called a meeting of the women about some ordinary difficulties regarding 'tidiness' and the seeming failure of the guests and applicants to have learned to 'clean well' from the staff workers. I had been bothered by this attitude so I called this meeting, only to have it blow up in my face like an atomic explosion. Out of the meeting came the idea, unmistakably expressed, that all those staff workers (even the seniors!) had not yet made the connection between 'little things in daily life' and *sanctity,* especially the incarnation of the very essence of the spirit of our Apostolate into daily life!

This, at first, seemed incredible to me; so I started probing. I began to talk about the courses they had taken here, the knowledge that has been given to them, all that I have shared with them myself. Here is where I got to the heart of the shock: they stated unanimously that they got 'very little' from their education here. They said they had forgotten most of it, that the only thing which mattered to them really was the personal contact with me and a few others they named (especially when we worked alongside them), and the help they got from the priests.

Even my own life, trials, tribulations, the graces of God to me, my efforts to implement the spirit of the Gospels in the most minute details of daily life ... it all seemed to have had very little effect. My biography was like any other biography they may have read: a nice story, romantic, colorful, full of adventure, but that's as far as it went. They all seemed to agree that there was no similarity whatever between what I did in the past, in the slums of big cities, and what I was doing now in Combermere.

They were obviously thinking of the physical setup, the numbers of people, the extreme poverty, etc. Father Briere asked them if they didn't see the same *faith and trust in God* supporting Madonna House today as it did

Friendship House of yore. I added that, surely, they could see the same reliance on 'begging from others' for our cash, soap, toothpaste, medicines, gifts of toys and clothing for the poor in our area ... that all this shouted of Faith and Trust.

Finally they began to see the connection; but only after Father Briere and I literally pointed to various objects in the room, as one would do to a kindergarten child, and asked where each thing came from and how it got here. It all added up to the fact that, with the growth of our Apostolate and the numbers of new people, I have a tremendous job of organizing and teaching. It also shows that the best method of teaching is *personal contact with the source of the teaching.* Unfortunately, I can no longer be in every department as I used to be, doing on-the-job training with examples and explanations, and showing how the spiritual aspect of life correlates with our work habits and the techniques for doing a job.

As if this weren't enough, I got another shock. Some of the staff said that, when they first came here, they got little out of the training because everything was so new that they hadn't remembered much. Some said that the work in the laundry (or wherever) wasn't connected to God at all. "It was just like it is in the world: Be tidy, do it well, etc." In so many instances, job techniques were not being correlated with the spiritual.

I came up for breath! I – who always tell you not to take even the obvious for granted – had taken it for granted that those who were helping me train would, in season and out of season, constantly *connect every task* with the spiritual aspect of the same. I had failed to train my key personnel! After this I had long talks with three of the people who work closely with me on the training. Openly and humbly, they acknowledged that they had utterly failed to make the connection. And here are the reasons they gave:

One said she was uneasy about it (though she knew she ought to do it) because she realized that, if she asked this of the little ones, then she would have to be an example herself. She was, as she put it, 'saving' herself from the pain of it all, by demanding only a natural efficiency, by talking about 'the tranquility of God's order' alone.

Another said she was very shy. It didn't sound right for her to be constantly reminding others that ironing, cleaning, shoveling snow, etc., had to be constantly connected with such august and holy ideas as God, Caritas, and other supernatural motives. She confessed it made her feel like a 'holy Joe' and she hated that. (She has begun to see the error of her ways since, and has become a good director.)

The third was really contrite. She knew that she should do it, but she somehow 'blocked' on that deal. She promised to do better. ... Now, *how are you in the fieldhouses* doing on this particular deal? Are you demanding only natural efficiency and order? If you do, you are 'way off-base.' For it is only love (in which all supernatural motives rest) that will make people implement our spirit of 'little things done well' and put thoughtfulness into daily living, connecting it all with the essence of our Apostolate – God! Examine your consciences very thoroughly, carissimi ... for I had to!

I examined myself and realized that I took the obvious for granted, so I now am turning over a new leaf and I am concentrating on my co-directors and key personnel: *YOU!* For if we miss the essence of our Apostolate – its very soul and heart – then we might as well fold up and close our doors.

Perhaps this may help to explain the trouble that some fieldhouses have so constantly. Those of you who trained with me when we were a very small house surely remember (I hope) how, in season and out of season, I connected all things to the essence and to the spirit. I hope that you haven't failed in this day by day. But I want you to examine your own conscience and give me a truthful answer on that subject.

The Need for Training

And that brings me to a second point. Your personal correspondence has developed into a sort of 'report' deal. You tell me about the progress or non-progress of your house, the sanctity or non-sanctity of your staff, and you

278

write (once in a while) about your own personal problems, difficulties, health, etc. I am perfectly satisfied with that part. But we have *both* forgotten that my main work as DG is to train you to be LDs, then to train the staff in general, then to train the newest members. I implore you to take advantage of my knowledge and experience of almost thirty years in the Apostolate, while I still live. Let us examine our consciences so that I might know where I have failed you, and you may know where you are in danger of failing the Apostolate (and God) by not handing on the spirit. Let us come closer in the Lord! Let us discuss things in depth and width and height in our letters with one another. Why don't you ask me to write out for you my ideas about your mission, foundation, or fieldhouse? What I think of how it should be ... how I visualize the fullness of its maturity ... what dreams that I dream in God about each.

I have a sense of deep urgency in this matter, for I have finally realized that I am running a training center and that one of my chief duties is that of training the LDs by mail. Do you wonder why this idea has impenetrated my poor soul, and heart and mind so late in the game? Well, I've never been in charge of a training center before! Toronto, Hamilton, Ottawa, New York City, Chicago, etc., were all *active* apostolates. All the training was done by *working* side-by-side with others, and indoctrinating them as we worked together.

But in September 1958, when I moved to St. Kate's cabin shortly after taking the vows of chastity with Eddie and simultaneously appointed Trudi Cortens to direct the work of our rural apostolate here, I think I had an emotional trauma. This latest separation connoted to me the surrender of my last 'baby' apostolate into the hands of others. I had to give up one more 'child.' I had already given up my country, my husband, my son, my second husband ... and twice, the Apostolate itself.*
Now the third time was at hand. I leave it to you to

* In the late 1930's, Catherine relinquished control of her Friendship Houses in Canada. In the late 1940's, she did the same with her Friendship Houses in the United States. The reasons for this are mentioned in Eddie Doherty's book *A Cricket in My Heart*, published in 1990 by the Blue House Press, San Antonio, Texas. Cf. pages 55-57, 107-116, 139-159.

evaluate the depth of this trauma.

With it came an emotional reaction. I think that, up to today, it was a subconscious reaction; anyhow, it was one I didn't want to face. From this time on, I was to be a desk-woman, an organizer, a teacher, all the things that I never in my wildest imagination considered that I was interested in ... and *not having any contacts with my passionately beloved poor!* So I subconsciously 'blocked' against this new and awesome and frightening job of being a Director General, and of taking hold of that office.

Slowly, in his mercy, God gave me the grace to see that this is what I am to do in my later years. I still have one passionate desire: to return to the slums once more before I die, and live there as "Katie Hook" again.* Twice I have asked Fr. Cal; twice he refused, saying that the time was not yet. Now I see why. I am needed in the DG Office, for there is some unfinished business to do ... the really big job of setting up the training, and seeing to the implementation of the spirit in our lives.

I cannot do it alone. Due to the growth of the Apostolate, that can only be done through key personnel now. That means, first and foremost, you who are LDs. And my assistants here in Combermere, and the directors of training, and the department heads. These key personnel must be of a certain type. That means they must *have* the spirit. Next, they must be able to *impart* the spirit to others. Then, of course, personalities matter ... but you know all this anyway. I hope, carissimi, that you get the picture of what I am trying to express so haltingly. All this is the result of my meetings with the women staff.

Sharing the Burden

I've already tackled in the above paragraphs the problem of LD correspondence, my side and your side of it, and why I am not satisfied with it. But in general, the letters from the other staff members in the field present a real problem and they have to be thought about.

Some of the staff show great sensitivity and a

---

* It was an easier name for people to pronounce than Catherine deHueck, and it hid her aristocratic origins so she could identify more easily with working-class immigrants.

cooperation with grace. Many of them carry a terrific burden on their young shoulders, as they witness the thoughtlessness and general negativity of other staff workers around them. This needs to be picked up somewhere, by somebody ... and clarified and shared by all of us, including the chaplains.

But such letters are rare. The majority of correspondence indicates the same thing that I heard at the women's meetings – a non-connectedness between the spiritual and the practical. We must 'preach the Gospel' as it were, by applying it constantly to our daily life in a mission house. We must take the little things that our life is composed of, and connect them somehow with the Gospel and the Author of the Gospel. It is high time that we realize that we are directing *all together.*

There is much difficulty in letting you know the answers that I write to the staff in the field in my personal letters to them. If at all possible (but without directly asking for it), you might get it from the individual under your care. Maybe that would help you to understand your staff better. But whatever it is, it lies in the topics I have written to you about, and which I discussed in the Staff Letter which I feel is so necessary to explain.

Now that I have faced my own emotional problem, and (shall we say) am really 'sinking my teeth into' this state of being a DG, I hope that I shall undo my own mistakes and lack of understanding. Forgive me if I have failed you, and let us begin all over again.

Lovingly in Mary,

LEARN TO BE A DIRECTOR

February 8, 1960

Carissimi,

I want to continue, today, with some thoughts on learning to be a Director. Your first duty as an LD is *to direct* – to direct souls to God, your own soul first. At no time must you dare to forget this *one primary verity,* even in the heaviest days of pioneering, when you are starting a foundation from scratch. Nor must you forget it in the flush of a well-run establishment, where you might have less worries about financial matters, or when your personnel might present less difficulties than in another foundation.

Let me repeat myself: the primary concern and work of an LD is the spiritual. But you must never forget that *grace works on nature!* So your awareness, the ingenuity of your love, must be directed toward the well-being of your staff. This embraces the entire framework of well-being, the emotional state of being as well as the physical and spiritual. In a word, the first concern of an LD is the 'whole person' – body, soul, mind, heart – of each one of the staff.

Into this effort must go all of your Pax and Caritas ... all of your empathy, your sympathy, your growth in understanding and leadership. The staff – and always the staff – is the primary concern of the LD. They have the first call on the your time and energy, for the care of their souls and bodies. This also embraces an appraisal of each person individually, and helping the person to grow and mature through various means ... changing the type of occupation, if possible; clarifying a talent or ability; trying always to see where these talents can best be developed, both for the sake of the person and for bringing the greatest 'fruits' to the Apostolate and to God.

This means that *recreation* is taken into consideration

and is directed into proper channels. Whenever possible, and where the environment permits (as in a larger city), various courses can be taken ... and other 'outside help' can be sought in order to develop those talents. Where these means are not available, care must be taken to provide sources – books, magazines, other materials – to foster 'true' recreation.

The second concern of the LDs must be the Apostolate itself. In this matter, too, the staff plays a major role. No apostolate, no matter how immense, will be successful unless everyone in it – the members and the director – have the proper motivation for their every action and every dealing with those whom they serve. It is better to start small and grow slowly ... but to do the thing right, at all times. The poor, the segregated, the sinned against, all those whom we serve must be *looked upon as Christ,* and treated accordingly. For if the LDs cannot connect those they serve with Christ, how in heaven's name can their staff do so? There will be conflict between their teaching and their true attitude, which will not be conducive to Pax and Caritas.

As 'little founders' and 'foundresses,' the LDs have the responsibility to continue in 'the marketplaces of the world' that spirit which God has so mercifully and generously entrusted to me, a poor sinner. There must be a continual appraisal of the work done, the service rendered, and an unceasing effort made to enlarge the Apostolate in width or (as always) in depth. Should any LD be content to 'remain in a rut' along these lines, it won't be long before the spirit will depart from that house.

The LDs must strive to be *good organizers.* They have been chosen because they definitely have that talent. This must be cultivated and increased. And one of the things that all LDs must be is shining examples (to their staff and to God) in *organizing their time.* Time is a precious commodity, the gift of God to us. To waste it is a mortal sin; it can never be recovered. The organization and reverent use of time redounds in the 'fruit' of order and peace. It is the climate in which charity grows, and in which the natural and supernatural expand.

The duties of LDs include the financing of their house

or foundation. Here again, *faith is of the essence.* The LDs must pray unceasingly for faith and trust in Divine Providence. But they must also be *doers* of the word! (Reread Proverbs 31.) They must use all their intelligence and imagination to find new ways of begging or of raising money (through means that have been checked with the DG), but never ceasing to pray for more ideas.

LDs are people who are completely free, ready to be 'eaten up' by the demands of life. They have no set hours, but can choose the time of their rest and recreation. They are also bound, within reasonable limits of care of health, to be "all things to all men" at all times. Again, faith plays a great role in this; and fear must be absent, to allow reason to play its proper part in this discernment.

LDs must believe that, if the 'duty of the moment' and the call of 'charity' demand many late hours (as may even the call of 'order' ... letter writing, bookkeeping, etc.), God will provide them with the health and strength to do it, if the work is imperative for the common good. In the LDs must dwell the essence of the spirit of our Apostolate: *charity, availability, hospitality.* They must exemplify these three qualities, together or each separately, in a living form.

LDs are *people of prayer.* They are contemplatives 'on the job' ... every so often lifting their hearts to God, and developing a constant habit of acknowledging His Presence in the midst of their work. They are people in love with God and, like a bride or bridegroom, always aware of The Beloved. There should be no effort or strain attached to this 'awareness.' It might not come in a day; but it is always to be prayed for, and hoped for.

LDs are to be *people of vision.* (This, too, must be prayed for.) Their vision must be The Vision of God, for they are working for the extension of His Kingdom. Love does such things; it is never static, but always dynamic!

LDs are *people of wisdom,* pliant in the hands of the Holy Spirit, unworried about incidentals. They are understanding, kind, gentle to others, and severe with themselves. Theirs is the wisdom of children ... for childlike simplicity and purity of heart see deeply.

This, briefly, are some of the duties of LDs. Perhaps it

is not so much their 'duties' as their 'state of loving' that we are talking about. This has been a real opus; but, as I explained to you, we have gone through God's wringer, and thoughts are flowing out of my heart like water wrung out of a garment that has been soaked in it. I hope that some of these thoughts will be of help to you. God love you and Mary keep you!

Affectionately in Mary,

BE COOL, CALM AND (RE)COLLECTED

June 20, 1961

Carissimi,

We have discussed again and again the dangers that can beset an LD (and often do). The greatest of these is the slow, insidious, almost unnoticeable shifting in the 'accent' of the spirit. What should be a manifestation of the spirit of the Madonna House Apostolate becomes *the spirit of a given house* ... with only superficial overtones (or overlays) of the Apostolate as it really should be. To put it a little more bluntly, an LD can become so immersed in the apostolate of a given house that he or she forgets (being so concentrated in the work at hand) that the house is part of a whole, and not an independent entity. Just as we are all members of the Mystical Body of Christ; so also, each mission house is a member of 'a body' called the Apostolate of Madonna House. At no time can LDs consider any house *their* house, or the works of it *their* work. (This has happened occasionally.) All our fieldhouses are but 'rooms' of Madonna House at Combermere; and every LD should always be 'in tune with' the spirit of the entire Apostolate.

The daily life and routine of each house, the tremendous needs and demands of those who live in that area, will tend to obliterate this fundamental concept, without which the Apostolate will die. Though a mission might have the 'appearance' of being a very successful undertaking, it will die in its spirit! This tendency has to be watched for constantly because, once this basic spirit is gone, all the rest is as if it were not. So I want to remind you once more of this life-giving principle of Oneness in Spirit. No matter how painful, how crucifying at times, the difficulties in your house might become (as well as in the times of peace and order), you must always consider all things from the high mountain of Pax and Caritas, from which the 'vision of the whole' is clearly seen.

Unless you do this, you will be constantly 'bogged down' by the needs of your house. And this concentration (at the expense of the Apostolate!) will exaggerate these needs, and magnify them out of all proportion. Then (without wishing to do so, and quite unconsciously) you will harm the Apostolate, or at least impede its 'growth in grace' before the face of God. As I have said before, this is where you must go prayerfully before the Blessed Sacrament, to regain your view of the whole Apostolate, and to examine yourselves in that light.

Over the years, I find two trends coming up one after the other, like the white and black keys of a piano; now one is pressed down, now the other. When all goes well with your house, you are somewhat remiss (perhaps that is too strong a word) in sharing with me your thoughts, plans, etc. Letters become farther apart and contain very little that matters. *But* ... should the slightest difficulty arise between you and your staff, or should the trend of the work pattern change for some reason, then letters and telephone calls to Combermere follow with a rapidity that is amazing!

The overall impression is something like this: When all is well, there is "no need to communicate" very much with Combermere; but when anything goes wrong, "Let's put this situation in the lap of Catherine Doherty (pronto!); *she* will solve the problem! ... If we can't handle a staff worker, let's send him or her back to the training center; *they'll* straighten the person out!" (The result is a series of crises, which could often be averted with an objective approach, along with much prayer and meditation.) It is always left for this person called Catherine Doherty to decide and solve. In one way this is quite right; but I am still waiting for a letter or letters that will tell me of a crisis and enclose two or three ways that it might be solved, and then ask me to choose the best.

There seems to be no such thing on your part as clear and objective thinking. It's important that you learn to 'get over' any emotional involvement of your own in a particular crisis and, above all, to adopt a prayerful approach that takes in the whole Apostolate and not just your house. Why don't you sit down in the chapel and ask yourself a simple question: "How will this, my crisis, affect the whole Apostolate? How can I solve it locally, without creating too much disturbance for the whole of which I am a part?"

One crisis that arises in all of the houses, from time to time, is 'the pressure of work' versus 'the amount of staff.' The obvious and simplest solution is to immediately ask for more help from Combermere. If you stop to think about this, however, you'd realize that you were 'cutting off your nose to spite your face.' Emergency demands at this distance are hard for us to evaluate; and you may get half-trained personnel, because there is no one else to send. Then you are even more unhappy because this has created new tensions in your house. (You must understand that, unless we in Combermere have time to train staff before sending them to the field, this problem will continue indefinitely.)

There are, however, a number of ways to approach to a personnel crisis in any fieldhouse; and many of these you can do by yourself. First of all, you need to make an objective appraisal of the work being done in your house. After that, you will be able to make an intelligent choice. For example:

1. You can decide to *redistribute* the work load. You may have to cancel some free days or have work 'bees' where everyone takes time to work together on some project. Or you can recruit some volunteers from the community. If the crisis is a true emergency (and not an exaggerated one), 'paid help' could be used until the situation is under control.

2. You can decide to *tighten up* on the work being done. Certain areas could be left undone for awhile, or cut back partially, or removed entirely from your work list. Some jobs – like office work, laundry, driving cars for errands, repair work, heavy work on the grounds, etc. – will have to be done at some point. But you could use 'hired help' temporarily to deal with the situation ... even for three to six months of the year, if need be. (Usually the crisis is over before that.)

I myself have gone through 'crisis' situations many times where I didn't have any source of supply, such as you have at Combermere. But I had to do something about it; and I did it. Perhaps you should examine your conscience on this, especially on your organizing potential. Is it being used to the 'nth' degree, or could it be improved? Do you immediately want to put the brunt of the whole situation on me? Or are you willing to take time to 'figure out' for yourself some new ways of reorganizing your house, and then to submit to me your plans for that? (If not, prepare yourself for disappointment and a delayed solution of your problems and crises.)

Please answer and give me your advice and counsel, dearly beloved, for we need to share our thoughts on these vital points.

Lovingly yours in Mary,

Catherine

LEARN TO TRAIN OTHERS

March 1, 1962

Carissimi,

I've been wanting to sit down and talk to you about many things. Our quite obvious growth necessitates communication and clarification all the time. We must make reappraisals of our training constantly, because nothing is static here. We are always moving to meet new needs, as well as old needs on new depth levels.

At present, we are busy with a complete reorganization of the Men's Section of Madonna House, to bring it into line with that of the Women's Section. More male vocations are coming in, enough to divide the work into different categories and to create separate 'departments' ... each with a permanent 'department head.' It is still at an embryo stage, but emerging well. Father Briere will be made available for a time to supervise the overall training of the men.

I am already having a weekly meeting with the two Directors of Training and their assistants, who are also houseparents in the dormitories. I have inaugurated short (ten-to-fifteen minute) morning meetings, right after breakfast each day, with all the heads of departments. By doing this, they can get acquainted with each other's needs and plan a better distribution of work and personnel. It is proving very helpful to them, because they learn the art of organizational management (and of decision-making) through the day-to-day solving of practical problems.

I won't go into the changes on the academic front, except one: I've been working on the final organization of the Archives. Since our training is directed to the sanctification of each individual person, and giving them a 'vision of the whole,' we obviously want to challenge them to do research into the Archives. More and more, we find that the best way for staff to acquire knowledge is to have them research a particular topic, working on their own (but with some supervision). We continue straight lecturing, of course, but we supplement it with much more research than before.

This means that the permanent staff that you will eventually get in your fieldhouse should have a better understanding of our vocation and spirit, and will have less emotional, academic, or technical problems to distract you from the direct apostolic works of your house. (Temporary staff, who are sent to you for a 'pupilship' year in your foundation, may or may not have these skills.)

The problems which are predominantly emotional have not been resolved in Madonna House, so now we are 'tightening up' the matter at this end. But all this tightening, all this deep examination and reexamination in so many areas of training will continue on at Combermere for some years. We need your help in this. Please pay special attention to those who come to you for 'pupilship' training. Remember that they will leave you at the end of a year. Please be sure to give them a chance to 'work out' in all your various little departments, so that they have a rounded-out picture of your particular mission house when they are done. And continue to help them grow in the spirit of Madonna House as applied to the realities of our Apostolate. We count on you!

Lovingly yours in Mary,

PUT ON THE 'CHRIST MIND'

June 11, 1962

Carissimi,

I've been spending many sleepless nights, thinking and praying about the Apostolate. Inexorably, time marches on; and I am not getting any younger. I realize that it behooves me to pass on to everyone, as much as is possible, what could be called the *Christ Mind* in me. I want to qualify this strange phrase by saying that it refers (theologically speaking) only to that part of me which pertains to the Apostolate and its foundation. Of myself, I have nothing! I shouldn't even be talking to you, except in the 'natural order' perhaps ... as a human being who has seen much, learned much, and would like to share it with her daughters and sons.

What I want to discuss is a sort of growing 'vision of the whole.' On the agenda of our next LD meetings will be the question of "how to prepare your staff in the field for going to the foreign missions." I know you will kind of smile at that. Some of you have enough difficulty training the staff for your own mission house ... but who can tell? Perhaps a wider viewpoint, an opening of other horizons, may also help the home missions.

We have learned much in the last couple of years from our own mistakes and shortcomings. In hindsight, I see that is it a mistake to appoint people to key training positions if they themselves are still unsettled. That 'uncertainty about life' can spread itself by osmosis, harming others ... or at least preventing a better training from being given them.

Another factor that militates against our ability to train is this: The senior members of our Apostolate have not had that fairly orderly training (physically speaking) that we were able to give the next generation of staff. The training of the very seniors was done in parts, not as a whole, and much slipped by them. It was a very hard time in the Apostolate back then, so it is understandable that this happened. Perhaps that is a reason for many of the difficulties in the fieldhouses that you experience so often. I submit to your consideration the thought that, slowly and judiciously, we should begin replacing the very senior people who are in the field. They can be brought back to Combermere for retraining and for 'refresher' courses, and will be replaced in the field with the new element, the new blood. Things will greatly improve, though you might not realize it right away. (The Men's Section here is greatly benefiting by the new and fresh reorganization which has been given to it.)

Speaking of the need for training, I see that some LDs have never been trained in bookkeeping and office procedures. Hire someone to teach you right now! Then order will reign in a very important part of our Apostolate. Remember that we are, in conscience, responsible – before God, before the hierarchy, and before civil authorities – to keep proper track of all moneys that are given us.

Some of you haven't been trained in the art of letter-writing or in our personalized way of begging for money. For many long years, I have been begging for money and clothing. And as a beggar, I am supposed to be 'one of the best' in the Church of America. My secret (if secret it be) is very simple: *I answer letters as fast as I can* ...never keeping them longer than one week but, even at the expense of my health and sleep, I try to answer them within forty-eight hours. My letters, too, are highly personalized, for I am truly interested in everyone, our donors included. And it is this highly personalized type of writing that (I think) has brought us our following and our money.

Procrastination in answering letters leads to a constantly narrowing source of supply. Above all, *it is not charitable* to keep people waiting for an answer! Nor is it *polite* (for politeness is a child of charity). Nor does it 'do justice' to the situation. Dignum and justum est* ... it is

* A phrase taken from the prayers of the Mass, which Catherine would heard spoken every day. "It is right and just, it is our duty, it is our salvation, always and everywhere to thank you, O God."

proper and fitting that we should thank those who do us good, and not leave our correspondence unanswered for weeks or months.

The ingenuity of love should be at work. If you answer those letters promptly, your relationship with others develops, your correspondence increases; and with it the income does likewise. But the motive is not simply utilitarian; so put on the *Christ Mind* when you answer letters.

As you notice, I allow my thoughts to ramble, and write to you as they come forth in my mind. As time goes by, I shall discuss one subject or another, whatever is dear to my heart and (in my estimation) important to the Apostolate.

Lovingly yours in Mary,

DEVELOP YOUR CRITICAL FACULTY

June 16, 1962

Carissimi,

I write you to ease the turmoil of my thoughts, which seem to increase as I write instead of decreasing. Still, I share them with you to ease myself of them, for a burden shared is a burden lightened. Take last night. I woke up at 4:00 a.m. and went swimming twice in the Madawaska River, trying to relax and to go back to sleep. But the

Apostolate – which is my life and love – kept coming back, sometimes in its total vision, sometimes in its partial vision. And once more I realized how many things I would like to share with you, but don't do so. Many questions arise in my mind, and no answers come to them because I postpone asking; so they get 'lost in the shuffle' as many things in our lives tend to do.

One of the things that I thought about last night was *television*. Not many of our houses as yet have it. But I want to clarify the attitude that should be taken toward TV. In letting your staff watch it for recreation, there are two approaches you might choose. The first approach is to let them see everything, telling yourself that there is no harm in it because lay apostles must know the good and the evil of our communications system, and that the technology of it is not alien to us either (... and nothing should be alien to us, except sin). With the second approach, you would be more cautious and would censor the programs, excluding some and keeping others.

But the matter of TV goes much deeper than that. First, it is an insidious influence which, if allowed to run freely, will become a hypnotizing thing that wastes time. It militates against using that time to better advantage, such as doing something more worthwhile that would help to promote the family spirit.

Let's face the fact that the usual excuse for having a TV set is that "There are such good programs available"; and the few good ones are constantly mentioned. We hear about serious music, and good plays, and news coverage. But let us also face the fact that that is often *not* what the staff is watching when we have a TV in the house. Perhaps they listen to the news; but that is followed by some drama, and they continue to watch it if their time is free. Often these shows are based on a very superficial value of life, and would have been rejected if one were to consider them by themselves.

Some censorship must, therefore, be exercised; especially as to the *amount of time* spent before a TV set. An evaluation, a careful evaluation, must be made between you and me as to the results of that viewing; and an analysis made of the programs available. You see, one of the key factors that you do not take into consideration (and you should!) is that many of the staff *lack a critical faculty* with which to judge the programs offered.

We have proof of this. Sometime ago we had a Leadership Course given here by some friends from the National Film Board of Canada. It dealt with movies, the critical faculty of the viewers, and the leadership of an audience. Since TV is simply a 'home movie' in a sense, it is very pertinent to discuss the results of that workshop in this letter. It lasted for two days and (I'm sorry to say) at the end of it, both specialists told our young people very frankly, almost brutally, that:

1. They lacked any critical faculty.

2. They did not know the first thing about critical analysis and points of order.

3. They were typical youth, sponge-like in the reception of knowledge given them. They never analyzed or criticized, but accepted facts as given or read. And they would make poor leaders unless they did something about it all.

4. They suffered from a malady of modern times, by which most of them were afraid to express their few opinions, criticisms that they may have had, lest they be 'out of line,' etc. Everybody waited for someone else to start, and nobody did.

Let me give you one other example ... though if I were to write out all the examples I have seen in my many years of experience, it would make a book. I will discuss the power of the written or printed word on the minds of our staff. X___ is a good example of it. In her gardening course, she learned all the latest modern methods of fighting harmful insects: DDT and company. There was no one more enthusiastic in the whole place. She pestered me to buy all the latest things.

When I pointed out to her that one had to have a critical faculty toward these things and not 'go overboard' without investigation, she obeyed me ... *but* ... I am sure she questioned my funny Russian mentality! It seemed to her that I didn't *ever* believe what I read. So I started her on research, gave her books to read about the adulteration of food, the dangers of DDT, etc. We got scientific films on the harmfulness of insecticides. Then I introduced her to some advanced ideas on what is called 'organic' farming. Over the months, she became very aware of the soil, the environment, the bad effects of pesticides and unnatural fertilizers, and has since matured into an excellent organic gardener with deep convictions about protecting the earth and working with nature.

This is what I call training the critical faculties of a human being – not to argue but give proper scientific data, the relevant statistics, and so forth. This took about a year, but it did develop the critical faculty of one staff worker. Today she is a person who can be trusted to weigh what she reads before she believes it.

I have had similar experiences with others in different departments here, such as the laundry, where the person in charge got interested in the whole chemistry of soaps and detergents so she could critically appraise the advertising and printed media regarding the use of bleaches and softeners. One of our duties, carissimi, is to constantly train our staff in critical appraisal, for this will lead them eventually to recognize *truth* when they see it, and to recognize *lies* when they encounter them.

Now back to the TV. One house told me the programs they watch and at least one of the shows I would say (for I took pains to see it) is most inane, extremely uninteresting, and downright nauseating – a soap opera with a new quirk. They mentioned it because a priest staying there watches it. I would say that priests are free to see what they desire to, but it isn't necessary that the staff watch it with him. They can simply inform the priest *why* they do not watch it. (I can't imagine this sort of thing to happen often; but if it does, it can be handled this way.)

Good programs of music or good plays can be watched if they are not on too late; though perhaps you could have a critical discussion about it so as to enable the staff to *watch critically* and develop this *ability to judge* what is good entertainment. Be careful about programs that skirt the limits of propriety, make light of marriage vows, show disrespect for in-laws, etc.

Many of these programs which I have examined from an apostolic point of view have been devastating enough to keep me awake the whole night wondering how it is possible for us to 'restore the world to Christ' with that kind of entertainment penetrating every home. The same is true of many of the comic strips in the newspaper, and many of the jokes that one hears. Only psychiatrists fully know the damage they can do to young minds and souls.

You should draw the attention of your staff to these situations; truly, it is a matter for crying, not laughing. I am sure that, if you critically examine many of the foregoing with your staff, the revelation will really stagger them. They have not been trained to evaluate entertainment this way, and they need help in developing this skill.

There is much to discuss regarding TV and other areas of the visual and audio arts. Let us discuss this among ourselves via letters, and we shall do so in more depth at the LD meetings. I have just barely skimmed the surface here to draw your attention to it all.

Lovingly in Mary,

Catherine

FOSTER THE FAMILY SPIRIT

June 20, 1962

Carissimi,

You begin to realize that I have a veritable Niagara of thoughts I want to share with you! They've been running fiercely and furiously in me during the last year, giving me not only many sleepless nights but a good dose of colitis as well ... and, at times, a deep feeling of guilt. Ora pro me! [Pray for me.] But as I look back on the past year, I do not regret the sleepless nights. And I would be willing to have colitis again and again, if the slow clarification that came from it (and which enables me to write this letter) would be of any help to you.

I look upon our Apostolate as a fleet of canoes bobbing up and down on the stormy sea of life, and I desire to help guide and strengthen your particular canoes. Today I want to speak of unity; not ecumenical unity, but apostolic unity – the unity among us. It is a hard subject to tackle because this unity is of God and is therefore *inward and mysterious*. It deals with intangibles, as well as the tangible fruits of those intangibles. I shall try to put into words what is in my heart.

We are all one Apostolate ... you not only know that intellectually but realize it deeply within your heart. As I have mentioned before, however, the works of a given house, the responsibilities of an LD, the 'daily grind' (if I may put it that way) are like sandpaper on a wooden floor, or like sand in a machine. They may sand our way to unity or, if we are not careful, they can stop the machine.

I have expressed in a childlike fashion that Madonna House in Combermere is like a house with many rooms. Those rooms are your houses, and some of them are in the missions. But an LD can become so engrossed in the work that he or she forgets about unity, and that 'room' becomes 'my house.' This intangible withdrawal, not really meant as such nor really desired, but brought about by the daily absorption into one's own apostolate, could be dangerous in years to come. We must be cognizant of that attitude and try to correct it.

Up to now, our method of fighting this tendency has been to remain united in the following ways: Newsletters from your house, sharing your activities. Reports on your staff meetings, which apprise us of the work habits and family patterns, the problems and solutions of various difficulties, etc. The correspondence of the staff with the DGs at Combermere. Frequent letters between the LDs and the DGs. The yearly meeting of all the LDs at

Combermere. The visitations of the DGs to the various houses. Occasional telephone conversations to Combermere, when considered necessary. These are all good methods of keeping us close to one another and of fostering unity. So let me review *why* it is we do these things, as I see it, and forgive me if I seem to discuss the obvious. Sometimes even the obvious bears repetition!

Newsletters

The primary idea is to keep in close touch. It establishes a communication in our family, and is a good link of unity. It shares what you are doing, but it also forms a 'slice of history' of the Apostolate. It serves as a part of our research work on the Apostolate, and is a good preparation for any staff going later to that fieldhouse and who will help you when they are assigned there.

The newsletters (which should not be a chore) make good reference material and good spiritual reading. They will, many years from now, be a weekly historical report of outstanding events in each house. They also help us by giving us a vision of the whole Apostolate.

Staff Meetings

These meetings are stupendous material for the DGs. They apprise us of the weaknesses and strengths of a house, the problems of a particular work, the needs of the staff in a house as well as those of the LD. Linked with the personal letters of all of you, they form our 'gospel' as it were, and in many ways our 'textbooks' and 'reference books' since they help us to deal individually with the staff, the LD, and the house.

They are irreplaceable, for they are our key to directing and helping you and the staff. They give us, much more profoundly and clearly than anything else could, the 'picture' of a given house. (I definitely I want to talk more about this at our next LD meetings.)

The original idea of a weekly staff meeting is not really well kept in some houses, and I feel that's a pity. Perhaps meeting each week is too much, or is impossible to achieve in some situations. Nevertheless, I hope that no less than two meetings a month will continue to be the rule, though I prefer to see three or four!

Correspondence with the Staff

Frankly, I hated to impose this 'obedience' to staff in the field of having to write the DGs in Combermere twice a month, but I continue it because many of our members are still filled with remnants of their emotional (negative, usually) 'transfer' onto me as a mother figure. They often have an unnecessary awe of me, which somehow develops into a false fear; and there is sometimes a tinge of hostility toward authority in general. I am aware of all this and I have prayed much about it. Although at first I receive unsatisfactory little letters, this 'obedience' of writing me has worked well.

The fact that the staff in the field don't have to confront me face-to-face seems to help. And oftentimes they feel my tenderness and love more easily in letters. It leads me to open my mind and heart more to them; and it enables me to still be of assistance to you, the LD, in their continued training. It also enables me to understand a given staff worker better; it shows me his or her progress, or lack of it. And it has proven to be extremely helpful, spiritually and psychologically, for the sake of unity among us.

Letters between the DGs and LDs

Your letters are beyond value to any DG; and I hope that my responses are also helpful to you. Some of you are very faithful to this and you are the joy of my heart. Others, though still a joy to my heart personally, write too spasmodically, unless you are in trouble – then come airmail letters and phone calls! If we could try to remain closer to one another, however, the Apostolate would benefit.

I plan to write more letters to you, sharing my thoughts. I hope they will reveal to you the hunger of my heart for a closer relationship with you, for it is in *working together* that we will really grow in unity. Another point in favor of this exchange of letters between you and me is the fact that anything of a personal nature will be burned at my death. The other letters will be a great help for any future DG.

The Yearly LD Meetings

The more I consider the needs of the Apostolate, the more deeply I realize the need for our Directors' Meetings. We feel very deeply the fact that we skipped one last year. I hope it will never happen again, for nothing can take the place of this unifying factor – a discussion face-to-face, in common – not only between the DGs and the LDs, but among the various LDs as they exchange ideas and experiences among themselves. Unless a great emergency precludes it, we will try to hold them yearly from now on. I am truly looking forward to this year's meeting when we will all be together again.

The Visitation of a House by DGs

At present, making a visit to all of your houses unfortunately presents great difficulties; and as the Apostolate grows more widespread, I see that it will present even greater ones. But, technically speaking, visitations are certainly one of the best ways to promote unity, efficiency, and mutual understanding.

As we begin to go to the foreign missions, I foresee a problem arising, and that is: "Where am I most needed?" Is it at the training center, the fieldhouses here in North America, or at the overseas houses? I can foresee that I shall be 'as one crucified' between the needs of these two branches of home and foreign missions. That is because of the need of much reorganization of the Apostolate along physical, mental, intellectual and spiritual lines. All of this will be very time-consuming. Too, there is much to be written down of the experience and history of the Apostolate that is known only to myself. This will help to clarify things for the future. All of this has to be done before my death.

At the same time, I know that a visitation by me is still important to the Apostolate (and maybe to you personally, my dearly beloved). The time is coming, however, when I will have to send proxies whom I have trained; and I will evaluate with them, later on, the results of their visitation. (Yes, there will be a lot to discuss when you come for the annual LD meetings in Combermere.)

Emergency Telephone Conversations

These are, of course, exactly what they are supposed to be – emergencies. This is a good way to deal with the occasional crisis, however, as it gives both of us the security of knowledge that, if worse comes to worse, there is a speedy way of communication already tested and at hand. This, too, helps greatly with the unity we are discussing.

But the *great unifying principle* between us is, of course, *CARITAS* – an intense love between us! We are teaching our youngest members that they will not be good lay apostles in 'the marketplaces of the world' unless they begin their tremendous Apostolate of Love by *loving one another*. In this we who are Directors should be a great example to them, to say the least! I know that we are; but perhaps we do not show it enough.

What is your way of fostering this idea of unity through the personalities in your house? I suggest that Madonna House in Combermere be always placed before your staff members as a unifying principle, for Combermere is 'the womb' of their vocation. It is the heart, soul, mind of the Apostolate. The staff must develop toward Madonna House in Combermere a great love and gratitude for having been trained here. Their memories of Combermere should be shaped by positive ideas, and by grateful feelings.

However, they must not slip into sentimental emotions about the place – either gooey, or hostile, or what-have-you. Neither should they make any comparison between their present challenges in a fieldhouse and their fond memories of the motherhouse. They must not think of Combermere as an 'escape' from the world, or a place to 'hide away from life.' The image of Combermere needs straightening out in the minds of some of the staff, and would be a powerful point of unity in your particular foundation (especially if it is clear in your own mind) and useful in the day-by-day hurly-burly of mission life to help others see the 'vision of the whole.' Otherwise, one can get overly absorbed in one's apostolate of the moment.

Please do not feel that you have to take all of these letters from me as Gospel Truth, my dearly beloved, or even as papal pronouncements (smile!). I mean them to be challenging and provocative, springboards for discussion and further examination, and a stimulant to our correspondence.

Lovingly in Mary,

SEE THE LARGER PATTERNS

June 19, 1962

Carissimi,

The avalanche continues. Thoughts that are clamoring to be shared with you knock at the door of my brain constantly and loudly. They tumble over one another, pushing each other out of the way so as to be the one that gets out first! ... I think, however, that I shall continue to discuss a topic that pertains to my previous letter: on unity among ourselves and how to strengthen it; and on the growth of the 'vision of the whole' ... which is never static but always dynamic, for grow it should.

I hope that you especially – the ones who are still the pioneers of our Apostolate, who are so busy building and organizing and coping with growth and many other things – will never be so busy that you have little time to consider your house or your work from those two important points of 'unity' and of the everlasting 'vision of the whole.' Getting too enmeshed in the 'needs of the moment' can kill both the unity and this vision, or at least stifle it at birth.

Let us examine, at close range, what I mean. It will reduce itself to very simple and ordinary things, for such is the warp and woof of our days and our lives. One has to remember that *every day* in the Apostolate is an important day for the whole of it. The strands of yesterday form the cloth of today, and today weaves the pattern of our tomorrows. To lose those patterns is a great tragedy, for generations yet unborn need those foundational patterns. I repeat, *they need them vitally!*

Consider Arizona. It is one of the cradles of American anthropology, and has one of the richest deposits of minerals. It is a veritable paradise for sociologists, archeologists, and geologists. It is a place with a flamboyant and important historical past. All of these subjects, these scientific disciplines, this background form tremendously important strands and patterns of life which are of value to *all* of the Apostolate.

What price would Madonna House in Combermere pay for a collection of newspapers, magazine cuttings, bibliographies, letters, and what-have-you about all of those strands among which our Arizona team has lived since 1957!

If only I had informed the LD right at the beginning, who in turn could have trained the staff there to open their minds, souls, hearts, ears and eyes to the background among which their daily lives were being lived out! Their close contact with the Mexican and Indian peoples would have swelled our knowledge of all those subjects which are so vital these days.

This brings me to the keeping of files that could be literal textbooks for the training center. We could borrow them as a source of important local information, and they would add to the knowledge of your own team there. They would make your personnel better 'instruments of the Lord' to the people around you.

Some of the other houses are uncovering information which has helped much in understanding the customs and ways of life of the people whom they serve. Each house would profit by obtaining this information about their locale, organizing and filing it. The gathering of data and filing of it creates a common interest and enhances the family spirit that you are all trying so hard to create. It is good to have personal hobbies, of course; but it is better to have a common one.

We should introduce throughout the entire Apostolate the study of missiology. It is a 'must' now for every lay missionary going out to missions, for that is becoming a very challenging situation – this adaptation of Americans and Canadians to the mission lands. They suffer especially from a lack of cultural knowledge, much more profoundly than do people brought up in European countries. Missiology, as given today in the universities for missionaries, comprises: anthropology, geography, history, psychology, sociology, and miscellaneous subjects. By 'miscellaneous,' I mean the close examination and practice of certain ways and customs of the people in order to give you an up-to-date knowledge of foods, dress, social relationships, etiquette, and cultural mores.

Perhaps you LDs could introduce some sort of study like this on Sundays, while just one of you cooked some food that would be representative of the region studied. Another way to broaden yourselves for the missions would be to subscribe to magazines; perhaps you could beg some subscriptions. One of the best sources is the *National Geographic* magazine of the U.S.A. You could make it known that you would like back copies of this, and use it for cutting out and filing pertinent articles for future historical and geographical lessons. These would be of great importance for the growth of family spirit and the unification of your group.

Another thing which would help in expanding your cultural interests would be to start collection of postcards and of clippings about art. We have such a section in our files, filled with articles from magazines that were donated to us. Be aware of the possibilities of expanding your cultural interests in this way, and realize how much of it will contribute to making you become better missionaries. Slowly, through begging and perhaps personal gifts of art books from families of the staff, you can build up a good collection of art. Need I say more about how this sort of activity can increase local knowledge and what an interesting exchange could be made with the other houses?

Have you considered Christmas cards? One of our staff came here on a visit and said she was stymied for material for catechetical classes, things that could be used for activities and instruction. We showed her our scrapbook of Christmas cards. There is need to appraise them for their usefulness to you; I tend to divide them by subject matter: applique, designs, angels, shrines, embroidery, etc. One of our staff got ideas for her candle making from the pictures of candles which we had saved.

One can also get filmstrips, movies and other visual aids in order to teach various hobbies and handicrafts. Right now our anthropology class is using many films, and we invite friends to participate in viewing them.

A well-thought-out program of the various things I have suggested will go a long way to raise the level of knowledge in your foundation. We in Combermere are experimenting with them all. *Are you?* They are also great means of growth in holiness and in enhancing the 'vision of the whole.' Please give it all some thought.

Lovingly yours in Mary,

CHECK AND RECHECK

September 1, 1962

Carissimi,

By now you must be used to the fact that you are going to receive many "LD Letters" from me. I suggest that you put them in a binder so that you have them handy for reference. They will, I hope, be of help to you in your training of the staff. I dislike the word 'training,' but I hope that these letters will help with such problems as you may have in trying to give the spirit of our Apostolate.

In our discussions here, we see a number of problems arising. The first one that faces the Department Heads can be summed up in several words: *Take nothing for granted.* Check and recheck; and then check again! The second problem seems to be that the Department Heads aren't explicit enough in giving directions for a given job, believing that the person has understood when, in fact, he or she hasn't! *Check to see if the person has understood the directives given.*

Be Ready to Correct

As for 'taking nothing for granted,' it may seem a silly thing to discuss; but believe you me, my dearly beloved friends, all of us make this mistake because we often *overestimate the experience* of the staff worker we are training. We have to bear in mind also that many people today have emotional problems, and our staff is no exception. One of the primary results of this is: though the person *seems* to be listening, oftentimes he or she is *not* absorbing! We must take this into account.

We have to be very explicit or detailed in our instructions on whatever the job is, until we are sure that the person understands every movement in it and all that goes with it (such as the preparation of tools and their proper use, like: hammer, saw, rake, shovel, typewriter, ironing board, bucket and mop, whatever is needed). Teach them to assemble all their equipment before they begin work. Later you will teach them how to put it away when finished. Make sure that all of this is familiar to the person. Then, check and recheck. Be ready to teach and correct *as needed,* not at some future time.

During the first few days of a given job, check as to the quality and timing of their work. Timing is important. Encourage a slow but steady speedup in the work. We see a great slowdown in people with emotional problems. Although at first we make allowances for this, eventually we must teach them to work at a normal rate. Where you can, try to work with them for a while on jobs that are new to them. This will often be of great help in instructing them by your example and bringing about better use of time.

You must always be ready to connect each job with the spiritual, and a nice way is to explain that is that Christ often used the words 'arise' and 'hasten.' It would be interesting to underline in the Bible the passages where God spoke to the great prophets (such as Moses, Jeremiah, etc.) and made them do things *BUT FAST!* It would be especially interesting to do this in the New Testament.* We suggest having a project like this because (unfortunately) people in our modern world will work faster for good pay than they will for God! We talk about the 'rat race' in the world, but nobody talks in a positive way about a 'rat race' in the service of God! Men will kill themselves working for cash; but they will barely live for God, as far as work is concerned anyhow.

This means, of course, that you will have to examine *your own* 'distribution of time' and become more efficient in this. As the saying goes, "a busy person can always do more," but it takes an intelligent and disciplined person to make good use of *every* minute. You must also be aware that your emphasis has to shift slightly from the work you

---

* Catherine especially liked *The Gospel of Saint Matthew* (a 1964 movie by the Italian film director, Pasolini) because it showed Christ preaching urgently over one shoulder as he hurried from one town to another.

now are doing yourself to your 'primary' work – your spiritual family, the staff! (We have discussed this many times; now is the time to implement it.)

On-The-Job Training

I have already touched on this point in previous paragraphs, but it can stand a few more clarifications because I am dealing with minute details here. I want to remind you that your staff may appear to be listening, but they don't; may appear to be absorbing, but they aren't. So a good technique when giving explicit directions for a job is to have them repeat the instructions back to you.

One thing I want to add here is this: let the atmosphere be unhurried. Your own tension can be transmitted to the staff you wish to train and they will become confused. Show them that you are kindly disposed toward them, and want to help them as best you can. Take a deep breath, untense yourself, and begin to speak in a clear peaceful voice, remembering to smile with your eyes as well as your lips. Be peaceful and take your time. Even though you are hurried and may have to dash somewhere, don't show it.

At times you can have a short 'bull session' with your staff, focusing on the jobs being done, analyzing them a little, asking for advice on how to do them better, faster, more efficiently. This is good for morale, and should be done outside of staff meetings. (Depending on the type of jobs being discussed, it might be better to have talks with the women separately, and talks with the men separately, if you have a 'doubleheader' like that in your house.)

This constant 'taking nothing for granted,' this checking and rechecking, this explaining and re-explaining, this timing and encouraging, will subject you to a certain crucifixion, but it will pay dividends and will be worth the pain.

One more word: I suggest that you read these letters of mine in some quiet corner, at some quiet time (if you can find it), perhaps before going to sleep. My love will be in them and, I hope, a lullaby and a blessing for you.

Lovingly yours in Mary,

MAKE THE CONNECTION

September 1, 1962

Carissimi,

In our last letter, we discussed two problems of Department Heads: the need to check and recheck, and the need to be explicit in giving directions. A third problem, more important and more delicate than the others just mentioned, is the need to *teach the spiritual dimension* of all the problems and difficulties that arise in the various departments. There seems to be a strange psychological inhibition about giving the spiritual dimension of a job. That partially stems from the fact that many department heads are in about the same age group as the people they are called upon to direct.

Let us talk for a bit about the difficulty in making spiritual connections with little things. This is not a new situation. We belong to a Jansenistic, puritanical society that is quite divorced from God; and so God and the things of God are seldom mentioned. So it is difficult for you (all of you) to use a predominately spiritual approach when you teach and correct others. You LDs have often said to me: "We cannot talk about God, and gratitude, and all that, and express it the way you do. But we want to learn how to do so." And, dearly beloved, this *has* to be done, or our training and its results will never amount to anything.

Let me give you a example which may be of help: I was passing through the kitchen and the young ones were being taught how to make cookies. One had burned a batch of them and she was laughing about it. The staff worker in charge of the kitchen didn't seem to mind. I must admit she said: "You must be careful. Cookies cost money and we get that money from other people." But this was said in a natural tone of voice that didn't carry much conviction. It was exactly the tone of voice that a tired teacher might use remind her class, "Now, children, sit up straight."

I stopped the proceedings and gathered everyone around me. With tears in my voice (I couldn't help it!) I spoke to them for half an hour on the spirit of poverty, on Nazareth and Our Lady and her spirit of poverty, on the care of creatures: dough, butter, lard, sugar, raisins, etc. For these are creatures of God and must be used reverently and efficiently for his glory.

I continued, telling them about the poor who send us their pennies, about a farmer's wife with seven children who had helped a neighbor clean house so she could give us some money. I connected it all with burnt cookies and discussed the virtue of concentration on a given job, the duty of the moment, the spirit of our Apostolate – little things done well for the love of God. Cookies are very little things. I showed them that *every act has a spiritual connotation*. I don't think that this group burned many cookies after this.

Next, I asked the staff worker in charge of the kitchen why she hadn't given these young people that connection. She gave the usual answer: "Catherine, it is so hard. I never think of it ... perhaps because I don't *want* to think about it." Now I ask myself: Is it a lack of motivation, or is it just her cultural background? It is probably the latter because her motivation is high. *How about you?* What are you doing with your staff in this regard?

Unless we make this connection, we are building our houses on sand and not on the Lord, and that will be our responsibility. Let us concentrate on this area of passing on the spirit. I will help in every way I can, if you will give me a picture of what each of your staff needs. If you ask me to help you in breaking that hesitancy, that 'fear' of making this spiritual connection, I will (with the grace of God) do all I can. But please, dearly beloved, let us discuss it *now!* We cannot dillydally anymore. We have to put order in our training center, and we have to eliminate many things in your attitudes too, so that our next meeting of the LDs will find us talking about God, the Apostolate, and all of these important things, and not only about the efficiency or deficiency of the staff.

Speaking of imparting the spiritual answers to everything, I want to say this: if a staff worker tends to whine or complain, or is discouraged somehow, one thing I have found helpful is to say to them: "Come here. Look at the crucifix and repeat what you said. This crucifix is the *only* reason why you are here. And all of this untidiness, forgetfulness, complaining, is against this crucifix." I do not impose any methods on you, but this is one I have found helpful.

I am the first to blame for their faults, and yours; but let each of us take his or her share. Let's examine our consciences. Let us discuss this. Let us 'get cracking' so that God will be known and loved in our houses by our staff and us! And every little thing that happens during the day will be connected with Him. Let us do it if it kills us!

Some of you teach powerfully by example; but words are necessary too. Let's talk it over. *The time is now!**

Lovingly yours in Mary,

LET YOUR LIGHT SHINE SOFTLY

September 10, 1962

Carissimi,

I would like to talk to you about *missions*. I know that your mind is not always occupied with this topic, and most of you do not think of yourselves as *missionaries*. Because you have been very busy building your respective foundations, the whole idea of the missionary spirit of

---

* An allusion to the book *Our Time is Now: a study of some modern congregations and secular institutes,* written by Mary O'Leary (London: Burns and Oates, 1955).

Madonna House Apostolate has (perhaps) escaped you. That is understandable.

But my mind is forever thinking of the future growth of our Apostolate. As a foundress, I owe it to the Apostolate (and to God) to do this, so that such lights as God gives me about our later expansion into the missions will be yours to meditate upon in that future which is yet to be. Obviously I am concerned with what could be called theological or spiritual principles. On these I meditate, applying them (according to the grace of God) to our Apostolate.

To me, the true 'mission field' is the cave at Bethlehem, the climb to the top of Mount Tabor, and the hill of Golgotha with its burial niche carved on one side. To put it another way: our mission field is the Incarnation, the Transfiguration, the Crucifixion, and the Resurrection. Let us examine these ideas slowly, reverently, prayerfully.

We live in an age of tremendous upheaval and change, an age of war, nationalism, and hatreds. Any team of Madonna House going to the missions today will meet these things head-on. Any child, in fact, any simple person with little education realizes that, in the foreign missions today, Western ideas and white skins are *not* a passport to human hearts. On the contrary, they are often a tremendous handicap to the giving of the Glad News that God loved us first and calls us to a life of love with him ... a handicap to the job that God has given us to 'preach the gospel' to all nations!

One doesn't have to have a Ph.D. to understand that the old missionary methods – which simply brought Western culture, Western habits of thinking, Western architecture and Western philosophy – will not work in our age and time. The mission teams of Madonna House should not be too concerned with what is known as the 'intellectual aspects' of mission work. Though we prepare you (and hope to prepare you even better) to know the anthropology, geography, history, and mores of the people to whom you will go, nevertheless, your main weapons will always be Pax and Caritas. Though you will be learning their language (perhaps at great pain for you) as you walk the village pathways, your silent example will speak louder than your tongue can ever do.

All of you realize that love *identifies* itself with those it serves, that you do not arrive at a mission station as a Lady Bountiful (or Lord Bountiful). You walk in great humility, with a heart filled with gratitude that you have been permitted to come and serve your brothers and sisters in another part of the world.

You also know that you have to *walk softly,* and never act or look (or even feel, if it can be helped) disgusted or astonished at the ways of the people you have come to serve. They may seem 'ignorant' to you, for you evaluate them according to your narrow tastes and ideas, which are Western. But you must remember that some of their civilizations were ancient when European civilization was barely beginning, and your ancestors were then barbarians. So walk reverently, with eyes and ears wide open, studying the ways of ancient cultures, even though they may seem strange to you, especially in the area of hygiene, family attitudes, etc.

The Cave of Bethlehem

We begin with Christmas, the feast of the Incarnation. Like Christ – who became a little child in Palestine and grew up to be a Jewish man of a certain type, with certain habits and mores – so you, too, will incarnate yourselves and be 'born' like a little child into a new civilization and a new people who will be 'your' people. Like Ruth in the Old Testament, you will leave your country and your people and you will incarnate yourself (as much as it is spiritually possible) into the ways of your new country.

You will adopt the good ways of your newly-found people to the nth degree! Yet, like Christ, you will – with great love, gentleness, understanding, pity and compassion – firmly reject for yourself that which is incompatible with Christianity. Through your quiet example, and occasionally by word of mouth, you will show your newly-found family better ways to do things; and later on, better thoughts and beliefs.

The whole process is gentle, never violent. It never comes from one who thinks himself 'better than' those whom he teaches or serves. Yes, incarnation – which is another powerful word for identification – is your first step.

It is one that can shake the foundation of the world, change it, and restore it to the Christ whose incarnation is the motivation for yours.

The process is long, tedious and painful. In a way you must 'change into' the Hindu you serve, the West Indian you serve, the African you serve, inasmuch and insofar as love will enable you to do. This has to be done without any compromise with Christian principles. This is a deep incarnation, and it will require much work, prayer, fasting, meditation, silence, and a 'dying to self' to achieve it.

The Ascent of Mount Tabor

If you succeed in this painful/joyful process, then the place where you are will change. Some of you will certainly journey to Mount Tabor ... and the feast of the Transfiguration will enter your life, because you have transfigured yourself (as far as it was in your power) into the environment to which you have come. Because you have done it *out of love,* because of that love and that incarnation, you have been enabled by the grace of God to truly 'preach the gospel.' I feel sure that God will allow you to be transformed, even as he was allowing his light to shine as it did on Mount Tabor. He will do that *through* you! And because you did all this, there will be no obstacle in you to his work for those you serve and love ... and they, too, will be transformed!

The Hill of the Skull

But do not forget for a moment that the price of transfiguration, the price of taking another step in that incarnation of yours ... or which will be yours, when you go to the missions, either foreign or at home. The price is Golgotha. The cost of souls is high – as high as a cross on which you must hang. For unless you do so, there will be no success ... because you do not love enough; because humility (which is truth) is not fully part of you; because passionate love (the kind that leads to Golgotha) has not yet begun to consume you. So Golgotha it must be.

But if you go to the Hill of the Skull (which is what the word *Golgotha* means), and if you hang there with Christ on the other side of the cross, naked of 'self' as he was naked of body, and if you are buried with him in the tomb of obedience and total surrender, then will come your resurrection. And with your resurrection will come the resurrection of a whole countryside, maybe a whole nation. Then will come your Easter, and the Easter of those you have come to serve. Then will Easter *Alleluias* ring out in new tongues in the hearts of many. Then your missionary efforts will be crowned with success.

Christmas, the Incarnation, Mount Tabor, the feast of the Transfiguration, Golgotha, the Passion, the Crucifixion, Easter, the Resurrection ... These show me the spirit in which Madonna House Apostolate and its members must go to the missions. I see no other.

Lovingly in Mary,

TAKE TIME FOR SOLITUDE

September 11, 1962

Carissimi,

I would like to know your reaction to having a poustinia in each of your houses.* For several years now, I have been making poustinias in St. Kate's cabin, in the same room where I normally work and sleep. But psychologically speaking, for a poustinia to be really

---

* At the time Catherine wrote this, the very first poustinia of Madonna House was being readied for use, a few miles outside of Combermere.

effective for our young staff (and for all of us), it should be one room in a house which is kept just for that. The walls should be absolutely bare, except for a cross (which is easily made out of two pieces of wood). The cross should be without a corpus, to remind us that *we* are the one who is going to 'hang' there for this twenty-four hours of prayer and penance.

The furnishings of such a room would be a small table with a Bible on it, a simple cot with wooden planks on the bedsprings, a hot plate on which the person can boil water for tea, and some bread without butter. This will constitute the fasting and penance. Generally speaking, the person will go there to be in solitude and silence before God, with just the Bible and a bare cross. There is to be no human contact, for solitude is essential. It must be as though the person were far away from anyone. I don't think this is impossible to achieve in the fieldhouses, do you?

For instance, Portland could use one of the smaller rooms in that empty school next door for such a purpose. Surely Whitehorse with its immense basement could set aside some space, or maybe go to a room at Maryhouse. At Aquia, one of the cottages could serve this purpose. The Casa has Miss Miller's little cabin, which might be ideal. It is conducive to prayer and penance; with very little arrangement it could be used as a poustinia. I don't know about Carriacou; perhaps a little shack could be rented on a quiet beach far from the house itself. Edmonton could rent a room somewhere in the downtown area, or perhaps find a small cottage somewhere for this purpose. Think about it, all of you.

Once this practice of 'going to the poustinia' for short periods of prayer and penance becomes established in Madonna House, future generations of staff workers will feel the need for 'the desert' in their lives.

Lovingly in Mary,

PLAN YOUR DAY

November 28, 1962

Carissimi,

As you know, we are making tapes for you to have in the field. They will bring you a wealth of history on the Madonna House Apostolate, important lectures by our priests, guest lecturers here (for instance a whole set of Russian History by Helen Iswolsky who taught it at Fordham University for twenty years) and others. Tapes are not like people; they will not intrude themselves on you; and, in the pressure of things, you may forget them. *Don't!* Do plan well at the beginning of your year and make sure that this wealth coming your way is not buried like the talent of the man in the Gospel.

This brings me to a thought that has been with me a long time: *the proper use of time.* Bear with me, dearly beloved; I am not critical of you, but I do feel that some of you have not yet mastered that know-how, that tremendously important know-how for an LD (or any executive for that matter) of the proper use of time. The key to it, of course, is planning. Strange as it might seem, we of the Apostolate must *plan our day.* We must plan it well, knowing all the while that a telephone call, a visitor (or a group of them), the need of an individual person (or of several people) will shatter those plans as a sharp blow shatters glass. Nevertheless, we must still plan daily, or preferably the night before, for the next day. It is good at the end of the day to jot down whatever was not accomplished, because of circumstances beyond our control, and try to fit it into the next day.

Into this daily planning must enter the firm conviction, understanding and knowledge of a very simple fact: that an LD is not one who does everything herself or himself, but one who knows how to *delegate both jobs and authority.* That is the second key to being a successful director who knows how to use to good advantage this precious commodity that God gives us – *time!*

While you plan, you must appraise your staff and decide which person can do what job best. Let me illustrate: Some members are good at jobs that require no decision-making. You can give them work that is most useful, but does not require any decisions to be made, such as: ironing clothes, folding laundry, scrubbing floors, peeling potatoes, stamping envelopes, running errands, etc. They can assist others who do make decisions, and work together as a team. You must take into consideration the emotional and physical state of a person on any given day, and plan accordingly.

There should be clear-cut outlines of the day's work (or week's work) and a rotation schedule so that different people 'take a turn' at various household jobs such as sacristan, cooking, cleaning, etc. If your house has jobs that are particularly monotonous or onerous, be sure to rotate these jobs occasionally. It will be a great help in promoting efficiency, and be therapeutic for the individual. Always bear in mind what is good for the person at the time. You will have to 'roll with the punches' and know that there will be a thousand jobs that are never done, and you must try to 'squeeze them in' when they will be good for a staff worker at that time.

Another key, of course, is *your own* use of time. You also are a worker and have your duties. You too can go into any department and assist for a while, becoming 'one of the gang' for a bit. But, above all, you are the schedule maker, the planner, the counselor, the busy person who always finds another hour, another half hour to finish that which was left unfinished.

Let us discuss a little this planning of time. There is so much more that can be said of it.

Love,

PUT FIRST THINGS FIRST

December 20, 1962

Carissimi,

I know that many of you have been very busy this past year. Some have been busy building; others with programs for children and adults; some with added pressures because of sudden necessary changes of staff; some with endless telephone calls and doorbells ringing all day in a chaotic order of charity.

Yes, there is no denying that there has been great pressures in your work. The cry for action, the seemingly inescapable need for it, is almost beyond the description of human words. Well do I know those pressures, for I have been subjected to them for more years that I care to count ... in Toronto, Harlem, Chicago, etc. Nevertheless, I call your attention, carissimi, to the needs of *yourself* – your soul, your mind, your heart – and those of your staff.

One LD wrote me that she had 28 newsletters and sermons from Combermere (and I presume Staff Letters as well) that were unread. She suggested that each house write a monthly newsletter instead of a weekly one. I know that you are all under pressure from the literature that comes to you from all sides, but the answer to this is that weekly newsletters keep the family spirit up as nothing else does.

We already have so little contact with one another that (if it were not for myself telling you about the newcomers, and them about you) you would be an unknown quantity to most of them. As it is, you are becoming an unknown quantity to the majority of the staff in many ways. It is always amazing to watch senior staff members return to Combermere and almost shyly renew their ties with a member of their own class, with another staff worker they had once known so well, not to mention the newcomers. So it is for the good of all of you that we insist upon these letters.

Monthly newsletters would reduce our contacts, and with them our family spirit to practically a nonexistent quantity. They would become mechanical. At times I am afraid that the weekly ones are already that way, and those who write them consider it a 'chore.' (That is a horrible word that I dislike intensely; it changes work from the prayer that it is into sort of a dark type of slavery.)

No, a newsletter should be written with a heart *full of love,* one that desires to share the little happenings of the week from one house to another. It should be read with reverence and joy, too. It should be read with concentration so that everyone would know what their brothers and sisters are doing. Try to read even *between* the lines about the difficulties that aren't mentioned, and pray for each other after you have read them. Things that happen in your house are the history of God's mercy to us, of his graces and of our spiritual and physical growth.

I am afraid that you LDs are neglectful at times with the reports of your staff meetings. I cannot direct without knowing what is happening. And when a house leaves a wide gap between these reports, I am like one who looks into a void. I fear that the fieldhouse will suddenly have an emergency 'in full bloom' and we have to try, by airmail letters and telephone calls, to get some clarity and understanding into a situation, which (if we had seen it coming) we might have been able to prevent.

I warn you, carissimi, with that intuition that I think God has given to me, that you who neglect these things are walking a dangerous path. Newsletters, private letters to me, reports of staff meetings, etc., should be full of news. They are a 'must' if our Apostolate is to survive, if you are not to fall into the error of 'functioning on your own' as it were, in a vacuum, separated from Madonna House in Combermere. Some of you have experienced the tragedy of that terrible vacuum, that emptiness, that 'cut-off'ness.

This temptation comes on soft feet. It begins by skipping one week of these documents, and then another, until finally you are *alone* ... dealing with 'your house' and not a house of the Madonna House Apostolate. If you need to, it is better to take a full day off and go away (as I told the LD mentioned) and read and write those letters, than it is to accumulate some twenty of them and get sucked into a whirlwind of activity that suddenly dethrones God and puts an idol in his place – the idol of 'actionitis.'*

We have to be watchful of these things. We have to always keep in mind *first things first*. And the first thing is prayer. The second thing is growth in virtue, and attention to the staff. The third is work. And it is concerning work that, whenever possible, you should cut down and rearrange schedules. For this I suggest the poustinia; it will put things into the right perspective.

I feel that we are sitting down and talking as sisters and brothers in the Apostolate. I hope that you will realize that I consider you as a team, working *with me* and not so much as under me. I believe that you have the whole Apostolate at heart, that you are concerned with it and its totality first, and your house next as a part of it. I believe this because, tomorrow, any one of you might be elected DG and you will know what I mean. You will know it in blood and sweat and tears beyond telling, and a joy beyond expressing. And I must make you ready for that too, that strange and lonely place which is the DG Office. It is a place where you can live only because you are sustained by God and your LDs.

Yes, my intuition is alerted. And I confess that I am just a wee bit worried, for anything that threatens the family spirit, the closeness of us with each other, and your closeness with me alerts me before the Lord, and I want to talk to you about it. So let us be watchful, dearly beloved. Those endless letters, sermons, reports, newsletters, and so forth, that you have to read and write are the strongest links between our growing family. Do not break those slender threads, or we will have no family of Madonna House Apostolate.

Lovingly yours in Mary,

Catherine

* Cf. *Dearly Beloved*, Vol. 2, pages 154-160.

322

PUT YOUR HAND TO THE HELM

January 17, 1963

Carissimi,

There are so many things I want to share, but somehow the pressures of the day and of the Apostolate have eaten deeply into my limited time. Two new additions in the writing field have done the same because, at the request of our priests, I have (in a manner of speaking) 'imposed upon myself' the task of writing the History of our Apostolate and a Commentary on the Mass.

Then again, I still have a fear of overburdening you with too many letters. Often, in the quiet hours of the late evenings – when I pray for you so very specially and think of you so lovingly – I hunger to share with you many, many thoughts. But the next day, that little fear of overburdening you begins nagging at me; and I postpone the whole affair. And yet I don't know if I should. I am uncertain on this point, for some strange reason.

I want to share with you a beautiful letter that one of the staff wrote me. I hope she doesn't mind if I pass along some of her shining thoughts for your encouragement:

> This morning at Mass, when I was praying for different people in the Apostolate, I began to realize what a 'test period' we are going through again. I lifted up each of our staff to the Lord, thanking him for their love, and for being with them in their great suffering, illness, weariness, aches, pains, doubts, trials, and rough times.

> In going over in my mind the roster of names, I seemed to be completely filled with peace. I thought of the rocking boat, and Jesus sleeping peacefully in it. What a wonderful way to have him in our midst, awake or asleep! I thought of the foreign missions and how much God must want us to go overseas; and how the devil must want to drown us all. I also felt

how stable and secure the 'boat' of Madonna House must be, to have God allow it to be subject to such pounding.

Isn't it a beautiful letter? And aren't those consoling and true thoughts? They brought me much joy and peace, for I feel the same way as the writer of this letter; only more so, because I am writing the History of the Apostolate. There is only one thing I have to say, as I probe my memory and write chapter after chapter (I'm on Chapter Thirty, describing Harlem), and that is: The words of this letter are indeed the naked truth. And we can rejoice in them because the hand of God *is* strong on the Apostolate and guides its tiny boat over very stormy seas. I am witness to this so very specially, after all my years in the Apostolate.

I can't describe the feeling of strength I've had all this morning ... not in myself (for I am still floundering around, both physically and spiritually). This feeling of solidarity is not about myself but about the Apostolate. (Blow me down, if I don't seem to have latched onto a little more of the 'vision of the whole'!)

This letter should give courage to all of us, but especially to you who are at the helm of such little boats (the tiny 'rooms') that make up the fleet (the 'house') of Madonna House Apostolate. These words should guide us all into the calm seas of a perfect faith, and peace, and love of the Lord. I felt the words were too true, too beautiful, too shiny to keep to myself alone.

But I must remind you, my dearly beloved LDs, of one thing: Though Christ sleeps in our boat, though he guides it by his very Presence, *he has put you at the helm* of your little boat. Though you must live by faith, as so beautifully expressed in that letter I just quoted, you and I must also *do our share in guiding that boat* in faith!

Because you and I are the Directors of this Apostolate, our concern should be constantly, ceaselessly, directed toward the staff. We should be elder sisters and elder brothers to them. We should be fathers and mothers to them. And we should be their friends! Their struggles are great; so are ours. But they are not DGs nor LDs nor heads of departments; and so they haven't the graces we have. And it is our job to be 'all things' to all our children, in all our houses.

I feel this strongly because it is so obvious that the young ones depart from our training center to go into the missions with their needs unfulfilled. For example: X___ informed me how fearful she is in her new assignment. Everyone in that mission house is a 'senior' to her, and she has never worked with any of them before. But she puts up a brave front and goes on with life, though she is quaking inside. That same week (from the same fieldhouse), Q___ confessed that she couldn't stand X___ "because of the front she puts up."

I contacted the LD of that house, because the LD has the tremendous job of knowing these currents and undercurrents that make the little 'boat' unsteady. How can any LD know them? By talking to the people involved, by being observant and watchful, by being gentle and affectionate ... yet firm and strong.

Whenever a newcomer arrives at a mission station, the whole staff should go out to that person for a few weeks or month. (As LD, you must take the responsibility to 'train' your staff to do this.) Remember that the newcomer is both frightened and excited, and a bit confused as to where everything is. The person needs gentleness, tenderness, compassion (coupled with your firmness, and clarity of direction, and uncompromising attitude on the spirit of Madonna House) until he or she is 'settled' into the routine of the house.

Well, I guess I shared some of my thoughts with you, and I feel all the better for it. Pray for me. When the History is finally written, I will be 'emptied' ... for it is quite an opus, and it takes quite a bit out of me because I have to walk back along the lane of painful memories. But I don't mind, because there is much joy in it too.

Lovingly Yours in Mary,

Catherine

BE ALIVE TO LIFE

March 13, 1963

Carissimi,

I feel it is time for me to sit down and talk to you. I have such need of you these days. There is no denying that Madonna House is progressing in wisdom and grace. And I see divine grace coming to all your houses. So let us thank God together.

At the same time, the very growth of our Apostolate demands more growth in individual souls, more cooperation ... for the ways of spiritual life are never static but always dynamic. That is where my need of you comes in. As I read the letters of the 'children,' I see those needs reflected there too. For instance, one young staff worker writes me as follows:

> Some days I think I am getting picayune. At breakfast the other day, the kids complained about the stuffiness in the chapel. Ye gads! I can't understand this! The LD installed a fan; and still people are not satisfied. So I said to them: "What's the matter with you guys? What would you do if you were in the heat of India? Did they have fans in Harlem Friendship House? I know my parents couldn't afford a fan. I sweltered many nights and days, growing up in Canada."

Probably she herself has been guilty of negative remarks at times, but it is surely a grace that she realized what was being said by others. And she is not picayune; she is right. I want you LDs to be aware of this tendency toward negativity. It is no sort of preparation for our foreign missions. The attitude of not only 'taking things for granted' but demanding more and more in the way of little comforts certainly doesn't go along with that 'identification with the poor' that I write about with so much depth of feeling.

In another fieldhouse, one member questioned why they were celebrating February 14th. She wondered what had happened on that day! Granted that she wasn't concentrating too well when she was listening to my lectures on our history given some years ago. But surely she should have remembered a major event like Harlem Foundation Day. Could it be that the LDs under whom she has worked (and she is in her third mission) did not accentuate our family history enough? Do you LDs really remember it? Do you remind others? If this precious heritage is not 'in your bones,' how can you show it to those under your care?

In another house, one of the staff is like 'a fish out of water.' She is amazed that there are no 'corporal works of mercy' there. She must have missed all the Staff Letters I've written and the many newsletters written by various houses about 'life in the field.' (Or is it that these letters are not read very attentively in the houses?)

Make sure that your staff read and discuss these letters. It's for your own benefit. Tomorrow, you may be in charge of that other house; and you may be getting a staff worker from another house. How difficult it will be if that person doesn't know anything about you or the particular apostolate of your mission. It also breaks the unity of Madonna House if the staff 'haven't got the picture.'

More importantly – and we are all to blame for this situation – it is quite evident that we didn't give this person the facts of the spiritual life, namely: that to 'feed the hungry' means to feed people *spiritually* as well bodily ... and sometimes much more spiritually than bodily! (You see how I need you to continue that training that we carry on so flexibly in our Apostolate.)

The LD of that house writes: "I have come to realize that I made a huge mistake when I first met this person. I just assumed that she would be *alive, aware, interested in life* and what goes on. I expected her to be familiar with our history, aware of what happens in other houses, and in the Apostolate in general. It took me quite a little while to discover that these things were 'not there' in that person. Or if they were, they were still latent and not expressed."

Why aren't people alive, alert, aware, interested in

life, in what goes on? *That's the sixty-four-dollar question!*
Is it possible that some of our houses don't understand the
need for having staff who are alive, aware, etc., etc.? If so,
perhaps an examination of conscience is indicated of the
LDs.

I don't mean to censure you or correct you. I am so
happy about you that I could shout and dance! But these
things come to me, and I have to share them with you.
Alone, I cannot carry them. I ask you to help me, carissimi.
And I know you will. (Well, I have expressed myself and it
has helped me. Thank you for listening.)

Lovingly yours in Mary,

Catherine

SHARE YOUR PROBLEMS

November 6, 1964

Carissimi,

I want most of all to communicate with you as a
person, a friend, an equal in so many many ways, for I have
need of you as you have need of me. Our last LD meeting
was that type of communication! We all felt it. We were of
one mind, heart, emotions even; and there was an openness
and simplicity among us; and we all felt, at least for the
moment, greatly strengthened and happy about it all.

But something happened after that meeting. Perhaps it
was the question of facing oneself, rethinking what had
happened and being frightened again by the fact that unity,

love, understanding, and openness are all inexorably connected with *the cross*. And all of us fear the cross! We forget that once we reach the point of acceptance of that cross, we begin to love *with Christ's heart* ... with his peace and joy lifting us 'out of ourselves' as it were, and making us truly instruments of his love.

I cannot tell you how deeply I share your daily problems, how profoundly I love you and how much I trust you. Each one of you, I hope, has experienced in some manner and in some way this love and trust, this sharing of your joys, sorrows, work problems, staff problems and what-have-you.

Tell me truthfully if I am wrong, but it seems to me that between us there are still some strange barriers, probably most of them psychological. In some of you, I sense a fear of me ... a fear not of my person, but of my office. Somehow or other you have, in your minds, mixed me up (so it seems to me) with some mother figure or other authority in your lives who (you feel) rejected and punished you. I'm not that figure.

Some of you, because of fear or guilt (I don't really know the motivation), do not really share with me that which is 'of the essence' both for us personally and for the Apostolate. And in order to make the Apostolate one in mind, soul and heart, *we* must be one. Now don't misunderstand me, dearly beloved. I know that in so many ways we *are* one, but there are still some recesses in ourselves that pertain to our apostolic unity and the strengthening of the bonds of our family at the top level. It is like a piece of unfinished business. Why should that be so? I wish it weren't.

If there are some among you (if I am right about this) whose feeling of guilt and fear is still present in regard to me because of some transference from another picture, could you not begin to use your insights (you know quite a bit of how to use those insights now) and get rid of those feelings by sharing very openly and truthfully with me whatever you feel about me?

Are you afraid, perhaps, that I will not accept you as you are? We discover more and more ... as we study psychology, scripture, and liturgy ... that few of us really believe with a deep faith that *God loves us*. That is because we really do not love ourselves. We do not accept ourselves. And from this non-acceptance stems all that guilt, all those fears, all the pain and difficulty of sharing and of being really open to one another. We find this especially true on the top level, such as the relations of the LDs to us.

If you don't really believe that God loves you (at least you don't accept that fully) and if you do not accept and love yourselves as you should, you will consequently imagine that I (as a person who matters to you) do not accept and love you fully either. Hence comes the reticence; hence the non-sharing of your deep personal problems in which I might be of some assistance to you in the dispelling of those murky emotions.

The truth of the matter is that I know you very well (I think) with all your strengths and weaknesses, with all your beauty of soul, mind, and heart. In community life nothing stays hidden very long, dearly beloved. And the truth is that – knowing all this – I do love you and accept you as you are. My heart hungers to help you to get rid of all the unnecessary burdens so that you might be 'free as a bird' to love God better. But I do wish that you understood this in a real depth, and trusted me more! Then our communication would enter a new phase, and a great peace and joy would flow to you from God and affect your house and the whole Apostolate.

Forgive me for belaboring the point, but I still have this intuition which lies heavily on my heart. The intuition is that we have not yet established a final depth of openness, a final unity; and it should exist between us if we want it to exist between us and the staff. Humbly, I beg your pardon if I am wrong. But I thought it another proof of my love and acceptance that I would write you this letter. Let me hear what you have to say in return.

Lovingly yours in Mary,

MARSHAL YOUR TIME

April 12, 1965

Carissimi,

All of us have to reexamine our attitudes toward time, but even more so *the primacy of values*. No one knows better than myself the pressures of a particular apostolate, but it would be unrealistic to give in to them. If you were stricken with appendicitis and rushed to the hospital, then had to spend a month in convalescence, your apostolate would not collapse. Would it collapse if you went for a day in the poustinia, to take stock of your life and to stop your whirlwind activities? Would it collapse if you paused to be recharged in God's silence and solitude?

I'm not going to multiply examples, but I will say this: that *organizing time is a HOLY occupation!* On a recent visitation, one LD complained to me that he had "so little time" to do things. I sat him down and, with Father Briere at the typewriter, we went through the entire day from the rising hour to the retiring hour. After this close analysis of the day, an awful lot of time was found to do 'what had to be done' ... and much was left for prayer, meditation, reading, rest, etc.

Each LD must really sit down and honestly review his or her *set of values* in regard to time. Having done that, review some values doubly so, for 'values' fit into the reevaluation of time too. Your first priority here is to *ask yourself some questions*. For example: "What is most important in a given apostolate?" My answer would be the preservation and growth of the Madonna House spirit. "Where is that spirit found?" In our history, letters, work-outlines, books, courses (written and tape-recorded). We have a list of those, and so do you.

Another set of questions to ask yourself: "What is the primary duty of an LD?" To train and form the staff workers in the field. "For how long?" New waves of staff workers will always be coming. And the training of a Christian to grow into sanctity continues until death. "What is the greatest problem that *inhibits* people from 'growing in the Lord' ... and even may *destroy* that ability to grow?" The answer stares us in the face; it is the subject of innumerable books, articles, TV programs – *neurosis.* "What are the causes of the problem?" Rapid historical changes, great mobility of population, new technological advances. "What are the consequences?" A sense of uprootedness, a breakdown of family relations, the threat of hot and cold wars, the fear of atomic annihilation ... a sense of 'valuelessness' as the advance of science demotes man (and the earth itself) from being the 'center of the universe' and reveals new galaxies, other universes.

Having asked yourself some key questions, what should be the *next* priority in your evaluation of time? I have mentioned various helps and tools, but IDEAS must come first. You can nurture 'ideas' within you only if you set aside quiet time to do so. Here the marshalling of time must be inexorable! Even if you are in the midst of a group of people who need your services and attention, you should still retire for an hour. (You explain to them that this is a sacrosanct hour; they will not object.) Or else you find some other method of 'making time' ... by going away, closing the house or whatever, according to the possibilities before you. You *must make time* for these 'ideas' to ferment, and for the intelligent discussions that should follow them.

If this is not done, the blind will continue to lead the blind. The narrow vision of our early youth in the Apostolate will 'guide' (if this word can be used; it should be 'misguide' instead) a particular mission house or the entire Apostolate into a historical time, an 'aggiornamento' time, in which we will (at best) be the cow's tail instead of being the leaders.

At this point, it may appear to some of you as if I lessen, decry, or denigrate the 'works' of the Apostolate. This is very far from the truth. When you organize yourself first, and then your crew next, and establish the values and priorities of your house, then the rest will fall into place. There are umpteen thousand ways by which 'the ingenuity

332

of love' and the use of natural intelligence (strengthened by prayer) will help you organize your time.

The 'works' of your particular house, far from suffering a setback, will on the contrary be better performed, with a greater spirit of joy, with a deeper spiritual motivation, and in less time. As to the burden of backlogged work, you can organize bees, or call in volunteers, or even hire people (on rare occasion) to do the type of jobs that will 'liberate' your house so that this 'proper priority' can be established.

My letter to you is getting very long, but I have this question much at heart and am worried about you. So, after lots of prayer and meditation in the night, I have written what is in my heart. I wish to share with you the increasing burden of directing souls to God and serving our neighbor.

Lovingly in Mary,

Catherine

KEEP ON GROWING

[1958 through 1967]

Editor's Note: The following insights were found scattered throughout Catherine's letters to the LDs, as she told them of the comings and goings in Combermere and other news of the Apostolate. They are presented here, to remind us to 'keep on growing.'

All of us must begin in God, continue in God, depend on God, and be led back to God, all the while attending to our outward duties and responsibilities. We must not act as if we were God. We must not impinge our personal ideas upon the Apostolate. We must be flexible. We must be objective ... not attached to our own will but always listening to God's Will. We must pray much, asking God for the strength to bear the weight of our staff, while we try to lead them to him. He will grant it to us.

Learn to read, pray, see, and think! *READ* the history of our family, consecutively, no matter what the pressure. Read every line, and between the lines. It's a blueprint for building a community of love, and will answer many questions. *PRAY* before the Blessed Sacrament, and go to the poustinia as the need arises. Community prayer must be bolstered by private prayer. *SEE* everything that exists in you and around you, and whatever happens during your day, *with the Eyes of God*. Meditate on what you see, and a great and wondrous transformation will take place in yourself and your house. *THINK* simply, directly, boldly. Always begin with the essence, not with what stems from the essence. Don't go from effects; start from the causes. This will help you avoid rationalization and false thinking.

There are a thousand rationalizations (and a million other excuses) ready at hand to remind you why you can't take time out to read or pray. The pressure of work is the most common one. But the cornerstone of your life is meditation and prayer. It is vital that you remember this. For a life of action (and action only), of allowing yourself to be dominated by action, will result in your *worshiping* action – the Good Works of God – instead of God himself.

Immerse yourself in the essence of our Apostolate. Do not engage yourself in the 'heresy' of Good Works. Some of you 'go overboard' without noticing it, and the next thing is that you are all tense, exhausted, nervous. And the essence of our Apostolate is lost somewhere along the line. What is this essence? To give love and peace ... person to person.

You have difficulty with your staff, or they have difficulty with each other. The house is upset; and your explanations, clarifications, arguments, coaxing, discipline, etc., are to no avail. Send them away to the poustinia, at least for the day. Let the Holy Spirit work on them before you do. Don't let it 'throw' you that the house is busy (or overwhelmed!) with work. If a person were sick with a high fever or pneumonia, or had an accident, you would do without him or her for maybe longer than a day. Darkness of soul, whether emotional or spiritual, is more important than pneumonia. Act accordingly, and you will reap tremendous benefits. You yourself will also have time to 'cool off' and to open your soul to the Holy Spirit.

You think it is easy to 'identify' with the poor by living as the poor do. That's just kindergarten stuff. True identification is a tremendous spiritual act, which demands that you yourself take the lance (there is no Roman soldier to do it for you) and plunge it deep into your heart. You tear the spiritual muscles of your soul wide open. You open yourself to the other, totally, and let that person enter in. You use all your senses, your grace, your empathy, your sympathy, *all* of your being, to 'become' that other person.

You have to 'become' Mrs. X___. You have to feel yourself married to a man of his type. You have to be in that house with those children, facing poverty, lack of money, dirt, noise, crowdedness. You have to *be* her! Only then will you know her needs, as an apostle should know them. Only then will you be able to truly fulfill those needs, lovingly.

The time of psychiatric treatment is full of emotional doubts, mixed with spiritual ones, and of difficulties along many other lines. The treatment may prolong itself over several years. And it may have been begun just before the time of final commitment to Madonna House. It is unfair to staff workers and to the Apostolate to refuse them final promises while they are under treatment. Yet it also unfair to allow them to make that final commitment.

A case comes to mind: Y___ found that her neurosis worsened (or became fully blown) after final promises, creating quite a problem ... at least in her mind, though not in ours. It necessitated her leaving the Apostolate. She feels guilty, more guilty than she would feel otherwise if she were in temporary promises. She considered herself a fully-fledged member of our family, a trusted senior member, yet needing a 'leave of absence' when she should be at her apostolic peak. This complicates her treatment, and perhaps extends the time of it. And it certainly not a good example for the 'young ones' here. It gives them the idea that people can never be liberated from their problems. It is a distorted picture, and untrue; but you know how young ones are. (Of course, we don't want to give the opposite impression either: that taking final promises will automatically 'solve' a host of problems.) I think an insertion or addition to the Constitutions, allowing more flexibility in making final promises, would be good. I would like to have your mind on it.

I never suspected that I myself had emotional fears, like any other human being. The reason is that, in my conscious self, I am an aggressive personality ... or what the world calls 'courageous.' If I see anything threatening me, any problem, any unpleasantness, anything difficult to face, I not only walk toward it, I *run to face it* and get it over with. I have done so all my life. But the doctors at the Mayo Clinic helped me much to realize that my colitis, my stomach cramps and diarrhea, were basically due to unconscious fear. If I don't exercise some intelligent control over these subconscious problems, my colitis will reoccur ... and a host of other emotions with it.

One night when I couldn't sleep, I spent the time going into the depths of myself. To my amazement, I suddenly discovered seven different tensions ... or seven 'events' that seemed so enormous that they threatened my subconscious self and caused those tensions. My conscious self was unaware of the threats; so, following the desire of my emotions, I was steadily withdrawing from these fears instead of facing them. To say that it was an easy thing to do an about-face in this matter would be a lie. But I faced them and knew the truth about myself, a deeper truth than I had known before; and I thanked God for it. Now the staff are telling me that I am changing, I am much more peaceful, easier to get along with. I contribute to their own openness and help their fears vanish. They welcome the change with glee, because now we can really create that 'team spirit' we've been talking about.

Two very practical questions about poverty for LDs to think about: Those staff who go out on errands, donation pickups, etc., complain that the weather is often very cold and there is a need of the body to warm up. They'd like to get a cup of coffee, but have no money for this. Please investigate the situation properly. A panelled truck is never as warm as the small cab of an open truck. Take this into consideration, along with the severity of the weather and the length of the drive. Provide coffee money and, on long trips, money for lunch also.

It is very difficult for men (this is the consensus of opinion with everyone I talked to) to shave with ordinary 'bar' soap. Its lather is not strong enough to soften the stubble; and many men, especially those with a certain type of skin, go through agonies in shaving with it. Therefore, I instruct all female LDs to see that their male staff are provided with the proper shaving soap.

A practical question about order: We in Combermere are organizing our files just now; or rather, we are rethinking them and therefore changing them. People are not always aware that proper record-keeping or file-keeping requires an intelligent approach and a periodic rethinking, redoing, rearranging. I propose that you meditate for the next month on these questions: In what state of affairs have I left my files and other records? Are they so arranged that my successor will have no difficulty in taking over? Or is my office an 'unholy mess'? If it is, that will set the whole Apostolate, my particular foundation, and the person who takes over my job, at least six months behind ... or more?

In charity to others, we should remember that (1) we are all mortal, and might die within the next twenty-four hours; (2) we are all subject to obedience, the LDs included, and might be moved or transferred suddenly.

These are serious questions, and not to be lightly dismissed. Do not say to yourself that you are very busy *(so am I!)* ... or 'too busy.' That is not an excuse; it is more likely a rationalization. If you really want to, you can *make* time.

As the launching of Sputnik* has shown so vividly, the average American young person (male or female) suffers from a tremendous lack of general cultural background and education. Even people with the higher university degrees have pools of ignorance with regard to geography, history, and their own religion. These are barriers to the 'vision of the whole,' academically and intellectually speaking. Even if they are graduates in home-economic courses or in the nursing profession (which should put them in touch with 'service' and the normal problems of everyday life), they usually have a wrong approach to manual labor, the theology of which is 'terra rasa' to them ... which means an earth completely devoid of any living matter, an unknown quantity, a desert.

Frankly, I hate even to tackle the problem. But we must face the problem squarely at Madonna House. Where to start? In the *practical* areas, we must give them knowledge and experience. The lack of these skills can destroy the apostolate of a given fieldhouse, or at least stymie its growth. *Academic* education (at least on a basic level) will be given to all. Those with intellectual ability or artistic talents should be nurtured through specialized training. The more brilliant 'brains' can go on for higher degrees. You can see for yourself that this is a broad approach, and it will be a good one, I think. What is your opinion?

Another area of training is in 'current events.' We are beginning to feel that being cutoff from the news of the world is very bad for lay apostles. We've devised the

---

* On October 4, 1957, the world's first artificial satellite (Sputnik) was sent into orbit around the earth. This evidence of Russian technology caused American educators to redesign their teaching programs. It also gave rise to many soul-searching articles and books (why 'Johnny' can't read, and 'Ivan' can ... etc.) about the deficiencies of classroom learning. More recent comments on this topic can be found in *Cultural Literacy: what every American needs to know* by E. D. Hirsch, Jr. (Boston: Houghton Mifflin, 1987) and *The Closing of the American Mind: how higher education has failed democracy and impoverished the souls of today's students* by Allan Bloom (New York: Simon and Schuster, 1987).

following (it might help you): someone keeps track of events each day and makes a short oral report to the others at supper; a bulletin board in the front room is devoted exclusively to clippings from newspapers and magazines; for those who want to go deeper, copies of the *Christian Science Monitor* are on our magazine rack. (I highly recommend subscribing to this periodical; it's the best paper in the world as far as current events are concerned.) Something has to be done about this situation. We cannot live in the splendor of our present isolation.

It is important to pray that the Holy Spirit give you particular insights about individuals, for no two people are alike. To think about each person, to pray about each, to plan for each (short-range and long-range), all this is part of your job too. For instance, Q___ said to me: "How can I be involved with others when I don't want others to be involved with me? That's the way I'm made! That's my personality." She is right that she cannot get involved with others until she allows them to be involved with her. *Love is a two-way street.* I know that she has an emotional block, but she also has a very good brain and learns well.

Intuition and prayer, coupled with love and intelligence, told me that she needs to be freed from her emotional problem through *academic studies.* Her horizons must be wide open along that line, and would be the 'key' to unlocking the barrier within her. It will take much patience, love, kindness, and delicacy to bring her to the point where she will let others get involved in herself ... yes, a constant kindness. Not too much pressure, but a persevering follow-up.

Z___, on the other hand, is a gentle soul with a vivid imagination. With her emotional makeup, she needs as much patience as Q___ does, but with an entirely different approach to come to the same result. As for R___, he has a good intelligence, but his passion for details keeps him from seeing the whole picture. That passion of his must be slowly cooled down ... again, it must be done lovingly, kindly. W___ has a certain abruptness in tone of voice and in outward manner, yet inwardly has a gentle and loving personality. But W___ also has a brilliant mind and understands the problem, and loves God deeply through liturgical prayer. But a 'helping hand' must be extended to W___. ... And so on down the line with the rest of the staff.

The Lord desires you to grow a beautiful garden of souls for him. But you must learn to be a good gardener; to know that each flower needs a different kind of fertilizer, another type of treatment, perhaps a transplanting into new soil. But to make each flower bloom at its best, and to produce the fruits that the Lord wants it to bear, you have to tend that garden according to his rules of 'diversity in unity.' Like all gardening, this is best done 'on your knees.' Use all your spiritual and intellectual faculties, and then more prayer. Ask the Holy Spirit and Our Lady for ever-deeper personalized insights for each of your staff.

It has become apparent that often those of us involved in the training spend time in the evening perhaps preparing for the next day or putting the finishing touches on some jobs. But it also became evident that often there are people who are lonely in the evening, for they may be the type who don't put themselves forward, and so nobody seems to pay attention to them.

Obviously, the ingenuity and love of those doing the training must go out to those people, and the eyes of the soul, as well as those of the body, must be aware of them. For love does such things – love is always aware of needs. We must pray to the Holy Spirit that we find new ways of thinking about these people and loving and planning how we can lead each soul to God in love and friendship. All of this is part of your job in the field too.

If people operate without spiritual motivation, but just on the natural level of 'getting the work done' or of inculcating good training habits (order, cleanliness, punctuality, efficiency) ... important as these might be ... we will be wasting our time and achieving nothing. Our goal is a spiritual one, that of answering the call of God to a specific Apostolate that has a specific accent and spirit. To have this spiritual motivation, Christ must become a *personal God* ... and God the Father really a *Father* ... and the Holy Spirit likewise ... all in the reality of faith, deep faith.

We've come to the conclusion that, for the majority of people who come to us, God is *an abstraction!* He is someone with a big stick, a frightening judge who sends one to hell if his commandments and the precepts of his church are not obeyed. So people respond by living more in the letter of the law than in the spirit, and emotional crises keep recurring. The right motivation, and a desire for heroic sanctity, would help to cure them. Without a personal God, without the supernatural motivation of loving and glorifying God, and serving him and (for him) loving our neighbor as ourselves – and loving ourselves well! – the vocation of Madonna House cannot be implemented.

Then many of the differences and difficulties that we must face while we are members of this family will become too burdensome. The challenges of our life will cease to have rhyme or reason. We will put more emphasis on counseling techniques than on spiritual verities. Not that we should cease to clarify emotional problems, however; we must help an individual solve them, or at least alleviate them. But emotional problems are a part of life. We must encourage everyone to accept these difficulties realistically. They are the normal average 'cross' that all men have to bear, who are born of women.

Recently G___ wrote me that she was concerned about the (seemingly) punitive dismissal of X___. She was especially upset that I had suggested that this matter be discussed in each house. She was also upset that any staff worker needed the spur of fear to keep in line.

I answered her personally; but it is a good theme to pick up on. You realize that it was with a deep sadness that I made that suggestion that X___ be separated from the Apostolate. Yet you LDs were all present when the matter was discussed, and it was unanimously decided that X___ would have to go. The reasons were clearly stated: X___'s utter noncooperation with the spirit and the work load of a given house and disobedience to its rules could no longer be tolerated.

We have seen that, at times, a staff worker's problem is not simply one of emotional immaturity (so common today), but clearly a complete noncooperation, a deliberate desire to see how far the person can push the patience of an LD and get away with it; a person who is definitely regressing rather than progressing in the spirit and works of the Apostolate. Everything is tried: understanding, charity, patience, help of every kind. Nothing works. So, a couple of warning signals are sent to the person. In the case of X___, this brought no improvement in behavior whatever, and dismissal became necessary. You'd think the reception of such a warning would induce fear. And that fear would make the person reexamine the situation, for "fear is the beginning of wisdom."

Others of our staff who received similar warnings have changed their ways and improved. They had needed a strong reminder like that. X___, however, did not respond in this way. The letters that we sent were like 'water off a duck's back.' So separation from the Apostolate resulted. Since X___'s actions were in the 'open forum' as we say, all the staff are entitled to know what happened to this person and why. Also, we of the DG Office desired to show that a staff worker can go 'so far and no further' ... and that we must implement our Constitutions when everything else has failed. I agree with G___ that it has a 'punitive' effect, in a manner of speaking; but at the same time, it was a wise and charitable action. Charity consists in using all the means that are allowed in the Constitutions to bring souls to God; among them are 'punitive' measures.

There is a great danger in considering discipline and disciplinary action as cruel. I am afraid that it stems from educators who decried the corporal punishment of children, so much so that the pendulum swung back until *any* punishment was considered cruel and unfair. You can see the results all around you. Youth has no respect for authority, or age, or wisdom, but especially authority. Many Catholic psychiatrists feel strongly that a child must be punished corporally, when he deserves it, because the 'little human animal' who is a child does not always understand words but *does* understand action. And since the principle of emotional life lies between pleasure and pain, pain (justly applied, without anger, and when the child deserves it) is a corrective which leads eventually to a inner self-discipline. It also makes the child realize that there are certain things one cannot 'get away with,' and this will redound to the good of the child and the good of society.

The same applies to any community. There must be discipline; and there are what you might call 'disciplinary measures.' One of them was what was used regarding X___. Telling the truth about the reasons for anyone's being discharged from the Apostolate might put 'the fear of the Lord' into the hearts of others, who then realize that they cannot get away with a prolonged lack of cooperation, who will begin to examine their consciences and see wherein they have been wrong. In this particular instance, some have seen the error of their ways. So our approach brought new insights and new graces.

Spiritual motivation must be gently, firmly, warmly, and austerely handled. The members of our family must look at its Directors and *see Christ in us.* How are they going to do that if they don't know a personal God? If they don't believe in God or trust him somewhat? We must really probe the depths of this question. One answer lies in a book called *Heroic Sanctity and Insanity* by Thomas Verner Moore, who is a doctor, Carthusian monk, and psychiatrist. His thesis is that if we practice heroic sanctity, we might cure ourselves of neurosis and even (in a manner of speaking) 'help ourselves' out of deep psychosis. Another book I highly recommend is *The Enemies of Love* by Dom Aelred Watkin of Downside Abbey. We are reading it aloud each day after the noon meal, and it is penetrating quite deeply into the general consciousness.* Life is composed of 'little things.' But if they are connected with God, and done with the intention of rendering glory to God, the sum total of it will be the fulfillment of our destiny: to be united with him through love!

This is a good time to speak again on what I have written a lot to you about – the family spirit. I want especially to stress the fact that you have to train your staff

---

* Moore's book, subtitled *An introduction to the spiritual life and mental hygiene*, was published in 1959 by Grune and Stratton of New York and London; Watkin's book, in 1958 by Burns and Oates of London.

and help them towards *openness*. I find that the staff is not open (in the sense that I mean it) to one another. They are like islands in the midst of a sea, standing there close to one another, outwardly within reaching distance, but inwardly they are islands. Unless we are open to one another, unless we cast aside a fear of one another, unless we are ready to show our weaknesses to one another and stop wearing masks that hide us from one another, we will never know one another ... and, therefore, not be able to love one another.

So I would like you to be very open with your staff in many ways. Do not be afraid to let them know your weaknesses; for, once *we who are Directors* are open, we can begin to train our spiritual children in that openness. This will lead them to loving one another and to having the family spirit, without which our Apostolate will fail. For we are part of the Mystical Body of Christ, the vivifying principle of which is the Holy Spirit. This closedness or 'closed-up'ness, so characteristic of modern men and women (youth or adult), is one of the greatest obstacles to the circulation of the Holy Spirit throughout the members of the Mystical Body. We must break that down. May the Lord inspire you – each one of you – as to the ways and means of doing it in your house.

A letter is going out to all of the Apostolate dealing with the recent separation of a staff worker. All of us are, of course, prepared for such an eventuality. We realize, at least statistically, that a certain percentage of our membership will depart at various points of their training, and even after they have received the staff-worker cross. The first worries us only a little, because we expect a certain percentage to find out that this is not their vocation. For this we have the various preliminary stages to help our mutual clarification. It is obvious, however, that we are going to feel much more deeply the departures and defalcations of anyone already under promises ... even though Mother Church gives them a right to depart in peace on the day when their promises are up, or earlier if they become officially released from them.

We are all deeply affected, though, when members of our family leave – especially so when it is obvious that

Satan had a hand in their leaving. It is extremely painful when it is a blatant, complete refusal to obey. This is a denial of the Madonna House spirit, a challenge to a whole setup which is from God. It is a rebellion of spirits which culminates in the classical sentence of Satan: *non serviam* ... "I will not serve!" Besides being a sin of disobedience as far as facts show (none of us can judge the inner person, ever; for God told us not to judge or we would be judged ... except inasmuch as it is in the office of the DGs to do the judging) it also indicates a complete lack of loyalty, of dedication, of surrender. As local directors, how is your obedience and loyalty to the DGs? Are you of one mind with us? Of one soul? Of one heart? Is your loyalty deep and inward, first to the Apostolate as a whole? Or does your house come before the rest of the Apostolate? We have discussed this at our meetings, but now is a good time to make a new examination of conscience.

This may be an unpleasant letter to read because there seems to be implied a question (on my part) of your loyalty, unity and trust of me. It isn't quite so, and yet it is. Such questions have to be asked in order to clarify this vital issue. So it behooves us *all* to examine our consciences. I have done so in regard to you and I find that I do love and trust you completely. Do you do that in reverse? My loyalty is yours; is yours mine? It is not so much to me 'as a person' that I ask your loyalty and trust – your obedience, dedication and surrender – as to 'the figurehead that I am' in representing the whole Apostolate. And I have to go a step further and ask if you will give the same loyalty, trust, and obedience to the *next* DG who will follow me. In this way I am paving the way for her because this has nothing to do with personalities, but with principles only.

Yes, I think a collective examination of our consciences has to be made, and it is important that we do so. Forgive me for asking, but I felt I had to for the sake of the Apostolate, for the sake of the Lord, and for the sake of yourselves and the staff.

Even now, when I am up half a day, my mind works overtime. My thoughts are of the Apostolate as they seldom have been before. I am examining my conscience in regard to every little thing that we do in Madonna House as far as training is concerned. I draw and draw on past experience and try desperately perhaps (and yet peacefully) to make a synthesis. It is not as easy as it seems.

New happenings, unexpected setbacks ... they all come forth like stones do every year on the fields at our farm. Every year we 'stone the fields' during the summer, when the earth is soft, malleable, plowable, diskable. Then comes the winter. Whatever it does, perhaps we do not quite understand ... but the 'crop of stones' is back again in the spring. I have meditated on this often. Perhaps the devil sows such stones in the spiritual fields of our Apostolate, and in those of the Church itself; for all over the world we are battling with that kind of crop!

Pay attention to what is happening in your house. Watch ... pray ... watch again ... check and recheck. Keep up posted by letter or by phone (as you feel the need of same) of any difficulty that arises. Do not allow little problems to pass you by. Pick up every breach against poverty, chastity, obedience (especially obedience). Be aware of the efficiency of your house, and watch for laziness, excuses, lack of openness. Souls are at stake; and our aim is sanctity!

CARRY ON THE SPIRIT

October 13, 1962

Carissimi,

Because I am on a program of partial rest these days, I have time to do much thinking, hoping, praying. My prayers are lifted to the heart of God for our little Apostolate; for the wings of time are brushing heavily against me, and I realize more and more its fleetingness. Therefore, I implore God to illumine my mind, to fill my heart and soul with *his* desires for our Apostolate.

Carefully, I go back over the years and remember what it was that came to me during the time preceding the foundation of our Apostolate. I do this with a flaming desire to hand over to you, my successors, the true spirit of our Apostolate as it came to me in such a simple and unglamorous manner over three decades ago.

Here are some of these thoughts that persistently stay with me and, by their tremendous clarity and simplicity, make me realize that in truth the Holy Spirit is again renewing all these words that I have been cherishing in my heart all these years. How well do I remember the years of 1927 and 1928! They were years of comfort, of good jobs with high earnings, and yet of a restlessness of spirit that would not allow me to enjoy the fruits of wealth and comfort, or even to sleep.

Suddenly, almost out of the blue, I was possessed with one idea: "Go, sell what you possess. Give it *literally* to the poor. Take up your cross. Follow Me! Follow me into the slums of the big cities, to which I brought you when you first came to this country from Russia." It seemed at the time as if the 'voice of God' were clear in my ears, though naturally I didn't hear anything with my ears. With a devastating clarity, it came to me that *for this* the Lord had saved me from the Russian Revolution and brought me to a land which was so difficult for me to adjust to. (It was hard for me because North American ways and mores and background were so different from Russia.)

Quite frankly, I must admit that I shrank from the thought at first! Young as I was, I had an inkling (a premonition, if you will) of what would happen to me if I embarked on this strange call, this inner call that opened up before my soul. You know the story from then on. You know my strange pilgrimage to some ninety different priests. You know of their refusal to even listen to what I had to say, because my primary duty was so evident to them in a little son named George. You know of Bishop Neil McNeil of Toronto and his decision ... and the rest is history.

You know that, following the bishop's direction, I obeyed the call of God. What you may not realize is that, by doing so, I entered a truly extraordinary and strange 'novitiate' of God himself. At that time there was no one else to lead me in this unusual vocation. Slowly, as a flower opens under the ray of the sun, the spirit of what today is the Madonna House Apostolate clarified itself. Needless to say, the price was high. You know some of its highlights. But only God will ever know its heights and depths, for there are no human words to express all that goes into obeying the Lord in this unusual fashion. I was led *only* by his light, which (as you know) can suddenly become dim and seem almost lost through dark days and darker nights.

But it was all worthwhile. It was all worthwhile because *you are here now.* The humble storefront on 129 Portland Street in Toronto has become the 'birthplace' of Madonna House in Combermere, and of all its missions. It has brought hundreds of lay people into its heart, courageous young men and women from so many nations. And (miracle of miracles!) it has brought priests to live at Madonna House and become a part of it, and associate priests to spread its spirit around the world, and seminarians to be ordained expressly for the Madonna House Apostolate. And it has brought Our Lady of Combermere here!

Yes, it was all worthwhile. And I would do it all over again if the Lord asked me to. But you and I will have to face a few simple truths. To none of us is life on this earth eternal. How many more days and months and years God has in store for me is not too important. What's important is that, when I die, your hands will have to *take up the flame* he has put into mine. Your mind, heart, and soul must obediently follow the path he has laid out for me ... for all of us. You must follow it without deviation; for heavy will be the responsibility of anyone who strays from that path. Truly the anger of the Lord will descend upon them, and the tears of Our Lady will make their life heavy.

It is true that you have a Constitution to guide you now, and a great deal of knowledge has been poured into you – knowledge that took me decades to acquire, in great pain and difficulty, and against terrific opposition. Be that as it may, I want to put down on paper the things that (to me) form the 'spirit' of Madonna House Apostolate. Perhaps they are all contained in two words: *Pax* and

348

Caritas. For those who are able to enter into them fully, that would be enough for me to say. But only God knows who they are (I can't), so I have to spell them out a little more carefully.

The Call to Radical Poverty

Let us begin at the beginning. With this strange call to arise and follow the Lord in poverty, I sold all that I possessed and gave it *literally* to the poor. Let us understand from the beginning that I did just that. Piece by piece, I sold all my belongings. And any time I received any amount of money for them, I gave it to some poor family I knew. I either gave it to them in cash or as a signed cheque. I did it literally. There was no quibbling about it in my mind or in my actions. There was no rationalizing, no arguing.

The things I could not sell, such as shoes and undergarments, I gave away. And I have kept it that way always, throughout the years. If I were to die today or tomorrow, there would be only secondhand clothes to return to the clothing room, or books to return to the Madonna House library. I have no personal possessions. There is no gold or silver belonging to me. All that I have, all that I wear, is 'on loan' you might say. None of it can go to my family, as far as blood relatives are concerned, for I only have the temporary 'use' of it ... on loan from Madonna House.

Fervently, I pray that this will always be the spirit of every LD and every staff worker. I pray that you will inculcate that spirit of detachment, of *non-possession*. For there is great danger in our Apostolate that the very charity of the people, who provide us with even luxury items, may be 'taken for granted.' Let there be poverty and simplicity in the hearts of our staff! And remember: it is your responsibility as an LD to teach them by your example and word. Watch out, dearly beloved, or the insidious creeping-in of a dark mist that comes from hell will blur our eyes to the literalness of holy poverty.

"Take up your cross." Here is a deep lesson for all of us; it was for me. What fashioned my cross, as it does yours? We must, all of us, unhesitatingly show you that; if we hesitate, we are lost. Its weight is made up of many components, the first of which is your own position of authority. Then it is your staff, for they are not easy to carry, no more than you are easy for Christ to carry; then your responsibility to the poor; then your responsibility to the world of our brethren wherever you are living, whatever you are doing.

Your cross might take the shape of illness. It might take the shape of intolerable situations in your house. You will fall many times under it. You will be 'sure' that this is the last time and you can't get up. But if you do not let go of the cross, the Lord will lift you up himself, because there is yet much he wishes to do with you. You have to be 'identified' ... 'become one' with the cross, as with the poor you serve. And there is only one way to do it – in love, in caritas, to be nailed on it for them.

"Follow Me!" Faith is of the essence here ... faith and hope that must not dim, but grow through the years. And the years may be heavy and dark, bringing intolerable conditions in which faith might appear to be shrinking and dying. Never believe that. When it is darkest, the Lord of faith is closest. You have to follow him wherever he leads – follow him through strange roads, incredible ascents and fearsome descents. But follow him you must.

It will bring you into the darkness of misunderstandings. It will bring you into the midst of persecutions. These days, it might bring you into death by martyrdom. Wherever he leads you, you follow. Follow him in utter faith, in complete trust and shining hope, even though (perhaps) in fear and trembling. But follow him, wherever he leads.

"Arise and Go." These three little words should mean a lot to our Apostolate, especially to you who direct it. You should be like the bride in the Canticle of Canticles: "I sleep, but my heart watcheth." In a manner of speaking, you should also be like the friends of the bridegroom who wait for him night and day, ready to serve him.

Be Both Martha and Mary
You cannot lie down on your job. You must stand up! And, standing up, you cannot remain still (except in your

soul); you must be about his business. For our Apostolate demands that you should be both active and contemplative, both Martha and Mary. Make no mistake; the stillness of Mary is an even bigger 'action' than the action of Martha. And so your life is in a constant 'arising,' a constant 'going.' Both are about your Father's business and that of your tremendous Lover, Jesus Christ.

How are you going to do all this? You will do it in grace and humility, realizing your utter poverty. You will do it by depending exclusively upon God. You will do it by walking hand in hand with Mary, through whom you will always find Jesus. You will do it in an utter simplicity of faith, seeing to it that you have the heart of a child. You will do it by making Mass (the liturgy in general) and Scriptures the twin lights of your life ... its foundation, its essence, its center. You will do it by having recourse (preferably daily) to the Sacrament of Penance, thereby seeing to it that your conscience is clear, crystal clear, like that of a child. (For confession presumes examination of conscience.)

You will do it by daily spending at least a half hour (and more, if need be) in silence before the Blessed Sacrament; by being faithful to the prayers outlined in the Constitution. They form the framework of our Apostolate. You will do it by fasting and prayer, under the rigid direction of your spiritual director (and, of course, by *having* a spiritual director, without whom you can do nothing.)

Go into Hearts ... Souls ... Minds

If you do these things I mention, if you really meditate on the words that came so clearly to me more than three decades ago and that were the heart of the foundation of our Apostolate, then you will understand. You will know that the 'works' of the Apostolate are contained in the words (which were added for me, seemingly by the Lord): "Go into the slums of the big cities." I understood them to mean the slums of men's *hearts,* the jungle of modern *souls,* the chaos of modern *minds.* But I also understood them as the slums of the big cities and the hidden slums of rural areas. To me it meant *the world,* the whole immense world of our earth! I hope it will mean the same to you in years to come, when you have to examine the invitations that will come to us. It will help you, in that light, to know when to open foundations.

So much for that first vivid sentence that came to me 'out of the blue' as it were, long ago and far away. Now for a few thoughts on the long 'novitiate' that God put me through. Out of it came the spirit of Madonna House Apostolate, that spirit which you must guard and cherish and pass on to others. Out of it, too, came that sentence that you know so well. We must 'live the gospel without compromise' ... at all costs, even that of our lives. When I searched more, seeking his help for further clarification, I also understood another part of our lives, of our spirit: Let us do 'little things,' humble things, ordinary things that all people have to do. Let us do them 'exceedingly well and with great love of God' and offer them up as our humble contribution of love to him. Glorify him through them; and use them as means of atonement for our sins and those of mankind.

Out of that novitiate, too, came the tremendous sentence that certainly isn't mine, but his, for I couldn't have thought of it all by myself: that it is important first to *be* before the Lord, and then to *do* for him. This expresses in yet another manner that, in our Apostolate, we are to be 'contemplatives in action.'

Then came that simple and lovely sentence: We are to witness to Christ 'in the marketplace' ... witness by loving and doing, not so much by speaking. Later, it was summed up for us even better by Charles de Foucauld when he said, "We must cry the gospel *with our lives*." (The same idea came to us both from God, I guess, in almost the same way.)

Many other things I learned in the novitiate of God, and I hope to share them with you, but there is one that I must add here. I know that you know this already, but we must never forget it, especially those of you in authority. Remember that 'to govern is to love.' Remember that there is one example that you can make yours unto the end of your days: Christ on Holy Thursday, washing the feet of his disciples and saying, *I have come to serve*. That means to govern well. It is your privilege, your joy, your duty.

Never put things before people! Never put works before souls! And remember: your primary duty is always to your staff. Teach by example. Do not ask anyone to do something you haven't done too, unless you are sickly and unable to do it. Have little thought for yourself (God will look after you); and let all of your thoughts be for others. Be concerned about the needs of the Apostolate in general, your apostolate in particular, and your staff very specially. Then shall you know – or perhaps I should say *begin to know* – the depth of the meaning of those words etched on your cross: *PAX* and *CARITAS*.

Lovingly yours in Mary,

Writings of Catherine de Hueck Doherty

Apostolic Farming
Dearly Beloved – Vol. 1 & 2 & 3
Dear Father
Dear Seminarian
Doubts, Loneliness and Rejection
Fragments of My Life
The Gospel of a Poor Woman
The Gospel Without Compromise
I Live on an Island
Journey Inward
Lubov
Molchanie
My Heart and I
My Russian Yesterdays
Not Without Parables
Our Lady of Combermere
Our Lady's Unknown Mysteries
The People of the Towel and the Water
Poustinia
Re-entry into Faith
Sobornost
Soul of My Soul
Stations of the Cross
Strannik
Urodivoi

by Eddie Doherty

Cricket in My Heart
Gall & Honey
The Secret of Mary
Splendor of Sorrow
True Devotion to Mary
Tumbleweed

by Fr. Emile Brière

I Met the Humbled Christ in Russia
Katia
The Power of Love

Available through Madonna House Publications
Combermere, Ontario, Canada
K0J 1L0